EDMONDS

SURE

SURE TO RISE

100 YEAR
EDITION
1908–2008

COOKERY
BOOK

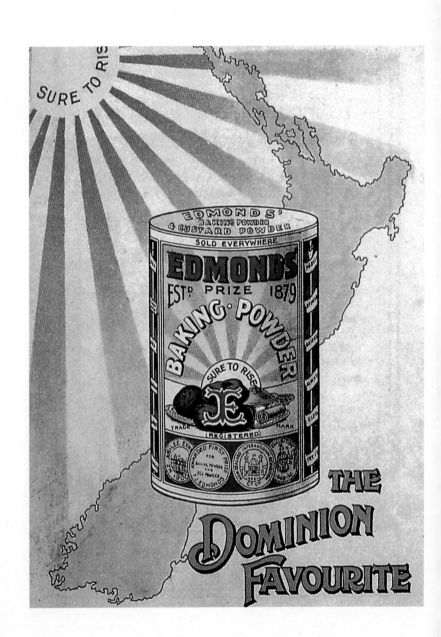

EDMONDS COOKERY BOOK TURNS 100

The *Edmonds Cookery Book* has been part of almost every New Zealand home for the past four generations. The first edition was published in 1908 by Thomas Edmonds in thanks for the support given to his products, particularly Edmonds Baking Powder. The popularity of the *Edmonds Cookery Book* is one of the great Kiwi success stories.

Almost 130 years ago, young Thomas John Edmonds stepped off the sailing ship *Waitangi* at Lyttelton. Thomas soon opened a small grocery store and learned from his customers of their dissatisfaction with the unreliable baking powder products they were able to purchase at the time. In response to their comments Thomas began making his own baking powder out the back of his shop, drawing on his blending experience gained working for a confectioner in London. His first batch of 200 tins went on sale in 1879. One customer reputedly questioned the superiority of the product over the one she was currently using. Edmonds is said to have replied 'It is sure to rise Madam' and so the famous Edmonds promise was born. From this comment the iconic rising sun logo and Sure to Rise trademark were developed, both of which still appear on Edmonds Baking Powder today.

Demand for Edmonds Baking Powder slowly grew until its popularity spread from the housewives of Canterbury to span the whole of New Zealand. As the 19th century drew to a close Edmonds moved to Ferry Rd, Christchurch and in the expanded premises increased production of Edmonds products. In 1908 the first *Edmonds Cookery Book* was published in thanks for the support given to Edmonds products. Housewives could receive a free copy by sending a written request and young couples were sent a complimentary copy on announcement of their engagement. The first edition contained 50 pages of 'economical everyday recipes and cooking hints'. Many of the original recipes are still part of the *Edmonds Cookery Book* today and are marked in this anniversary edition for your interest.

Thomas Edmonds was not only a successful businessman but a pioneer in industrial policies, during the Depression the company was the first to introduce a 40 hour week which meant redundancies were avoided. When the Edmonds company turned 50 in 1929 Thomas Edmonds generously gifted the city of Christchurch with a clock tower and band rotunda.

Today the Edmonds range has grown to include not only baking ingredients but flour, cake mixes and pastry. The *Edmonds Cookery Book* remains our first point of reference for cooking and baking. With sales estimated at over 3 million copies, it is not only our most popular cook book but New Zealand's most popular book.

De Luxe Edition		Printings	De Luxe Edition		Printings
1st	1955	120,000	26th	1989	30,000
2nd	1956	120,000	27th	1990	30,000
3rd	1957	120,000	28th	1990	30,000
4th	1959	120,000	29th	1990	30,000
5th	1962	80,000	30th	1991	16,000
6th	1964	80,000	31st	1991	19,000
7th	1966	80,000	32nd	1992	35,000
8th	1967	80,000	33rd	1992	27,000
9th	1968	80,000	34th	1993	27,000
10th	1969	80,000	35th	1993	27,000
11th	1971	80,000	36th	1994	27,000
12th	1972	100,000	37th	1994	30,000
13th	1973	80,000	38th	1995	20,000
14th	1974	100,000	39th	1996	30,000
15th	1976	200,000	40th	1996	30,000
16th	1978	200,000	41st	1997	30,000
17th	1980	100,000	42nd	1998	30,000
18th	1982	50,000	43rd	1998	15,000
19th	1983	100,000	44th	1998	35,000
20th	1985	30,000	45th	1999	35,000
21st	1985	54,000	46th	1999	35,000
22nd	1986	54,000	47th	2000	35,000
23rd	1986	50,000	48th	2001	35,000
24th	1987	50,000	49th	2001	35,000
25th	1988	30,000	50th	2002	35,000

De Luxe Edition		Printings
51st	2003	35,000
52nd	2003	35,000
53rd	2004	35,000
54th	2005	35,000
55th	2005	35,000
56th	2006	35,000
57th	2006	35,000
58th	2007	35,000
59th	2007	35,000
60th	2008	10,000
61st	2008	50,000

© Copyright Goodman Fielder New Zealand Limited

Published by Goodman Fielder New Zealand Limited
Avanti Finance Building, Block A, 65 Main Highway,
Private Bag 11 913, Ellerslie, Auckland

Distributed by Goodman Fielder New Zealand Limited and
Hachette Livre New Zealand, 4 Whetu Place, Mairangi Bay, Auckland.

ISBN 978-0-646-49451-7

Recipes developed by Goodman Fielder New Zealand Limited
and Robyn Martin & Associates Ltd, Auckland
Photography by Robyn Martin & Associates Ltd
Cover by Cowan
Typeset by Graphicraft Ltd, Hong Kong
Printed in Hong Kong through Bookprint Consultants Ltd, Wellington

CONTENTS

EXCELLENCE WITH EDMONDS

USING THE RECIPES

The *Edmonds Cookery Book* has been designed to make cooking simple for new and experienced cooks.

- **Read through a recipe carefully before starting**. Check that you have all the ingredients you require before preparing the recipe.
- **Easy Reference** — recipes are arranged alphabetically in each section.
- **Helpful Hints** — found at the beginning of some sections and at the bottom of recipe pages. Read these before starting to make a recipe from that section.
- **Information About Ingredients** — can be found on pages 10 and 11.
- **Ingredients are listed in the order of use.**
- **Terms Used in Recipes** — are explained on pages 12 and 13.
- **Prepare tins, dishes or trays before cooking.**
- **Preheat the oven before you start cooking**. Remember to check the oven rack positions (see page 9).
- **Cooking temperatures and times**, **number of serves** and **quantities made** are given at the end of each recipe.

WEIGHTS AND MEASURES

- **New Zealand Standard metric cup and spoon measures are used in all recipes.**
- **All measurements are level.**
- **Easy measuring** — use measuring cups or jugs for liquid measures and sets of 1 cup, ¹/₂ cup, ¹/₃ cup and ¹/₄ cup for dry ingredients.
- **Brown sugar measurements** — are firmly packed so that the sugar will hold the shape of the cup when tipped out.
- **Eggs** — No. 6 eggs are used as the standard size.

ABBREVIATIONS

L	=	litre
mL	=	millilitre
cm	=	centimetre
mm	=	millimetre
g	=	gram
kg	=	kilogram
°C	=	degrees celsius

STANDARD MEASURES ARE:

1 cup	= 250 millilitres
1 litre	= 4 cups
1 tablespoon	= 15 millilitres
1 dessertspoon	= 10 millilitres
1 teaspoon	= 5 millilitres
¹/₂ teaspoon	= 2.5 millilitres
¹/₄ teaspoon	= 1.25 millilitres

APPROXIMATE METRIC/IMPERIAL CONVERSIONS IN COMMON COOKING USE

WEIGHT

30 g	= 1 ounce
120 g	= 4 ounces
240 g	= 8 ounces
450 g	= 1 pound

VOLUME

1 kg	= 2¹/₄ pounds
1 litre	= 1³/₄ pints

MEASUREMENTS

2.5 cm	= 1 inch
20 cm	= 8 inches
30 cm	= 12 inches

WEIGHTS AND MEASURES — APPROXIMATE EQUIVALENTS

ITEM	MEASURE	WEIGHT
breadcrumbs (fresh)	1 cup	50 g
butter	2 tablespoons	30 g
cheese (grated, firmly packed)	1 cup	100 g
cocoa	4 tablespoons	25 g
coconut	1 cup	75 g
cornflour	4 tablespoons	25 g
cream	1/2 pint	300 ml
dried fruit (currants, sultanas, raisins, dates)	1 cup	150–175 g
flour	1 cup	125 g
gelatine	4 tablespoons	25 g
golden syrup	1 tablespoon	25 g
milk	1 cup	250 ml
nuts	1 cup	125–150 g
oil	1 tablespoon	15 ml
rice, sago	2 tablespoons	25 g
	1 cup	200 g
salt	2 tablespoons	25 g
sour cream	1 cup	250 g
sugar, white	2 tablespoons	30 g
	1 cup	250 g
sugar, brown	1 cup (firmly packed)	200 g
	(loosely packed)	125–150 g
sugar, icing	1 cup	150 g
standard No. 6 egg		weighs about 50 g

BEFORE AND AFTER EQUIVALENT MEASURES

APPROXIMATE AMOUNTS NEEDED TO GIVE MEASURES:

1/3 cup uncooked rice = 1 cup cooked rice
1/3 cup uncooked pasta = 1 cup cooked pasta
2–3 chicken pieces = 1 cup cooked chicken
100 g cheese = 1 cup grated cheese
75 g mushrooms = 1 cup sliced = 1/2 cup cooked
4 toast slices bread = 1 cup fresh breadcrumbs
200 g (two) potatoes = 1 cup mashed potato

A GUIDE TO OVEN TEMPERATURES AND USE

PRODUCT	°C	GAS No.	DESCRIPTION
meringues, pavlova	110–140	1/4–1	slow
custards, milk puddings, shortbread, rich fruit cakes, casseroles, slow roasting	150–160	2–3	moderately slow
biscuits, large and small cakes	180–190	4–5	moderate
roasting, sponges, muffins, short pastry	190–220	5–6	moderately hot
flaky pastry, scones, browning toppings	220–230	6–8	hot
puff pastry	250–260	9–10	very hot

OVEN TEMPERATURE CONVERSIONS

165°C = 325°F
175°C = 350°F
190°C = 375°F
200°C = 400°F

OVEN HINTS

- **Oven Racks** — position before turning oven on.
- **Oven Positions**
  Bottom of Oven — use for slow cooking and low temperature cooking
  Middle of Oven — for moderate temperature cooking
  Above Middle — for quick cooking and high temperature cooking
- **Fan-forced ovens** — refer to the manufacturer's directions as the models vary.
- **Preheat oven to required temperature before food preparation.**
- Cooking temperatures and times are a guide only as ovens may vary.

INFORMATION ABOUT INGREDIENTS

Baking powder is a mixture of cream of tartar and baking soda plus wheat flour, which helps the baking powder to flow easily.

Baking soda is also known as bicarbonate of soda.

Bouquet garni is a mixture of parsley, thyme and bay leaf which is tied together with cotton if fresh herbs are used, or enclosed in a muslin bag if dried herbs are used. Bouquet garni is used as a flavouring for stocks. It should be removed once the cooking is completed.

Clarified butter (frying butter or ghee) is prepared by melting butter in a pan until the milk solids settle to the bottom. The clarified butter layer can then be poured into a container leaving the milk solids behind. Can be used for frying as it heats to a high temperature without burning.

Coconut throughout the cookbook means desiccated unless otherwise stated. Coconut can be toasted by heating it in a frying pan over a moderate heat. Shake the pan from time to time. Remove pan from heat when coconut just starts to colour.

Coconut cream or coconut milk is available canned, or can be made by mixing 1 1/4 cups of coconut with 300 ml of boiling water then straining through a sieve and reserving the liquid. This will give about 1 cup (250 ml) of coconut milk.

Cornflour is made from maize and is a starch used to thicken products such as sauces and desserts, or it can be used in some baked products.

Curry powder is a mixture of spices and you can combine different spices in different amounts to make your own blend. Some of the basic spices might include cumin, coriander, ginger, cloves, fenugreek, turmeric and cinnamon. Whole spices can be ground with a mortar and pestle or prepared ground spices can be used.

Edmonds, Diamond and **DYC** products are used throughout this book.

Eggs should be at room temperature when making sponges and other baked goods as this produces a cake with better volume. Egg whites for making meringues and pavlovas should always be at room temperature.

FLOUR TYPES:

Edmonds standard plain flour is ideal for most cakes, sponges, biscuits and sauces. It has a lower protein (gluten) content which helps give tender baked products.

Edmonds high grade flour has a high protein (gluten) content. This is important in breadmaking to ensure that the dough, when kneaded, has sufficient strength to give the bread good volume and texture. It is ideal for a heavy fruit cake (keeps the fruit evenly distributed).

Edmonds self-raising flour is a blend of standard flour with raising ingredients. Self-raising flour can replace the flour and baking powder in scones, muffins, pikelets, pancakes and many cakes and slices.

Edmonds wholemeal flour is made from all parts of the wheat grain — the white flour, bran and wheat germ. Wholemeal flour contains more fibre than white flour. It can be used in muffins, breads, pie-crusts, crumbles and fruit loaves.

Fresh ginger is root ginger. This is available from the fruit and vegetables section of the supermarket and should be stored in the refrigerator crisper or frozen for easy grating. The ginger root can be peeled before using if desired.

Herbs throughout the cookbook means dried herbs unless fresh herbs are specifically listed. When substituting dried for fresh herbs in a recipe, use half the quantity of fresh herbs.

Jalapeño peppers are peppers that come in a variety of degrees of hotness and are used widely in Mexican cooking. They are available canned or in jars from the supermarket.

Low-fat options can be used in recipes calling for sour cream, cream cheese, cream and cheese if desired. Low-fat cream will not whip. Substitute only in recipes where whipping is not required.

Margarine can replace butter, giving a similar result. Extra flour may need to be added in some baked recipes to give the required consistency.

Nuts can be roasted in the oven or in a pan on top of the stove. To roast nuts in the oven, place in an oven dish and cook at 180°C for 5–15 minutes depending on the nuts. To roast on top of the stove, place nuts in a frying pan and cook over a moderate heat until just starting to colour. Toss nuts during cooking to prevent burning.

Oil can be used to replace butter in some baking with the amount of oil being equal approximately to between two-thirds and three-quarters of the amount of butter. There will be texture and taste differences.

OIL TYPES:

Canola Oil is a general purpose oil. It is lower in saturated fats than all commonly used vegetable oils and has a clean flavour.

Sunflower Oil is also a general purpose oil. It is high in polyunsaturates and mild in flavour.

Peanut Oil is perfect for Asian style cooking. It is high in monounsaturates and has a subtle nutty flavour.

Vegetable Oil is best used as a general purpose cooking oil. It is cholesterol free and has a clean taste.

Olive Oil is available in a variety of types. Light olive oil has the least flavour with the deeper green virgin olive oils having a distinct flavour. Use extra virgin for salads and dipping. The other varieties are great for everyday cooking but take care not to overheat olive oil as it will smoke at a lower temperature than many oils.

Pot measure refers to the size of the whole pot. When a 250 g pot measure is given it means use the whole pot.

Prepared mustard is wet mustard that has already been made or bought. **Wholegrain** or smooth varieties are available.

Sambal oelak is a paste made from hot chillies and salt.

Soft breadcrumbs are made from stale bread. They are not toasted.

Softened butter makes creaming butter and sugar easy. Butter can be softened in the microwave, left to stand in a warm place or softened over hot water. Softened butter is not the same as melted butter.

Sour milk or cream is made by adding 1 teaspoon lemon juice or vinegar to 1 cup of fresh milk or cream and leaving to stand until thickened. The commercial product will be thicker than homemade.

Stock can be homemade or bought in cartons as a liquid, in pots as a powder or as foil-wrapped cubes. One stock cube is the equivalent of 1 teaspoon of stock powder.

Tahini is a paste made from toasted sesame seeds and it is widely used in Middle Eastern cooking. It has a toasted nut flavour.

Tomato paste is concentrated tomato purée.

Tomato purée is available in cans or can be made from fresh tomatoes in a blender or food processor.

White sugar can be replaced with brown sugar to give a different flavour and, in baking, a slightly different texture.

Yeast — is used to raise bread. 1 tablespoon Edmonds active yeast (dried granules) can be replaced with 2 tablespoons of Edmonds Surebake yeast.

TERMS USED IN RECIPES

Al dente: Used to describe cooked pasta that is firm to the bite.

Bake blind: Loosely cover an unbaked pastry case with a sheet of baking paper larger than the size of the tin. Fill with dried beans, pasta or rice, and bake. This ensures the pastry base is cooked sufficiently for holding moist fillings. Baking blind beans or rice can be stored and re-used.

Baking paper: Suitable for lining cake tins and trays. Does not need to be greased although may need a smear of butter to adhere the paper to the tin.

Baste: To spoon juices over foods being roasted to prevent drying and to give a glossy surface.

Blanch: To place fruit and vegetables in boiling water for 30 seconds then remove to cold water to ease removing of skins or prepare for freezing.

Blend: To mix ingredients thoroughly to get an even consistency.

Boil: To cook at boiling point with large rolling bubbles forming.

Braise: To gently fry in oil then cook slowly in very little moisture, covered.

Cream: To beat softened butter with sugar until light, fluffy and creamy in colour.

Cut in: Use a knife, pastry blender or food processor to combine fat with flour to get a crumb-like consistencey.

Fold: Combining a delicate mixture with a heavier one by using a metal spoon in a cutting action, cutting down through centre and bringing bottom mixture to top. Used for additions of whipped cream and beaten egg whites.

Frothy: When making white sauce heat butter and flour until mixture appears frothy with small bubbles before adding liquid.

Jelly bag: A muslin or fine cloth bag that can be hung to allow jelly to drain through when preserving (refer to page 231 for more details).

Knead: Non-yeast doughs — press together quickly to combine, eg pastry, biscuits and scone doughs. Yeast doughs — are stretched and folded to develop elasticity.

Marinate: To leave meat, poultry or fish in a tenderising or flavouring liquid (the marinade) for a period of time.

Mash: Food is crushed until soft. This can be done with a fork or a potato masher.

Pan-grill — To heat a dry, heavy-based frying pan until very hot. Add oiled meat.

Purée: Mashed or sieved cooked fruit or vegetable to give a smooth semi-liquid product.

Rub in: To mix fat into flour by rubbing with fingers to get a crumb-like mixture.

Sauté: To fry food in a small amount of hot oil quickly, shaking and stirring the pan to get even cooking.

Setting test for jam: Jam has reached its setting point and is ready for bottling when a small amount is placed on a cold saucer and left to cool. The surface wrinkles when touched and will hold a channel when a finger is dragged through it.

Sieve: To pass through a mesh to get an even consistency.

Sift: To pass dry ingredients through a mesh to remove lumps, foreign matter or to mix evenly.

Simmer: To cook just at boiling point, not a full rolling boil.

Skim: To remove fat or scum from the surface of a liquid with a slotted spoon, spoon or absorbent paper.

Spoons: A wooden spoon is used for stirring a heated mixture, as it does not become too hot to handle. It does not discolour pale mixtures as a metal one can do by scraping against the metal of the saucepan. Metal spoons, solid or slotted, are used for transferring foods; slotted ones will allow liquids to drain from solids. Slotted spoons are useful for folding mixtures together.

Steep: To leave food or flavouring to stand in liquid to absorb flavours.

Stir-fry: To stir and toss prepared ingredients in hot oil very quickly, resulting in moist meats and crisp vegetables.

Stiffly beaten egg white: Beaten until peaks formed hold their shape, but tips bend over. Mixture should be glossy.

To cover steamed puddings: Tear a sheet of foil about 5 cm larger than the top of the basin. Make a pleat right across the sheet of foil. Cover basin with foil. Tie string very tightly around pudding basin just under the lip. Take a separate piece of string about 40 cm in length and fold in half. Secure the string at opposite ends of the basin to make a handle. This helps to get the pudding basin in and out of the saucepan.

HYGIENE IN THE KITCHEN

Poor hygiene and poor food storage can cause illness and waste. Here are some simple rules to follow:

- **Wash hands** before starting to prepare food and ensure that your work area is clean.
- **Clean chopping board** with hot soapy water after cutting raw meat.
- **Clean knives** that have been used for raw meat or fish before cutting other food. This prevents bacteria from uncooked food being transferred to cooked food.
- **After cutting onions and garlic**, wash knives to prevent transferring of flavours. If possible keep one board separate for chopping strong-flavoured foods.
- **Cooked meats and fish** must be cooled quickly and refrigerated without delay.
- **Egg dishes and custards** must be refrigerated without delay once cool.
- **Always reheat food thoroughly**. When reheating food ensure it is brought to boiling point, not just warmed.

STORAGE

- **Perishable foods** such as fish, meat, poultry and dairy produce should be stored in the refrigerator. Keep raw meat separate from cooked meat, ie store raw meat at the bottom of the refrigerator to stop liquid from dripping onto cooked food . Remove plastic wrapping from pre-packaged meats to allow air to circulate and cover loosely.
- **Cover food** to avoid drying out and the transfer of strong flavours.
- **Green and soft vegetables** should be stored in the crisper section of the refrigerator. Soft and short-life fruits should also be stored in the refrigerator.
- **Potatoes and kumara** should be stored in a cool, dark place.
- **Do not store** potatoes, kumara, bananas or unripe avocados in refrigerator.
- **Store pantry goods** such as rice, rolled oats, dry breadcrumbs and flour in clean sealed containers.
- **Edmonds products** should be stored in a cool, dry place.
- **Freezer storage** — see pages 248 and 249.

GOOD NUTRITION

Food is vital to life. It supplies the materials necessary to grow, gives us energy for activity, replaces worn out and damaged parts, and allows us to function normally. Good nutrition makes a difference to how we work, play sport and enjoy our lives. There is no magic food for good health and no supplement can replace a normal balanced diet.

Many people are confused about diet, nutrition and weight loss. It has long been assumed that if people ate enough food they would receive all the nutrients they need. Scientific studies now tell us we can no longer think this way. Currently the New Zealand diet is not only too high in fat and salt but too low in fibre and complex carbohydrates (wholegrain cereal), calcium and iron.

There are many theories about what we should and should not eat. The problem is often too much of the wrong food rather than not enough of the right kind. Excess kilojoules (or calories) and high intakes of salt and fat are common problems. The 1990 Hillary Commission 'Life in New Zealand' survey reported a decrease in the amount of fat and cholesterol eaten by the New Zealanders involved in the survey. However, levels remain above those recommended for optimum health even though many of us have attempted to improve our diets by cutting back our intake of fat and eating more fruit and vegetables. People now are prepared to make changes to their diet because they want to feel better.

Our meal patterns have changed over the years. Many people no longer eat three meals a day. Some people eat small amounts throughout the day (grazing) and a fried cooked breakfast is no longer common. Instead, cereals and milk or toast provide the start to the day. People who skip breakfast may eat high fat, high sugar, high kilojoule snacks mid-morning because they are hungry. This is not recommended. Breakfast should provide carbohydrates from bread, cereal (preferably wholegrain varieties) and fruit, protein from dairy foods such as milk or yoghurt (preferably low fat) and a small serving of fats (preferably unsaturated).

Lunch may vary greatly depending on what foods are available at the school canteen, local dairy, or coffee shop. Food choices can be very limited if lunch is late. But remember that lunch should provide you with about one-third of the day's energy intake. Some people skip lunch, or eat very lightly, then arrive home in the evening feeling hungry and with low energy levels. Often a large 'snack' is eaten at this time.

Many people feel guilty about snacking. However, healthy snacking can provide valuable nutrients. The bottom line is what you eat. Fruit, plain popcorn, low fat yoghurt, low fat milk drinks, sandwiches, juice, muffins and soup provide more useful nutrients than soda drinks, lollies, ice blocks, and candy bars. Active people find snacking a useful way to meet their increased energy needs, as do growing teenagers. Choose the right snacks and do not wait until the last minute before deciding what to eat. Plan ahead just as you would plan your day. Make snacks part of your eating plan, not an added extra.

Healthy eating cannot guarantee good health. Illness and disease result from many factors. Good health relies on family history, lifestyle, environment, mental health and exercise. Good nutrition equips the body to fight attacks from disease. Healthy eating does not mean one has to become a fanatic or deny oneself favourite foods. But remember that no one food provides all the nutrients needed for adults. No single food will cause weight loss or weight gain. The total intake is what counts. Good nutrition means balance, variety and moderation.

BALANCE

The body needs over 40 nutrients to function properly. These include carbohydrates (starches and sugars), protein (meat, eggs, milk), fats (oils, margarine, butter), and vitamins and minerals. While the body can produce some vitamins (Vitamin D from the action of sunlight on the skin and some Vitamin K from gut bacteria), the vast majority need to be supplied by the food we eat. While no food needs to be forbidden, some foods do need a higher profile than others. For example, women should consume adequate intakes of calcium-rich foods (dairy products, tinned fish) to reduce the risk of developing osteoporosis (thinning of bone) and they should eat foods high in iron (lean red meats) to prevent anaemia (low levels of iron in blood).

Food and Nutrition Guidelines for New Zealanders (from the NZ Ministry of Health)
1. Maintain a healthy body weight by eating well and by daily physical activity
2. Eat well by including a variety of nutritious foods from each of the four major food groups each day
   - vegetables and fruit
   - breads and cereals, preferably wholegrain
   - milk and dairy products, especially reduced or low fat varieties
   - lean meats, poultry, seafood, eggs or alternatives
3. Prepare foods or choose pre-prepared foods, drinks and snacks that are low in fat (especially saturated fat), salt and sugar
4. Drink plenty of liquids each day, especially water
5. If choosing to drinking alcohol, limit your intake
6. Purchase, prepare, cook and store food to ensure food safety

HEALTHY FOOD PYRAMID

New Zealanders should eat more from the fruit, vegetable, bread and cereal group (especially the wholegrain types). These foods should be balanced with moderate servings of lean meats, skinned chicken, fish, low-fat dairy products, eggs, dried beans, nuts and seeds. Sugar, added fat, salt, and alcohol should only play a small role. It is not necessary to totally ban these foods.

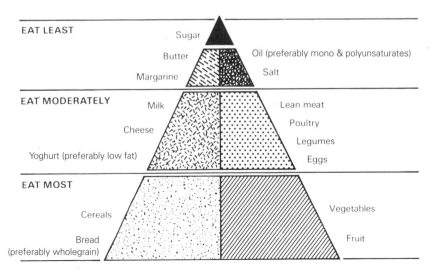

VARIETY

New Zealand has a plentiful food supply. To obtain the balance of nutrients for the body to function and perform correctly, a variety of foods is essential. The body must receive a regular supply of all nutrients. Different foods provide different nutrients (see table). Some nutrients taken in large amounts can even be harmful (this can occur with high doses of some supplements such as Vitamin A). Variety helps to keep food and meals interesting. People become bored eating the same food day in and day out. While everyone needs to eat to survive, food should also be enjoyable. There are many tasty new ways to prepare old favourites and new foods now available. Studies suggest people are prepared to change their diet if they can be convinced it will still taste good.

FOOD GROUP	MAJOR NUTRIENTS	MINIMUM DAILY AMOUNTS
Bread, cereals, rice and pasta (especially wholegrain varieties)	Carbohydrate, dietary fibre, Vitamins E and B group vitamins thiamin, riboflavin, niacin, B6 and folate. Some iron, calcium, zinc and magnesium	6 servings (more for active individuals) — include wholegrain foods E.g. 1 bread roll, 1 slice bread, 1 cup pasta
Fruits and vegetables (fresh, canned, frozen, dried)	Carbohydrate, dietary fibre, some potassium, calcium and iron. Magnesium, Vitamins A and B group Vitamins riboflavin, niacin, biotin, B6 and folate	3 servings vegetables (at least one green leafy vegetable) 2 servings fruit (at least one citrus fruit) E.g. 1 apple, orange, banana, pear, 1 medium potato, $\frac{1}{2}$ cup cooked vegetables
Lean meat, eggs, fish, chicken, dried beans or nuts and seeds	Protein, fat, iron, zinc, copper, selenium, calcium, phosphorus, riboflavin, protein, zinc, Vitamin A and B group Vitamins niacin, pantothenic acid, biotin, B6, folate and B12	1 serving (75–100 g) 1 egg 1 half chicken breast 2 slices cooked meat
Milk, cheese, yoghurt (particularly low or reduced fat varieties)	Calcium, phosphorus, protein, zinc, Vitamin A, D and B group Vitamins riboflavin and B12	Choose 2 servings Adults 1 large cup milk Children 2 large cups milk 2 slices cheese (40 g) 1 tub yoghurt
Margarine, spreads, oils (particularly mono-unsaturated or poly-unsaturated varieties)	Fat soluble Vitamins A, D, E. Essential fatty acids Omega 3 and 6	2 to 4 tablespoons daily

MODERATION

Moderation, in this case, means portion control. Select smaller servings of food that are higher in kilojoules, fat or salt. Examples include buying portion packs (helps control intake), sharing a serving of treat foods with a friend, adding salads and fresh vegetables to takeaway meals served at home, diluting alcoholic and soda drinks with lots of ice, having a drink of water in between each alcoholic drink and drinking water before getting thirsty.

For changes to be permanent they must be made slowly. Too often people make a radical abrupt change to their 'unhealthy' diet. They may deny themselves favourite foods, suffer torment while others eat treats and feel guilty after eating even the smallest nibble. As a result of the way they feel these people are unlikely to stick to their new eating habits. It is easier to make changes gradually by cutting back on serving sizes and limiting treats to once a week or one small serving.

To assist with weight loss and reduce the risk of developing heart disease, high blood pressure, diabetes and some types of cancer, reduce the intake of fat added to foods and limit foods high in fat or oils. You cannot avoid all fats.

Guidelines for preparing food with less added fat
- **Use low fat** milk, yoghurt and cottage cheese, and if using dairy products such as cheese, sour cream and cream cheese in cooking, choose the lower fat or 'lite' varieties.
- **Choose reduced or low fat dressings**, or use salad dressing and mayonnaise in smaller amounts
- **Steam, bake or microwave vegetables** for maximum flavour. Dry roast or use the minimum of vegetable oil and use herbs for additional flavour.
- **Grill, bake, steam, poach, stir-fry or microwave food** where possible rather than frying or roasting in fat.
- **Use vegetable oils** (such as olive, canola or sunflower) instead of animal fats (butter, lard, dripping) and use less.
- **Choose lean cuts of meat** such as trim pork, lean beef and lamb, and lean mince. Trim any visible fat from meat before cooking. Remove the fat and rind from bacon before cooking.
- **Remove the skin and fat from chicken** before eating.
- **Skim the fat off** stews, gravies and soups before serving.
- **Use small amounts** of oil, margarine or butter for cooking and as spreads.
- **When eating out**, ask for dishes that are not cooked in fat, avoid fatty sauces and ask for dressings to be served separately.

Guidelines to using less salt
- **Use herbs, spices, garlic and lemon juice** instead of salt, for flavour.
- Use sauces, packet soups, vegetable stocks, and salad dressings in small amounts occasionally, or choose lower salt types.
- **Add less or no salt to cooking**. Eat meals without adding salt at the table and try to taste your food before adding any salt.
- Choose **canned foods** such as fish and vegetables that are packed in water rather than brine.

Guidelines for reducing sugar
Many high-fat foods are also high in sugar.
- **Have cakes and biscuits only occasionally**. Fill up instead on fresh fruit, wholegrain breads and cereals.
- **Keep chocolate bars and sweets for treats.**
- **Read labels** and look out for sugars listed as fructose, glucose, sucrose and honey.

Guidelines for increasing iron
- **Choose lean meats, chicken and seafood**. The iron in these foods, and especially from lean red meats and organ meats such as liver, is easily absorbed. Iron from vegetables, cooked dried beans, peas, lentils and cereal grains is less easily absorbed.
- **Add fresh fruits and vegetables that are high in Vitamin C** (such as citrus fruits, kiwifruit and tomatoes) to meals to help absorb iron.

Guidelines for including more calcium
Calcium is important for strong bones and for reducing the risk of osteoporosis.
- **Cook with and eat a variety of low fat dairy products** such as milk, yoghurt and cheeses (edam, feta, goats cheese, mozzarella, ricotta and cottage cheese are lower fat). Other foods which will provide calcium are canned fish containing bones (e.g. salmon), wholegrains and green leafy vegetables and citrus.
- **Vitamin D** is important for helping the body absorb more calcium so getting plenty of fresh air and some sunshine (always wear sunscreen) and having foods rich in vitamin D from oily fish like sardines and tuna, liver, and butter, oils or margarine.

Food is fuel for the body — fuel for muscles, tissue growth and cell repair. Carbohydrate foods provide a more effective fuel source for muscle energy than fats. For busy lifestyles we need to eat more of these foods: rice, pasta, bread, potatoes, cereals, fruit, vegetables and less fats (butter, oil, margarine). Take time to develop a good attitude towards your nutrition and you will have more energy to cope with a busy lifestyle. Don't forget to exercise. The best part of exercising and eating a healthy diet is that it makes you feel good. You should and can feel full of energy. Upgrading your diet is a great way to start.

Spaghetti Bolognese (pg 106), Steamed Vegetables (pg 163) and orange juice

BREADS AND BUNS

HINTS FOR BREADMAKING

Edmonds High Grade Flour is recommended for breadmaking. This flour has a high protein (gluten) content and ensures that the dough has sufficient strength to give the bread good volume and texture.

- **Temperature** is important in yeast baking. Yeast works best at 37°C (blood temperature). A high temperature will kill the yeast and too low a temperature will cause the yeast to work slowly.
- There are three types of yeast:
  1. **Edmonds Surebake** — a mixture of active dry yeast and bread improvers blended specially for easy breadmaking. This gives homemade bread a soft, fine crumb. Surebake is also recommended for use in breadmaking machines.
  2. **Edmonds Active Yeast** — dried yeast granules which become active when water, heat and flour or sugar are added. The yeast then produces carbon dioxide gas which causes the bread dough to rise.
  3. **Compressed Yeast** — not readily available.
- **Conversions for yeast products:**
  1. Replace 1 tablespoon Edmonds active yeast with 2 tablespoons Edmonds Surebake.
  2. Replace 1 sachet of dried yeast with 1½ tablespoons of Edmonds Active Yeast or 3 tablespoons of Edmonds Surebake.
  3. Replace 25 g or 1 cake compressed yeast with 1½ tablespoons of Edmonds Active Yeast or 3 tablespoons of Edmonds Surebake.
- **Using Edmonds Surebake** — the traditional sponging method is not required.
  1. In a large bowl, mix half the measured flour with the Surebake and other dry ingredients.
  2. Add ½ the quantity of liquid cold (ie water or milk) followed quickly by ½ the quantity as boiling water. Add any butter at this stage. Stir to a smooth paste and stand 2–3 minutes.
  3. Mix in remaining dry ingredients and proceed with the method as directed.

Ingredients:
- **Ascorbic Acid (Vitamin C)** — can be added in yeast cookery to speed up the rising of the dough. The powder form is easier to use than tablets.
- **Sugar** helps feed the yeast and aids the browning and flavour of bread — white and brown sugar, honey, golden syrup, treacle or molasses can be used.
- **Milk and butter** improve the softness of bread and fresh-keeping qualities.
- **Spices, seeds, herbs and grated cheese** can be added with the butter before kneading. Fruits or nuts should be added towards the end of kneading.

Proving:
- **Using the oven** — preheat to 50°C after placing a dish of hot water on the bottom of the rack. Turn oven off. Brush the top of dough with oil or melted butter and cover. Leave to prove for about 30 minutes or until dough has doubled in size before taking dough out.
- **Using the microwave** — brush the top of dough with oil or melted butter and cover loosely with plastic wrap. Microwave for ten minutes on 10% power. Stand for 10 minutes then repeat until dough has doubled in size.

APPLE BREAD

3 cups Edmonds *standard plain flour*
1/2 teaspoon salt
3 teaspoons Edmonds *baking powder*

1 tablespoon sugar
1/2 cup grated apple
1 to 1 1/2 cups milk, approximately

Sift flour, salt and baking powder into a bowl. Stir in sugar. Add apple and enough milk to make a soft, smooth dough, mixing all together quickly. Place in a greased 22 cm loaf tin. Bake at 180°C for 1 hour or until the loaf sounds hollow when tapped on base of bread. When cooked, remove from tin and wrap in a teatowel or paper towels until cold.

CHEESE BREAD
Add 1/2 cup grated tasty cheese and pinch of cayenne to sifted ingredients. Replace apple with 1/2 cup grated potato.

BREADMAKER LOAVES

The following tested breadmaker recipe is designed to work in any machine. It will make a large white (750 g) loaf. Halve the ingredients to make a 375 g loaf. Use the recipe most appropriate to the size of your bread pan.

If the crust is not completely baked (soft and pale) on the top, reduce the water measurement by 2 tablespoons for your next loaf. If the crust is uneven and knotted on the top, increase the water measurement by 2 tablespoons for subsequent loaves.

4 teaspoons Edmonds Surebake
4 cups Edmonds *high grade flour*
1 tablespoon milk powder
2 teaspoons sugar

1 teaspoon salt
2 tablespoons butter
1 1/3 cups (330 ml) warm water

Put the ingredients into the bread pan in the order listed. Select the appropriate setting for a large white loaf. Press start.
Makes one 750 g loaf.

BROWN BREAD (NO-KNEAD)

1st EDITION RECIPE

1 cup kibbled wheat
1 cup boiling water
2 cups Edmonds *wholemeal flour*
2 teaspoon salt
2 tablespoons Edmonds *Surebake*

1 cup cold water
1 tablespoon golden syrup
1 cup boiling water
1 egg
3 cups Edmonds *high grade flour*

Combine kibbled wheat and boiling water. Set aside for 20 minutes. Put wholemeal flour, salt, and yeast in a bowl and stir together. Add cold water and golden syrup, immediately followed by boiling water. Stir to a smooth paste and stand 2 to 3 minutes. Mix in egg and flour, adding the last cup of white flour slowly (more or less than the cup may be needed to give a very thick batter, which is not quite as stiff as a dough). Beat with an electric mixer — medium speed for 1 to 2 minutes or by hand for 3 to 4 minutes. Cover and put in a warm place for 15 minutes. Stir well and pour into two 22 cm greased loaf tins. Put in a warm place until the dough doubles in volume. Bake at 200°C for 35 minutes or until the loaf sounds hollow when tapped on base of bread. If loaf is browning too quickly cover with foil.
Makes 2 loaves.

CHELSEA BUNS

1st EDITION RECIPE

$^{1}/_{4}$ cup warm water
$^{1}/_{2}$ teaspoon sugar
2 teaspoons Edmonds active yeast
3$^{1}/_{2}$ cups Edmonds high grade flour

1 teaspoon salt
1 tablespoon sugar
$^{3}/_{4}$ cup warm milk
3 tablespoons melted butter

FILLING
50 g butter, softened
$^{1}/_{2}$ cup brown sugar
1$^{1}/_{2}$ cups mixed fruit

1 teaspoon cinnamon
$^{1}/_{2}$ teaspoon mixed spice

GLAZE
1 tablespoon sugar
1 tablespoon water

1 teaspoon gelatine

Place warm water and first measure of sugar in a small bowl. Stir to dissolve sugar. Sprinkle yeast over and leave for 10 minutes or until frothy. Combine 3 cups of the flour and salt in a large bowl. Stir in second measure of sugar. Set the remaining $^{1}/_{2}$ cup flour aside. Make a well in the centre of dry ingredients. Pour in milk, butter and frothy yeast mixture. Beat with a wooden spoon until mixture forms a ball, adding more flour if necessary. Turn out onto a lightly floured surface. Knead dough until smooth and elastic. Lightly brush bowl with oil. Place dough in bowl. Lightly brush with oil. Leave in a warm place until doubled in size. Punch dough down in the centre. Lightly knead then roll dough out to a 30 × 25 cm rectangle. Spread dough with filling. Roll up like a sponge roll. Using string, cut into 12 even-sized pieces. Arrange in a greased 25 cm sponge sandwich tin, nine around outside edge and three in the centre. Cover and leave in a warm place until double in size. Bake at 190°C for 25 minutes or until golden. Brush with glaze while hot. Makes 12.

FILLING
Cream butter and sugar together. Stir in mixed fruit and spices.

GLAZE
Put all ingredients in a saucepan. Heat until sugar and gelatine have dissolved, stirring constantly.

HOT CROSS BUNS

1 1/2 cups milk
1 teaspoon sugar
1 tablespoon butter
2 teaspoons Edmonds *active yeast*
4 1/2 cups Edmonds *high grade flour*
1 teaspoon salt
1 teaspoon cinnamon

1/2 teaspoon mixed spice
1/2 teaspoon ground nutmeg
2 teaspoons sugar
3/4 cup sultanas
3/4 cup currants
1/4 cup chopped mixed peel

CROSSES
1/2 cup Edmonds *high grade flour*   6 tablespoons water

GLAZE
1 tablespoon sugar   1 teaspoon gelatine
1 tablespoon water

Heat milk until almost boiling. Stir in first measure of sugar and butter until butter melts. Set aside until lukewarm. Sprinkle yeast over and leave in a warm place for 15 minutes or until frothy. Combine 4 cups of the flour, salt, cinnamon, mixed spice and nutmeg in a bowl. Stir in second measure of sugar. Make a well in the centre of dry ingredients. Pour yeast mixture in. Beat to a soft dough, adding more flour if the dough is sticky. Mix in sultanas, currants and mixed peel. Turn onto a lightly floured board. Knead until smooth and elastic or until dough springs back when lightly touched. Lightly brush bowl with oil. Place dough in bowl. Brush top with oil. Cover and leave in a warm place until double in size. Punch dough down in the centre and knead lightly. Divide mixture into 16 even-sized pieces. Shape into balls. Place buns 2 cm apart on a greased oven tray. Cover and leave in a warm place until double in size. Pipe crosses on each bun. Bake at 200°C for 20 minutes or until golden. Remove from oven and brush with glaze. Cool on a wire rack. Makes 16.

CROSSES
Mix flour and water together until smooth and able to be piped. More water may be needed. Place mixture into a small plastic bag. Snip across one corner to form a hole for piping. Twist top of bag to hold dough firm, and squeeze to pipe.

GLAZE
Put all ingredients in a saucepan. Heat until sugar and gelatine have dissolved, stirring constantly.

WHITE BREAD

5 cups Edmonds *high grade flour*
1 teaspoon sugar
1 teaspoon salt
2 tablespoons Edmonds *Surebake*

³/₄ cup cold water
2 tablespoons oil
³/₄ cup boiling water
oil

EGG WASH
1 egg yolk

1 tablespoon water

Combine 2 cups of the flour, sugar, salt and yeast in a large bowl. Add cold water and oil, immediately followed by boiling water. Stir to a smooth paste and stand 2 to 3 minutes. Gradually mix 2 cups of flour into the yeast mixture.

When flour is mixed in, turn out onto a lightly floured surface, using part of the reserved cup of flour for this. Knead dough until smooth and elastic. If the dough is still sticky, add a little of the remaining measured flour, kneading until smooth and elastic, or until dough springs back when lightly touched. Lightly brush large bowl with oil. Place dough in bowl. Brush top with a little oil. Cover. Put in a warm place until double in size. Punch dough down in the centre. Carefully take dough out of bowl and turn onto a lightly floured surface. Knead for 5 minutes. Divide dough in half. Shape each portion into a ball. Place the two balls side by side in a greased deep 22 cm loaf tin. Cover. Leave in a warm place until double in size or until dough reaches top of tin. Brush surface of dough with egg wash. If wished, sesame seeds, oat bran or poppy seeds can be sprinkled on top. Bake at 200°C for 30 minutes or until loaf sounds hollow when tapped on base of bread.

EGG WASH
Combine egg yolk and water.

Use stale bread to make croûtons or melba toast. Store in an airtight container.
Serve with soups, pâtés or salads.

WHOLEMEAL BREAD

1¹/₄ cups hot water
¹/₄ cup honey
³/₄ cup milk
1 tablespoon Edmonds *active yeast*
4 cups Edmonds *wholemeal flour*

2 cups Edmonds *high grade flour*
1¹/₂ teaspoons salt
50 g butter

Combine hot water, honey and milk. Leave to cool until lukewarm. Sprinkle yeast over and leave for 10 minutes or until frothy. Combine 3 cups of the wholemeal flour, high grade flour and salt in a bowl. Set remaining cup of flour aside. Cut in butter until it resembles coarse breadcrumbs. Make a well in the centre of the flour. Add frothy yeast mixture. Stir until well mixed. Turn out onto a lightly floured surface, using part of the reserved cup of flour for this. Knead the dough until smooth and elastic. If it is still sticky, add a little of the reserved flour, kneading until smooth or until dough springs back when lightly touched. Lightly oil a bowl. Place dough in bowl and brush lightly with oil. Cover and leave in a warm place until double in size. Punch dough down in the centre, then lightly knead. Divide dough in half. Shape into ovals. Place dough into two greased 22 cm loaf tins. Cover and leave until dough rises to top of tins. Bake at 200°C for 40 minutes or until loaf sounds hollow when tapped on base of bread.

Top: Wholemeal Bread (pg 26), Centre: Chelsea Buns (pg 23),
Bottom Right: Muffins (pg 33), Bottom Left: Hot Cross Buns (pg 24)

BANANA LOAF

1³/₄ cups Edmonds *self-raising flour*
¹/₄ teaspoon Edmonds *baking soda*
¹/₄ teaspoon salt
¹/₂ cup sugar

2 eggs
¹/₄ cup milk
75 g butter, melted
1 cup mashed banana

Sift flour, baking soda and salt into a bowl. Mix in sugar. In another bowl beat eggs. Stir in milk, butter and banana. Mix quickly into dry ingredients, stirring until ingredients are just combined. Spoon into a greased and lined 22 cm loaf tin. Bake at 180°C for 45 to 55 minutes. Leave in tin for 10 minutes before turning out onto a wire rack.

BRAN MUFFINS

1 cup Edmonds *standard plain flour*
1 teaspoon Edmonds *baking powder*
¹/₂ teaspoon salt
¹/₄ cup sugar
1¹/₂ cups bran flakes

1 tablespoon golden syrup
1 tablespoon butter
1 teaspoon Edmonds *baking soda*
1 cup milk
1 egg, beaten

Sift flour, baking powder and salt into a bowl. Mix in sugar and bran. Melt golden syrup and butter together. Dissolve soda in milk. Add these with the egg to the dry ingredients. Mix quickly, just enough to combine. Spoon into cold greased muffin tins. Bake at 220°C for 12 minutes or until golden brown.
Makes 12.

CHEESY OAT LOAF

2 eggs
1¹/₄ cups milk
¹/₄ cup oil
¹/₂ teaspoon salt
1 tablespoon sugar
1 cup rolled oats

1 cup bran flakes
1¹/₂ cups grated tasty cheese
1 cup Edmonds *wholemeal flour*
¹/₂ cup Edmonds *standard plain flour*
4 teaspoons Edmonds *baking powder*

Beat the eggs in a bowl with milk and oil. Add salt, sugar, oats, bran, cheese and wholemeal flour. Sift in flour and baking powder. Mix well to combine. Spoon into a greased and lined 22 cm loaf tin. Bake at 180°C for 45 to 50 minutes or until loaf springs back when lightly touched. Leave in tin for 10 minutes before turning out onto a wire rack.

CORNMEAL MUFFINS

125 g butter
1 cup medium-ground cornmeal
3/4 cup milk
1 cup Edmonds *standard plain flour*

3 teaspoons Edmonds *baking powder*
1/2 teaspoon salt
1/4 cup sugar
1 egg, beaten

Put butter, cornmeal and milk into a saucepan. Heat until butter has melted, stirring occasionally. Allow cornmeal mixture to cool. Sift flour, baking powder and salt into a bowl. Stir in sugar. Add egg to dry ingredients. Stir in cornmeal mixture. Stir to just combine. Spoon mixture into greased muffin tins. Bake at 190°C for 15 to 20 minutes or until golden.
Makes 12.

CHEESE MUFFINS
Omit sugar. Halve the butter. Add 1/2 cup grated tasty cheese and pinch of cayenne pepper.

DATE LOAF

1 cup chopped dates
1 cup boiling water
1 teaspoon Edmonds *baking soda*
1 tablespoon butter
1 cup brown sugar

1 egg, beaten
1 cup chopped walnuts
1/4 teaspoon vanilla essence
2 cups Edmonds *standard plain flour*
1 teaspoon Edmonds *baking powder*

Put dates, water, soda and butter into a bowl. Stir until butter has melted. Set aside for 1 hour. Beat sugar, egg, walnuts and vanilla into date mixture. Sift flour and baking powder into date mixture, stirring just to combine. Pour mixture into a greased 22 cm loaf tin. Bake at 180°C for 45 minutes or until loaf springs back when lightly touched. Leave in tin for 10 minutes before turning out onto a wire rack.

APRICOT LOAF
Replace dates with apricots.

FRESH LEMON LOAF

125 g butter
3/4 cup sugar
1 teaspoon grated lemon rind
2 eggs

2 cups Edmonds *self-raising flour*
1/4 teaspoon salt
1/2 cup milk
1/4 cup chopped walnuts

GLAZE
1/4 cup lemon juice

1/4 cup sugar

Cream butter, sugar and lemon rind in a bowl until light and fluffy. Add eggs and beat well. Sift flour, salt and stir in alternately with milk. Mix in nuts. Turn into a greased and lined 22 cm loaf tin. Bake at 180°C for 45 to 50 minutes or until loaf springs back when lightly touched. Pour glaze over loaf. Leave in tin until cold.

GLAZE
Stir lemon juice and sugar in a saucepan over a low heat until sugar dissolves. Bring to the boil. Remove from heat and leave to cool.

Avoid overmixing muffins and gems as this produces peaked instead of rounded tops and a tunnelled rather than an even texture.

FRUIT LOAF

2 cups Edmonds *standard plain flour*
¼ teaspoon salt
2 teaspoons Edmonds *baking powder*
50 g butter
½ cup sugar

1 cup dried fruit — *e.g. raisins, dates,*
sultanas
1 egg, *beaten*
1 cup *milk*

Sift flour, salt and baking powder into a bowl. Cut in butter until it resembles coarse breadcrumbs. Add sugar and fruit. Make into a soft dough with egg and milk. Pour into a greased 22 cm loaf tin. Bake at 180°C for 1 hour or until loaf springs back when lightly touched. Leave in tin for 10 minutes before turning out onto a wire rack.

FRUIT MUFFINS

1 egg
¼ cup oil
½ cup sugar
1 cup *milk*
2 cups Edmonds *standard plain flour*

4 teaspoons Edmonds *baking powder*
1 teaspoon *cinnamon*
1 cup *fresh or frozen blueberries,*
blackcurrants or chopped apple
icing sugar

Beat egg, oil, sugar and milk together in a bowl. Sift flour, baking powder and cinnamon into egg mixture. Add fruit and mix lightly to just combine. Spoon mixture into greased muffin tins. Bake at 200°C for 15 minutes or until golden. Dust with icing sugar before serving.
Makes 12.

GEMS

25 g butter, melted
2 tablespoons *brown sugar*
1 tablespoon *honey*
1 egg
1 cup Edmonds *standard plain flour*

1½ teaspoons Edmonds *baking*
powder
pinch of *salt*
½ cup milk
extra butter

Preheat gem irons in oven at 200°C. Mix butter, sugar and honey together in a bowl. Beat in egg. Sift flour, baking powder and salt together. Add to butter mixture with milk. Mix lightly. Put ½ teaspoon pieces of butter in hot gem irons and spoon mixture into sizzling butter. Bake at 200°C for 12 minutes or until golden brown.
Makes 15.

GINGER GEMS

50 g butter
1/4 cup sugar
1 1/2 teaspoons ground ginger
1 egg
2 tablespoons golden syrup

1 cup Edmonds *standard plain flour*
1 teaspoon Edmonds *baking soda*
1/2 cup milk
extra butter

Preheat gem irons in oven at 200°C. Cream butter, sugar and ginger in a bowl until light and fluffy. Add egg, beating well. Beat in syrup. Sift flour into creamed mixture. Stir to combine. Dissolve soda in milk. Quickly stir into creamed mixture. Put 1/2 teaspoon pieces of butter into hot gem irons and spoon mixture into sizzling butter. Bake at 200°C for 10 minutes or until well risen and golden brown. Makes 12.

GINGERBREAD LOAF

1 cup Edmonds *standard plain flour*
pinch of salt
1 tablespoon ground ginger
1 tablespoon cinnamon
1 cup rolled oats
2 eggs

1/2 cup sugar
50 g butter
2 tablespoons golden syrup
1 1/2 teaspoons Edmonds *baking soda*
3/4 cup natural unsweetened yoghurt
1/2 cup sultanas

Sift flour, salt, ginger and cinnamon into a bowl. Add rolled oats. In a separate bowl beat eggs and sugar until thick and fluffy. Melt butter and golden syrup and cool slightly. Add to egg and sugar mixture. Fold in dry ingredients. In a small bowl dissolve baking soda in the yoghurt. Stir into the loaf mixture with sultanas until well combined. Turn into a greased 22 cm loaf tin. Bake at 180°C for 55 minutes or until loaf springs back when lightly touched. Leave in tin for 10 minutes before turning out onto a wire rack.

GIRDLE SCONES

1st EDITION RECIPE

1 cup Edmonds *standard plain flour*
2 teaspoons Edmonds *baking powder*
pinch of salt

1 tablespoon butter
1/2 cup milk, approximately

Sift flour, baking powder and salt together in a bowl. Cut butter in until it resembles fine breadcrumbs. Add sufficient milk to make a fairly soft dough. On a lightly floured board roll out to 1 cm thickness. Make into a round and cut into eight wedges. Cook on a hot greased girdle or non-stick frying pan for about 5 minutes on each side, or until browned and well risen.

HEALTH LOAF

$^1/_2$ cup Edmonds *standard plain flour*
$^1/_2$ cup bran flakes
$^1/_2$ cup Edmonds *wholemeal flour*
$^1/_2$ cup chopped dates
$^1/_4$ cup chopped walnuts
$^1/_4$ teaspoon salt
1 egg

2 tablespoons sugar
$^1/_4$ cup golden syrup, warmed
1 tablespoon melted butter
$^1/_4$ cup milk
$^1/_2$ teaspoon Edmonds *baking soda*
$^1/_4$ cup hot water

Sift flour into a bowl. Add bran, wholemeal flour, dates, walnuts and salt. In a separate bowl beat egg and sugar together. Add syrup, butter and milk. Mix into dry ingredients. Dissolve baking soda in hot water and add. Mix well. Pour into a greased 18 cm loaf tin. Bake at 190°C for 45 minutes or until loaf springs back when lightly touched. Leave in tin for 10 minutes before turning out onto a wire rack.

HONEY TEA BUNS

3 cups Edmonds *standard plain flour*
4 teaspoons Edmonds *baking powder*
$^1/_2$ teaspoon salt
1 teaspoon ground ginger
75 g butter
1 egg, beaten

2 tablespoons liquid honey
1 teaspoon grated orange rind
1 to 1$^1/_4$ cups milk
extra milk to glaze
sugar
cinnamon

Sift flour, baking powder, salt and ginger into a bowl. Cut butter through until it resembles fine breadcrumbs. Add egg, honey and orange rind. Add sufficient milk to mix to a smooth, firm dough. On a lightly floured surface roll out dough to 2.5 cm thickness. Cut into rounds using a 5 cm cutter. Place on a greased oven tray. Brush tops with milk. Sprinkle with sugar and cinnamon. Bake at 200°C for 15 minutes or until pale golden.
Makes 15.

MUFFINS

50 g butter, softened
$^1/_2$ cup brown sugar
1 egg
$^3/_4$ cup Edmonds *wholemeal flour*
$^3/_4$ cup Edmonds *standard plain flour*

1 teaspoon Edmonds *baking powder*
pinch of salt
$^1/_2$ teaspoon Edmonds *baking soda*
$^3/_4$ cup milk

Cream butter and sugar in a bowl. Beat in egg. Sift wholemeal flour, flour, baking powder and salt together. Return husks from sifter to bowl. Dissolve soda in the milk. Add sifted ingredients alternately with soda to the creamed mixture, mixing just to combine. Spoon mixture into greased muffin tins. Bake at 200°C for 12 to 15 minutes.
Makes 12.

APRICOT MUFFINS
Add $^1/_2$ cup chopped apricots to sifted ingredients.

SPICED MUFFINS
Add $^1/_2$ teaspoon cinnamon and $^1/_2$ teaspoon mixed spice to sifted ingredients.

OAT BRAN DATE LOAF

1 cup chopped dates
2 tablespoons golden syrup
1 cup boiling water
1¼ cups Edmonds *standard plain flour*

1 teaspoon Edmonds *baking powder*
1 teaspoon Edmonds *baking soda*
½ cup oat bran
¾ cup brown sugar

Put dates and golden syrup in a bowl. Pour over boiling water and stand for 15 minutes. In another bowl combine the flour, baking powder, baking soda, oat bran and sugar. Fold into date mixture. Spoon into a greased and lined 22 cm loaf tin. Bake at 180°C for 45 to 50 minutes or until loaf springs back when lightly touched. Leave in tin for 10 minutes before turning out onto a wire rack.

OATY APPLE LOAF

125 g butter
1 teaspoon mixed spice
½ teaspoon cinnamon
1 cup brown sugar
2 apples, grated
1 cup sultanas
1 cup water

1 teaspoon Edmonds *baking soda*
2 eggs, beaten
1 cup rolled oats
1½ cups Edmonds *standard plain
   flour*
3 teaspoons Edmonds *baking powder*

Put butter, spice, cinnamon, sugar, apples, sultanas and water into a large saucepan. Bring to the boil, stirring occasionally. Remove from heat and allow to cool. Add soda then beat in eggs and rolled oats. Sift flour and baking powder into the saucepan. Stir to combine. Pour mixture into a greased and lined 22 cm loaf tin. Bake at 180°C for 45 minutes or until loaf springs back when lightly touched. Leave in tin for 10 minutes before turning out onto a wire rack.

PIKELETS

1 cup Edmonds *standard plain flour*
1 teaspoon Edmonds *baking powder*
¼ teaspoon salt

1 egg
¼ cup sugar
¾ cup milk, approximately

Sift flour, baking powder and salt into a bowl. In another bowl beat egg and sugar until thick. Add with milk to the sifted ingredients. Mix until just combined. Drop tablespoonsful of the mixture from the point of spoon onto a hot, lightly greased girdle or non-stick frying pan. Turn pikelets over when bubbles start to burst on top surface. Cook second side until golden.
Makes 8–10.

Overmixing pikelet batter produces tough pikelets.
If pikelets brown unevenly, wipe the cooking surface with a paper towel to
remove excess butter.

SAVOURY CHEESE MUFFINS

1 tablespoon chopped celery
1 tablespoon chopped red or green
   pepper
$^3/_4$ cup grated tasty cheese
2 cups Edmonds standard plain flour
pinch of cayenne pepper

4 teaspoons Edmonds baking powder
$^1/_4$ teaspoon salt
1 egg, beaten
50 g butter, melted
$^1/_2$ cup milk

Put celery, pepper and cheese into a bowl. Sift flour, cayenne, baking powder and salt into the bowl. Stir to combine. Quickly stir in egg, butter and milk just to moisten. Spoon mixture into greased muffin tins. Bake at 200°C for 15 minutes or until golden.
Makes 12.

SCONES

3 cups Edmonds standard plain flour
6 teaspoons Edmonds baking powder
$^1/_4$ teaspoon salt

75 g butter
1 to 1$^1/_2$ cups milk, approximately
extra milk

Sift flour, baking powder and salt into a bowl. Cut butter in until it resembles fine breadcrumbs. Add milk and mix quickly with a knife to a soft dough. Knead a few times. Lightly dust an oven tray with flour. Press scone dough out onto this. Cut into 12 even-sized pieces. Leave a 2 cm space between scones. Brush tops with milk. Bake at 220°C for 10 minutes or until golden brown.
Makes 12.

CHEESE SCONES
Add $^3/_4$ cup grated cheese, pinch each of cayenne pepper and mustard to flour. Before baking top each scone with a small amount of grated cheese.

DATE SCONES
Add $^3/_4$ cup chopped dates, 1 tablespoon sugar and $^1/_2$ teaspoon cinnamon to flour. Before baking sprinkle scones with mixture of cinnamon and sugar.

SULTANA SCONES
Add $^3/_4$ to 1 cup sultanas to flour.

SULTANA OR RAISIN LOAF

1 cup sultanas or raisins
1 tablespoon butter
$^1/_2$ cup sugar
1 tablespoon golden syrup
$^1/_4$ teaspoon salt

1 teaspoon Edmonds baking soda
1 cup boiling water
2 cups Edmonds standard plain flour
1$^1/_2$ teaspoons Edmonds baking powder

Put sultanas, butter, sugar, syrup and salt in a bowl. Sprinkle baking soda over. Add water. When butter has melted sift in flour and baking powder. Mix quickly. Put in a greased 22 cm loaf tin. Bake at 180°C for 40 minutes, or until loaf springs back when lightly touched. Leave in tin for 10 minutes before turning out onto a wire rack.

SULTANA NUT LOAF
Add $^1/_2$ cup chopped walnuts to sifted ingredients.

WHOLEMEAL LOAF

1 cup milk
1 tablespoon golden syrup
100 g butter, melted
2 eggs
1 cup Edmonds *wholemeal flour*
1 cup Edmonds *standard plain flour*

¹/₄ cup Edmonds *wheatgerm*
¹/₄ cup oat bran
1 teaspoon Edmonds *baking powder*
1 teaspoon Edmonds *baking soda*
¹/₂ teaspoon salt

Put milk, golden syrup, butter and eggs in a bowl and mix well. Sift wholemeal flour, flour, wheatgerm, oat bran, baking powder, soda and salt into egg mixture. Return husks left in the sifter to the flour and mix well. Pour into a greased 22 cm loaf tin. Bake at 180°C for 30 minutes or until loaf springs back when lightly touched. Leave in tin for 10 minutes before turning out onto a wire rack.

WHOLEMEAL YOGHURT SCONES

1 cup Edmonds *wholemeal flour*
1 cup Edmonds *standard plain flour*
1 teaspoon Edmonds *baking soda*
3 teaspoons Edmonds *baking powder*
50 g butter

1 teaspoon sugar
¹/₂ cup fruit yoghurt
¹/₄ to ¹/₂ cup milk
extra milk

Sift wholemeal flour, flour, soda and baking powder into a bowl. Return husks left in the sifter to flour in the bowl. Cut butter into flour mixture until it resembles breadcrumbs. Stir in sugar and yoghurt. Add sufficient milk to mix to a soft dough. Lightly dust an oven tray with flour. Press scone dough out to a 20 cm round. Mark into eight wedges. Brush top with milk. Bake at 220°C for 10 minutes or until pale golden.
Makes 8.

AFGHANS

200 g butter, softened
$^1/_2$ cup sugar
1$^1/_4$ cups Edmonds *standard plain flour*
$^1/_4$ cup cocoa

2 cups cornflakes
Chocolate Icing (page 82)
walnuts (optional)

Cream butter and sugar until light and fluffy. Sift flour and cocoa. Stir into creamed mixture. Fold in cornflakes. Spoon mounds of mixture onto a greased oven tray, gently pressing together. Bake at 180°C for 15 minutes or until set. When cold ice with chocolate icing and decorate with a walnut if wished.
Makes 30.

AFGHAN SLICE
Press afghan mixture into a 20 × 30 cm sponge roll tin. Bake at 180°C for 25 minutes or until set. When cold ice with Chocolate Icing.

ALMOND BISCUITS

125 g butter, softened
$^1/_2$ cup sugar
1 egg
$^1/_2$ teaspoon almond essence

1$^1/_2$ cups Edmonds *standard plain flour*
1 teaspoon Edmonds *baking powder*
12 to 15 blanched almonds

Cream butter and sugar until light and fluffy. Add egg and almond essence, beating well. Sift in flour and baking powder. Mix to a firm dough. Roll pieces into balls. Place on a greased oven tray and press lightly with a floured fork. Press half a blanched almond on each. Bake at 180°C for 15 minutes or until cooked.
Makes 25.

ANZAC BISCUITS

$^1/_2$ cup Edmonds *standard plain flour*
$^1/_3$ cup sugar
$^2/_3$ cup coconut
$^3/_4$ cup rolled oats

50 g butter
1 tablespoon golden syrup
$^1/_2$ teaspoon Edmonds *baking soda*
2 tablespoons boiling water

Mix together flour, sugar, coconut and rolled oats. Melt butter and golden syrup. Dissolve baking soda in the boiling water and add to butter and golden syrup. Stir butter mixture into the dry ingredients. Place level tablespoonsful of mixture onto cold greased trays. Bake at 180°C for about 15 minutes or until golden.
Makes 20.

BASIC BISCUITS

125 g butter, softened
3/4 cup sugar
1 teaspoon vanilla essence

1 egg
2 cups Edmonds standard plain flour
1 teaspoon Edmonds baking powder

Cream butter, sugar and vanilla together until light and fluffy. Add egg, beating well. Sift flour and baking powder together and mix into creamed mixture. Roll heaped teaspoonsful of mixture into balls and place on an oven tray. Flatten slightly with a floured fork. Bake at 190°C for about 12 minutes or until pale golden.
Makes about 35.

CHOCOLATE BISCUITS
Add 2 tablespoons cocoa when sifting flour.

ORANGE BISCUITS
Omit vanilla essence and add 1 tablespoon grated orange rind to creamed mixture.

LEMON BISCUITS
Omit vanilla essence and add 2 teaspoons grated lemon rind to creamed mixture.

SPICE BISCUITS
Add 2 teaspoons mixed spice when sifting flour.

SULTANA BISCUITS
Fold 1/2 cup sultanas into creamed mixture.

BELGIUM BISCUITS

125 g butter, softened
1/4 cup brown sugar
1 egg
2 cups Edmonds standard plain flour
1 teaspoon Edmonds baking powder

1 teaspoon cinnamon
1 teaspoon ground ginger
1 teaspoon mixed spice
1 teaspoon cocoa

ICING
3/4 to 1 cup icing sugar
1/4 teaspoon raspberry or vanilla
  essence

few drops red food colouring
water

FILLING
1/2 cup raspberry jam, approximately

Cream butter and sugar until light and fluffy. Add egg and beat well. Sift flour, baking powder, cinnamon, ginger, mixed spice and cocoa together. Mix into creamed mixture to make a firm dough. On a lightly floured board roll dough out to 3 mm thickness. Cut out rounds using a 6.5 cm cutter. Bake at 180°C for 15 minutes or until golden. When cold, ice half the biscuits. Spread the un-iced biscuits with raspberry jam and place iced biscuits on top.
Makes 18.

ICING
Mix icing sugar with flavouring and colouring. Add sufficient water to make a pink icing of spreading consistency.

For crisper biscuits, flatten with a floured fork to about 5–8 mm thickness.

BRAN BISCUITS

125 g butter, softened
1/4 cup sugar
1 egg
1 cup bran flakes

1 cup Edmonds *wholemeal flour*
1 cup Edmonds *standard plain flour*
1 teaspoon Edmonds *baking powder*
pinch of salt

Cream butter and sugar until light and fluffy. Add egg and beat well. Mix in bran and wholemeal flour. Sift flour, baking powder and salt together. Mix into creamed mixture until well combined. Knead a few times. Take small amounts and roll out on a lightly floured surface to 5 to 7 mm thickness. Cut into pieces of about 5 × 8 cm. Bake on a greased oven tray at 180°C for 20 minutes or until set and lightly golden. Serve plain or buttered.
Makes 20.

BRANDY SNAPS

125 g butter, softened
2/3 cup sugar
1/4 cup golden syrup

1 cup Edmonds *standard plain flour*
1 teaspoon ground ginger

Cream butter and sugar. Add syrup, sift in flour, ginger and mix. Drop tablespoons of mixture onto a greased oven tray, no more than four at a time. Allow room for spreading. Bake at 180°C for about 8 minutes or until golden. Cool slightly until able to be removed without collapsing. Slide brandy snaps from tray with a spatula and wrap around the handle of wooden spoon to shape. Cool slightly and slide off. Leave to set.
Makes 30.

CHEESE BISCUITS

1 cup Edmonds *standard plain flour*
1 tablespoon icing sugar
1 teaspoon Edmonds *baking powder*
pinch of salt

pinch of cayenne pepper
25 g butter
1/2 cup grated cheese
3 tablespoons milk, approximately

Sift flour, icing sugar, baking powder, salt and cayenne pepper into a bowl. Cut butter into flour mixture until it resembles fine breadcrumbs. Mix in cheese. Add just enough milk to form a stiff dough. Knead lightly and roll out to 2 mm thickness. Cut into 4 cm squares and place on a greased oven tray. Prick each square with a fork. Bake at 200°C for 10 minutes or until lightly golden.
Makes 25.

CHOCOLATE CHIP BISCUITS

125 g butter, softened
1/4 cup sugar
3 tablespoons sweetened condensed
  milk

few drops vanilla essence
1 1/2 cups Edmonds standard plain flour
1 teaspoon Edmonds baking powder
1/2 cup chocolate chips

Cream butter, sugar, condensed milk and vanilla until light and fluffy. Sift flour and baking powder together. Mix sifted dry ingredients and chocolate chips into creamed mixture. Roll tablespoonsful of mixture into balls. Place on a greased oven tray and flatten with a floured fork. Bake at 180°C for 20 minutes.
Makes 25.

EASTER BISCUITS

2 cups Edmonds standard plain flour
1 teaspoon Edmonds baking powder
125 g butter
1/2 cup sugar

1/4 cup currants
1/4 teaspoon cinnamon
1/4 teaspoon grated lemon rind
1 egg

Sift flour and baking powder into a bowl. Cut in butter until it resembles fine breadcrumbs. Add sugar, currants, cinnamon and lemon rind. Lightly beat egg. Add to dry ingredients, mixing to form a stiff dough. Turn dough out onto a lightly floured board. Roll out to 4 mm thickness. Cut out rounds using a 7 cm cutter. Place biscuits on a greased oven tray. Bake at 180°C for 20 minutes or until lightly browned.
Makes 25.

FLORENTINES

125 g butter, softened
1/2 cup sugar
5 tablespoons golden syrup
1/4 cup Edmonds standard plain flour

1 cup sliced almonds
1/2 cup chopped glacé cherries
1/2 cup chopped walnuts
1/4 cup chopped mixed peel

ICING
150 g cooking chocolate

Cream butter and sugar, and beat in syrup. Sift in flour. Add almonds, cherries, walnuts, peel and mix. Place tablespoonsful of mixture onto baking-paper-lined trays, spacing them very well apart to allow for spreading. Cook no more than four at a time. Press each one out as flat and round as possible, using a knife. Bake in the oven at 180°C for 10 minutes or until golden brown. Remove from oven and leave on tray for 5 minutes before transferring to a wire rack. When cold ice with chocolate on the flat side of biscuit.
Makes 20.

ICING
Melt chocolate in a bowl over hot water.

GINGERNUTS

125 g butter, softened
1/4 cup brown sugar
3 tablespoons golden syrup
1 teaspoon Edmonds *baking soda*

1 tablespoon boiling water
2 cups Edmonds *standard plain flour*
pinch of salt
3 teaspoons ground ginger

Cream butter, sugar and golden syrup until light and fluffy. Dissolve baking soda in the boiling water. Add to creamed mixture. Sift flour, salt and ginger together. Add to creamed mixture, mixing well. Roll tablespoonsful of mixture into balls and place on a greased oven tray. Flatten with a floured fork. Bake at 180°C for 20 to 30 minutes or until golden.
Makes 25.

GINGER CRUNCHIES

125 g butter, softened
1/2 cup sugar
1 egg
1 1/2 cups Edmonds *standard plain flour*

5 tablespoons Edmonds *custard powder*
1/2 cup finely chopped crystallised
ginger
1 cup cornflakes

Cream butter and sugar until light and fluffy. Add egg and beat well. Sift flour and custard powder together. Mix into creamed mixture. Mix in chopped ginger. Roll tablespoonsful of mixture into balls. Roll in cornflakes. Place on a greased oven tray. Flatten with a floured fork. Bake at 190°C for 20 minutes or until golden.
Makes 25.

HOKEY POKEY BISCUITS

125 g butter
1/2 cup sugar
1 tablespoon golden syrup

1 tablespoon milk
1 1/2 cups Edmonds *standard plain flour*
1 teaspoon Edmonds *baking soda*

Combine butter, sugar, golden syrup and milk in a saucepan. Heat until butter is melted and mixture nearly boiling, stirring constantly. Remove from heat and allow mixture to cool to lukewarm. Sift flour and baking soda together. Add to the cooled mixture. Stir well. Roll tablespoonsful of mixture into balls and place on ungreased oven trays. Flatten with a floured fork. Bake at 180°C for 15 to 20 minutes or until golden brown.
Makes 22.

HONEY OAT BISCUITS

125 g butter, softened
1/2 cup sugar
2 tablespoons honey
1 cup Edmonds *standard plain flour*

1 teaspoon Edmonds *baking powder*
1/2 teaspoon cinnamon
1 1/2 cups rolled oats

Cream butter, sugar and honey together until pale. Sift flour, baking powder and cinnamon together. Add sifted ingredients and rolled oats to creamed mixture, stirring well. Roll tablespoonsful of mixture into balls. Place on a greased oven tray. Flatten with a floured fork and bake at 180°C for 15 minutes or until golden. Transfer to a wire rack to cool.
Makes 30.

HONEY SNAPS

50 g butter
2 tablespoons sugar
3 tablespoons honey

1/2 cup Edmonds *standard plain flour*
1 teaspoon Edmonds *baking powder*
1/2 teaspoon ground ginger

Melt butter, sugar and honey together in a saucepan. Remove from heat. Add flour, baking powder, ginger and stir until mixture is smooth. Drop teaspoon lots onto cold oven tray, leaving enough room for mixture to spread to double its size. Bake at 180°C for 10 minutes or until golden. Leave on tray a few minutes to cool before removing to wire rack.
Makes 20.

KISSES

1st EDITION RECIPE

125 g butter, softened
1/2 cup sugar
2 eggs
1 cup Edmonds *standard plain flour*

1 cup Edmonds Fielder's *cornflour*
1 teaspoon Edmonds *baking powder*
raspberry jam
icing sugar

Cream butter and sugar until light and fluffy. Add eggs one at a time, beating well after each addition. Sift flour, cornflour and baking powder together. Mix into creamed mixture, stirring well. Drop small spoonsful onto greased oven trays. Bake at 200°C for 8 to 10 minutes or until cooked but not brown. Sandwich two kisses together with raspberry jam. Sprinkle with sifted icing sugar.
Makes 20.

MELTING MOMENTS

200 g butter, softened
3/4 cup icing sugar
1 cup Edmonds *standard plain flour*

1 cup Edmonds Fielder's *cornflour*
1/2 teaspoon Edmonds *baking powder*
Butter Icing (page 76) or raspberry jam

Cream butter and icing sugar until light and fluffy. Sift flour, cornflour and baking powder together. Mix into creamed mixture, mixing well. Roll dough into small balls the size of large marbles and place on a greased oven tray. Flatten slightly with a floured fork. Bake at 180°C for 20 minutes or until cooked. Cool and sandwich two biscuits together with Butter Icing or raspberry jam.
Makes 16.

NUTTY GOLDEN COOKIES

125 g butter
1 tablespoon golden syrup
½ cup sugar
1 teaspoon vanilla essence
1 egg

1½ cups Edmonds *standard plain flour*
¼ cup Edmonds *custard powder*
1 teaspoon Edmonds *baking powder*
1 cup finely chopped blanched roasted peanuts

Gently melt butter and golden syrup in a saucepan. Stir in sugar and vanilla. Allow mixture to cool slightly. Lightly beat egg and stir into melted mixture. Sift flour, custard powder and baking powder. Add to the syrup alternately with the chopped peanuts. Allow mixture to cool for a further 4 to 5 minutes or until it is manageable to handle. Roll tablespoonsful of mixture into balls. Place on greased oven trays. Flatten with a floured fork. Bake at 190°C for 12 minutes or until lightly browned. Makes 30.

PEANUT BROWNIES

125 g butter, softened
1 cup sugar
1 egg
1½ cups Edmonds *standard plain flour*

1 teaspoon Edmonds *baking powder*
pinch of salt
2 tablespoons cocoa
1 cup peanuts, roasted and husked

Cream butter and sugar until light and fluffy. Add egg and beat well. Sift flour, baking powder, salt and cocoa together. Mix into creamed mixture. Add cold peanuts and mix well. Roll tablespoonsful of mixture into balls. Place on greased oven trays. Flatten with a floured fork. Bake at 180°C for 15 minutes or until cooked. Makes 20.

SHORTBREAD

250 g butter, softened
1 cup icing sugar

1 cup Edmonds Fielder's *cornflour*
2 cups Edmonds *standard plain flour*

Cream butter and icing sugar until light and fluffy. Sift cornflour and flour together. Mix sifted ingredients into creamed mixture. Knead well. On a lightly floured board roll out to 0.5 cm thickness. Shape into a circle or cut into pieces. Place on a greased oven tray. Prick with a fork. Bake at 150°C for 30 minutes or until pale golden.
Makes about 30.

SHREWSBURY BISCUITS

125 g butter, softened
½ cup sugar
1 egg
1 tablespoon grated lemon rind

2 cups Edmonds *standard plain flour*
1 teaspoon Edmonds *baking powder*
raspberry jam

Cream butter and sugar until light and fluffy. Add egg and lemon rind and beat well. Sift flour and baking powder together. Mix sifted ingredients into creamed mixture. Knead well. On a lightly floured board roll out to 4 mm thickness. Cut out rounds using a 7 cm cutter. Cut a 1 cm hole in the centre of half the biscuits. Place on greased oven trays. Bake at 180°C for 10 to 15 minutes. When cold spread whole biscuits with jam and top with biscuits with holes in them.
Makes 22.

YOYOS

175 g butter, softened
¼ cup icing sugar
few drops vanilla essence

BUTTER FILLING
50 g butter, softened
½ cup icing sugar

1½ cups Edmonds *standard plain flour*
¼ cup Edmonds *custard powder*

2 tablespoons Edmonds *custard powder*

Cream butter and icing sugar until light and fluffy. Add vanilla. Sift flour and custard powder together. Mix sifted ingredients into creamed mixture. Roll teaspoonsful of mixture into balls. Place on an oven tray. Flatten with a fork. Bake at 180°C for 15 to 20 minutes. When cold, sandwich together in twos with Butter Filling.
Makes 20.

BUTTER FILLING
Beat all ingredients together until well combined.

Top: Munchkin Bars (pg 68) and Loch Katrine Cake (pg 53),
Bottom: Melting Moments (pg 42)

Cakes

EDMONDS
SURE TO RISE
Premium Quality
High Grade
Flour
✓ All natural
✓ Unbleached
✓ No additives
✓ Triple sifted
WHITE FLOUR
1.25kg NET
Recommended for use in breads and buns, carrot and banana cakes, heavily-fruited cakes, puddings, pizzas and flaky and puff pastries.

HINTS ON CAKE MAKING

- **Preheat the oven** and **prepare cake tins** before starting to mix ingredients.
- **Grease the base of cake tins only**; cakes will pull away slightly from the sides of the tin when cooked. Run a knife around the sides to release the cake from the tin.
- **Sift dry ingredients**, using a sifter or sieve.
- **To cream butter and sugar**, use soft, but not melted butter. Creaming beats air into the mixture which helps the cake to rise.
- **Fold sifted dry ingredients in alternately with liquids**, beginning and ending with dry ingredients. Do not beat. Mix just enough to combine the ingredients. Over-mixing produces a tough, low volume cake.
- **Mix ingredients more quickly** by using a slotted spoon.
- **Two-thirds fill cake and patty tins** to allow for rising.
- **To test when a cake is done** — the cake will spring back when lightly touched with a finger.
- **Leave cakes to cool in the tin for 10 minutes** before turning out onto a cooling rack. This allows the cake to 'set' and helps prevent breaking when removed from the tin.
- **Leave cakes until completely cold** before filling and icing.

BANANA CAKE

125 g butter, softened
³/₄ cup sugar
2 eggs
2 cups mashed ripe bananas
1 teaspoon Edmonds baking soda
2 tablespoons hot milk
2 cups Edmonds standard plain flour
1 teaspoon Edmonds baking powder
Chocolate or Lemon Icing (page 77)
icing sugar (optional)

Cream butter and sugar until light and fluffy. Add eggs one at a time, beating well after each addition. Add mashed banana and mix thoroughly. Stir soda into hot milk and add to creamed mixture. Sift flour and baking powder. Fold into mixture. Turn into a greased and lined 20 cm round cake tin. Bake at 180°C for 50 minutes or until cake springs back when lightly touched. Leave in tin for 10 minutes before turning out onto a wire rack. When cold ice with Lemon or Chocolate Icing or dust with icing sugar.

VARIATION
The mixture can be baked in two 20 cm round sandwich tins at 180°C for 25 minutes. The two cakes can be filled with whipped cream and sliced banana.

Over-ripe bananas can be mashed then frozen
until ready to use for banana cake, muffins or loaves.

BUTTER CAKE

150 g butter, softened
1 teaspoon vanilla essence
³/₄ cup sugar
2 eggs
1¹/₂ cups Edmonds standard plain flour

3 teaspoons Edmonds baking
  powder
³/₄ cup milk, approximately
icing sugar

Cream butter, vanilla and sugar until light and fluffy. Add eggs one at a time, beating well after each addition. Sift flour and baking powder together. Fold into creamed mixture. Add sufficient milk to give a soft dropping consistency. Spoon mixture into a greased and lined deep 20 cm round cake tin. Bake at 180°C for 35 to 40 minutes or until cake springs back when lightly touched. Leave in tin for 10 minutes before turning out onto a wire rack. When cold dust with icing sugar.

LEMON SYRUP CAKE
Spoon Butter Cake mixture into a greased and lined 22 cm loaf tin. After cooking cake, spoon hot syrup over hot cake. Leave in tin until cold.

SYRUP
3 tablespoons lemon juice   ¹/₄ cup sugar

Gently heat lemon juice and sugar together, stirring until sugar has dissolved.

CARROT CAKE

3 eggs
¹/₂ cup oil
2 cups Edmonds standard plain flour
1 cup sugar
3 teaspoons Edmonds baking soda

¹/₂ teaspoon cinnamon
3 cups carrots, grated
¹/₂ cup walnuts, chopped
1 teaspoon grated orange rind
³/₄ cup crushed pineapple
Cream Cheese Icing (page 82)

Beat eggs until thick. Stir in oil. Sift flour, sugar, baking soda and cinnamon into the egg mixture and combine. Fold in carrots, walnuts, orange rind and pineapple. Grease and line the base of a 23 cm ring tin. Spoon mixture into tin. Bake at 180°C for 40 minutes or until cake springs back when lightly touched. Leave in tin for 10 minutes before turning out onto a wire rack. When cold ice with Cream Cheese Icing if wished.

CHOCOLATE BUBBLE CAKES

250 g vegetable shortening
1 cup icing sugar
1/4 cup cocoa

4 cups cornflakes or puffed rice
*   breakfast cereal*
1 cup coconut

Put vegetable shortening in a medium saucepan. Cook over a low heat until melted. Sift icing sugar and cocoa together. Add sifted ingredients, cornflakes and coconut to saucepan, stirring until well combined. Spoon mixture evenly into 24 paper patty cases. Chill until firm.
Makes 24.

CHOCOLATE CAKE

175 g butter, softened
1 teaspoon vanilla essence
1³/4 cups sugar
3 eggs
1/2 cup cocoa

2 cups Edmonds *standard plain flour*
2 teaspoons Edmonds *baking powder*
1 cup milk
Chocolate Icing (page 82) or icing
*   sugar*

Cream butter, vanilla essence and sugar until light and fluffy. Add eggs one at a time, beating well after each addition. Sift cocoa, flour and baking powder together. Add to creamed mixture alternately with milk. Pour mixture into a greased and lined 22 cm round cake tin. Bake at 180°C for 30 minutes or until cake springs back when lightly touched. Leave in tin for 10 minutes before turning out onto a wire rack. When cold ice with Chocolate Icing or dust with icing sugar if wished.

COFFEE CAKE

1 teaspoon instant coffee powder
1 tablespoon boiling water
175 g butter, softened
³/4 cup caster sugar
1 teaspoon vanilla essence
3 eggs

1¹/2 cups Edmonds *standard plain flour*
1¹/2 teaspoons Edmonds *baking*
*   powder*
3 tablespoons milk
Coffee Icing (page 82)
walnut pieces

Dissolve coffee in the boiling water. Cream butter, sugar, coffee mixture and vanilla essence until light and fluffy. Add eggs one at a time, beating well after each addition. Sift flour and baking powder together and fold a little at a time quickly into the creamed mixture. Stir in milk. Pour cake mixture into two greased and lined 20 cm sponge sandwich tins. Bake at 190°C for 20 to 25 minutes or until cake springs back when lightly touched. Leave in tin for 10 minutes before turning out onto a wire rack. Fill and ice with Coffee Icing. Decorate with walnut pieces if wished.

CONTINENTAL APPLE CAKE

250 g butter, melted
1¼ cups sugar
3¼ cups Edmonds *standard plain flour*
6 teaspoons Edmonds *baking powder*
4 eggs
2 large Granny Smith apples, sliced

½ cup sultanas
2 tablespoons sugar
2 teaspoons cinnamon
1 teaspoon almond essence
icing sugar
whipped cream or yoghurt

Put butter, first measure of sugar, flour, baking powder and eggs into a bowl. Beat with an electric mixer on high speed until smooth. In a separate bowl combine apple slices, sultanas, second measure of sugar, cinnamon and almond essence. Spoon two-thirds of the batter into a greased and lined 25 cm round cake tin. Arrange the apple mixture on top. Spoon remaining batter over apple mixture. Bake at 180°C for 35 minutes or until cake springs back when lightly touched. Leave in tin for 10 minutes before turning out onto a wire rack. Dust with sifted icing sugar. Serve with cream or yoghurt.

CUP CAKES

125 g butter, softened
1 teaspoon vanilla essence
½ cup caster sugar
2 eggs

1 cup Edmonds *standard plain flour*
2 teaspoons Edmonds *baking powder*
¼ cup milk

Cream butter, vanilla and sugar until light and fluffy. Add eggs one at a time, beating well after each addition. Sift flour and baking powder together. Fold into creamed mixture. Stir in milk. Place 18 paper patty cases in patty tins. Spoon mixture evenly into paper cases. Bake at 190°C for 15 minutes or until cakes spring back when lightly touched. Transfer to a wire rack. When cold decorate as wished. Makes 18.

BUTTERFLY CAKES
Cut a slice from top of each cup cake. Cut this in half. Place a teaspoonful of Butter Filling (page 81) or whipped cream in each cavity. Arrange wings on cakes. Dust with icing sugar.

QUEEN CAKES
Stir in ½ cup sultanas before adding milk.

ORANGE CAKES
Omit vanilla essence. Add 2 teaspoons grated orange rind. Ice with Orange Icing (page 77).

CHOCOLATE CAKES

1st EDITION RECIPE

Omit 2 tablespoons measured flour. Replace with 2 tablespoons cocoa. Ice with Chocolate Icing (page 82).

Soften butter in the microwave for easy creaming.

DATE CAKE

125 g butter, softened
1/2 cup sugar
1 tablespoon lemon juice
1/4 teaspoon grated lemon rind
2 eggs

1 1/2 cups Edmonds *standard plain flour*
1 teaspoon Edmonds *baking powder*
2 tablespoons milk
3/4 cup chopped dates

Cream butter, sugar, lemon juice and rind until light and fluffy. In a separate bowl beat eggs until thick. Sift flour and baking powder together. Add flour to creamed mixture alternately with the eggs. Stir in milk. Add dates and fold into cake mixture. Pour into a greased 18 cm ring tin. Bake at 180°C for 30 to 40 minutes or until cake springs back when lightly touched. Leave in tin for 10 minutes before turning out onto wire rack.

GINGERBREAD

125 g butter, softened
1/2 cup sugar
1 cup golden syrup
1 egg
2 1/2 cups Edmonds *standard plain flour*

1/4 teaspoon salt
1 1/2 teaspoons Edmonds *baking soda*
1 1/2 teaspoons ground ginger
1 teaspoon cinnamon
1 cup water

Cream butter and sugar in a bowl until light and fluffy. Warm syrup slightly until runny. Beat into creamed mixture. Add egg. Beat well. Sift flour, salt, baking soda, ginger and cinnamon together. Stir into creamed mixture alternately with water. Pour mixture into a greased and lined 20 cm square cake tin. Bake at 180°C for 45 to 60 minutes. Leave in tin for 10 minutes before turning out onto a wire rack.

GINGER CAKE

125 g butter, softened
1/2 cup sugar
3 tablespoons golden syrup
2 cups Edmonds *standard plain flour*
1 teaspoon Edmonds *baking powder*
1 teaspoon ground ginger
1 teaspoon mixed spice

2 eggs, beaten
1/4 cup chopped crystallised ginger
1/4 cup chopped walnuts
1/4 cup sultanas
1 teaspoon Edmonds *baking soda*
3/4 cup milk

Cream butter, sugar and golden syrup until light and fluffy. Sift flour, baking powder, ginger and mixed spice together. Add sifted dry ingredients to creamed mixture alternately with beaten eggs. Stir in ginger, walnuts and sultanas. Dissolve baking soda in the milk and stir into mixture. Line a 20 cm square cake tin with brown paper followed by baking paper. Pour mixture into tin. Bake at 180°C for 35 minutes or until the cake springs back when lightly touched. Leave in tin for 10 minutes before turning out onto a wire rack.

HONEY CAKE

1 cup honey
1 cup water
1½ cups chopped dates
50 g butter
1 teaspoon vanilla essence

2 cups Edmonds *standard plain flour*
4 teaspoons Edmonds *baking powder*
icing sugar
whipped cream
Caramel Sauce *(page 195)*

Put honey, water, dates and butter in a saucepan. Stir constantly over a medium heat until butter has melted. Remove from heat and allow to cool. Stir in vanilla. Sift flour and baking powder into the saucepan. Stir to combine. Pour mixture into a greased and lined 20 cm round cake tin. Bake at 180°C for 45 minutes or until cake springs back when lightly touched. Leave in tin for 10 mintues before turning out onto a wire rack. When cold dust with icing sugar or serve as a dessert with cream and Caramel Sauce.

LADYSMITH CAKE

175 g butter, softened
¾ cup sugar
3 eggs
1½ cups Edmonds *standard plain flour*

1 teaspoon Edmonds *baking powder*
2 teaspoons cinnamon
¼ cup raspberry jam
¼ cup chopped nuts

Cream butter and sugar until light and fluffy. In a separate bowl beat eggs until thick. Sift flour and baking powder together. Add to creamed mixture alternately with the eggs. Transfer one-third of the mixture to a bowl. Stir in cinnamon. Reserve remaining mixture. Spoon cinnamon mixture into a greased and lined 18 cm square cake tin. Spread surface with raspberry jam. Top with reserved mixture. Sprinkle the top with chopped nuts. Bake at 180°C for 50 minutes or until cake springs back when lightly touched. Leave in tin for 10 minutes before turning out onto wire rack.

LEMON SOUR CREAM CAKE

125 g butter, softened
2 teaspoons grated lemon rind
1 cup sugar
3 eggs

1 cup Edmonds *standard plain flour*
1 teaspoon Edmonds *baking powder*
½ cup sour cream
icing sugar

Beat butter, lemon rind, sugar and eggs together until light and fluffy. Sift flour and baking powder together. Fold sifted ingredients into egg mixture alternately with sour cream, mixing until smooth. Pour mixture into a greased and lined 20 cm round cake tin. Bake at 160°C for 45 minutes or until cake springs back when lightly touched. Leave in tin for 5 to 10 minutes before turning out onto a wire rack. When cold dust with icing sugar.

LOCH KATRINE CAKE

BASE

1 cup Edmonds *standard plain flour*
1 teaspoon Edmonds *baking powder*
50 g butter
3 to 4 tablespoons milk

1 to 2 tablespoons raspberry jam
1 cup currants
Lemon Icing (page 82)
chopped nuts

SPONGE

50 g butter, softened
$\frac{1}{2}$ cup sugar
1 cup Edmonds *standard plain flour*

1 teaspoon Edmonds *baking powder*
2 eggs, beaten
4 to 6 tablespoons milk

Sift flour and baking powder together. Cut in butter until the mixture resembles coarse breadcrumbs. Add just enough milk to form a stiff dough. Turn dough out onto a lightly floured board and roll to a rectangle large enough to line a 20 × 30 cm sponge roll tin. Thinly spread raspberry jam over dough. Sprinkle with currants. Cover with sponge mixture. Bake at 190°C for 30 minutes or until cake springs back when lightly touched. When cold ice with Lemon Icing and sprinkle with chopped nuts if wished. Cut into squares.
Makes 24.

SPONGE
Cream butter and sugar until light and fluffy. Sift flour and baking powder together. Add to the creamed mixture alternately with the eggs. Stir in just enough milk to form a smooth, spreadable mixture.

MACAROON CAKE

125 g butter, softened
$\frac{1}{2}$ cup sugar
3 egg yolks
1 teaspoon vanilla essence

$1\frac{1}{2}$ cups Edmonds *standard plain flour*
1 teaspoon Edmonds *baking powder*
pinch salt
2 tablespoons milk

MACAROON

3 egg whites
$\frac{1}{2}$ cup sugar

$1\frac{1}{2}$ cups coconut

Cream butter and sugar until light and fluffy. Add egg yolks and vanilla, beating well. Sift flour, baking powder and salt together. Add to creamed mixture alternately with the milk. Spread mixture into a greased and lined shallow 23 cm square cake tin. Spread with macaroon mixture. Bake at 180°C for 30 minutes or until an inserted skewer comes out clean. Leave in tin for 10 minutes before turning out onto a wire rack.

MACAROON
Beat egg whites until soft peaks form. Fold in sugar and coconut.

MADEIRA CAKE

175 g butter, softened
3/4 cup sugar
1/4 teaspoon grated lemon rind

3 eggs
1 1/2 cups Edmonds *standard plain flour*
1 teaspoon Edmonds *baking powder*

Cream butter and sugar until light and fluffy. Stir in lemon rind. In a separate bowl beat eggs until thick. Sift flour and baking powder together. Add to creamed mixture alternately with the eggs. Stir to mix. Spoon mixture into a greased and lined 20 cm square cake tin. Bake at 180°C for 40 minutes or until the cake springs back when lightly touched. Leave in tin for 10 minutes before turning out onto a wire rack.

MARBLE CAKE

3 eggs
3/4 cup sugar
1 cup Edmonds *standard plain flour*
1 teaspoon Edmonds *baking powder*

50 g butter, melted
2 tablespoons boiling water
1 tablespoon cocoa
2 to 3 drops red food colouring

Beat eggs until thick. Gradually beat in sugar until mixture is very thick and white. Sift flour and baking powder together. Fold into egg mixture. Fold in butter and boiling water. Divide mixture into three equal parts. Into one-third stir the cocoa, and to another third add enough red food colouring to make a pink mixture. Leave the last third plain. Spoon the three mixtures in diagonal stripes into a greased and lined 20 cm square cake tin. Using a knife twirl together the three mixtures. Bake at 190°C for 20 to 25 minutes or until the cake springs back when lightly touched. Leave in tin for 10 minutes before turning out onto a wire rack.

ONE EGG CHOCOLATE CAKE

50 g butter
1 tablespoon golden syrup
1 egg
1/2 cup sugar
1 tablespoon cocoa
1 cup Edmonds *standard plain flour*

1 teaspoon Edmonds *baking powder*
few drops vanilla essence
1 teaspoon Edmonds *baking soda*
3/4 cup milk
Chocolate Icing (page 82)

Melt butter and syrup in a small saucepan. Put melted ingredients into a bowl. Add egg and sugar and beat well. Sift cocoa, flour and baking powder together. Fold sifted ingredients and vanilla into egg mixture. Dissolve baking soda in milk. Fold into egg mixture. Pour mixture into two greased and lined 20 cm sponge sandwich tins. Bake at 190°C for 30 minutes or until cake springs back when lightly touched. Leave in tin for 5 minutes before turning out onto a wire rack. When cold ice with Chocolate Icing.

RASPBERRY DELIGHTS

50 g butter, softened
1/4 cup sugar
2 eggs
1/4 cup Edmonds standard plain flour

1/4 cup Edmonds custard powder
1/2 teaspoon Edmonds baking powder
raspberry jam

Cream butter and sugar until light and fluffy. Add eggs one at a time, beating well after each addition. Sift flour, custard powder and baking powder together. Mix into creamed mixture. Place spoonsful of mixture in greased patty tins. Bake at 180°C for 10 minutes. Place a teaspoonful of jam on top of each cake. Bake for a further 3 minutes.
Makes 15.

RICH CHOCOLATE CAKE

(A very moist and rich flourless cake. Suitable for dessert.)

175 g unsalted butter, softened
3/4 cup brown sugar
1 teaspoon vanilla essence
6 eggs, separated

150 g cooking chocolate, melted
2 x 70 g packets ground almonds
icing sugar
whipped cream

Cream butter, sugar and vanilla until light and fluffy. Beat in egg yolks. Fold in melted chocolate and almonds. In another bowl beat egg whites until soft peaks form. Gradually fold whites into chocolate mixture. Pour into a greased and lined 20 cm spring-form tin. Bake at 190°C for 20 minutes then reduce heat to 150°C for a further 35 minutes or until firm. Allow cake to cool in tin. Release cake and transfer to a serving plate. Dust with icing sugar and serve warm or cold with cream.

CHOCOLATE LIQUEUR CAKE
Omit vanilla essence and replace with 2 teaspoons chocolate, coffee or orange liqueur.

ROCK CAKES

1 cup Edmonds standard plain flour
1 teaspoon Edmonds baking powder
50 g butter
1/4 cup sugar

1/2 cup currants
1/4 cup mixed peel
1 egg, beaten
2 tablespoons milk

Sift flour and baking powder into a bowl. Cut in butter until it resembles coarse breadcrumbs. Add sugar, currants and peel. Add egg and sufficient milk to make a stiff dough. Place in rocky heaps on a greased oven tray. Bake at 200°C for 10 to 12 minutes.
Makes 15.

SEED CAKE

125 g butter, softened
1/2 cup sugar
1 tablespoon whisky or brandy (optional)
1 1/2 cups Edmonds standard plain flour

1 1/2 teaspoons Edmonds baking powder
2 eggs, beaten
1 tablespoon caraway seeds

Cream butter and sugar until light and fluffy. Add whisky or brandy. Sift flour and baking powder together. Add eggs alternately with sifted dry ingredients. Mix in caraway seeds. Place in a greased and lined 18 cm square cake tin. Bake at 180°C for 30 to 35 minutes or until cake springs back when lightly touched. Leave in tin for 10 minutes before turning out onto a wire rack.

TOSCA CAKE

2 eggs
1/2 cup sugar
3/4 cup Edmonds standard plain flour

1 teaspoon Edmonds baking powder
75 g butter, melted
2 tablespoons milk

TOPPING
3 tablespoons melted butter
1/4 cup sliced almonds

1/4 cup sugar
2 tablespoons milk

Beat eggs and sugar until pale and thick. Sift flour and baking powder together. Carefully fold into egg mixture. Fold in melted butter and milk. Pour into a greased 25 cm loose-bottomed flan tin. Bake at 180°C for about 30 minutes or until cake springs back when lightly touched. Remove from oven and quickly spoon topping over. Return to oven and bake for about 10 minutes or until topping is golden and caramelised. Leave in tin for 10 minutes before turning out onto a wire rack.

TOPPING
Heat butter, almonds and sugar in a saucepan. Stir constantly until sugar has dissolved. Add milk and bring to the boil. Boil for 5 minutes.

WHOLEMEAL CHOCOLATE CAKE

$^1/_4$ cup cocoa
$^1/_4$ cup boiling water
$^1/_2$ teaspoon vanilla essence
125 g butter
$^3/_4$ cup brown sugar
2 eggs

$^3/_4$ cup Edmonds *standard plain flour*
$^3/_4$ cup Edmonds *wholemeal flour*
3 teaspoons Edmonds *baking powder*
2 tablespoons milk
icing sugar

Dissolve cocoa in boiling water. Mix to a smooth paste. Add vanilla and allow to cool. Cream butter and sugar until light and fluffy. Add cocoa mixture. Beat eggs in one at a time, beating well after each addition. Sift flour, wholemeal flour and baking powder together. Return husks from the sieve back to the sifted flour. Fold sifted ingredients into creamed mixture. Stir in milk. Spoon mixture into a greased and lined 20 cm round cake tin. Bake at 180°C for 40 minutes or until cake springs back when lightly touched. Leave in tin for 10 minutes before turning out onto a wire rack. When cold dust with icing sugar.

FRUIT CAKES

HINTS ON MAKING FRUIT CAKES

- **Line tins for heavy or rich fruit cakes** with two layers of brown paper followed by one layer of baking paper.
- **Bake heavy or rich fruit cakes** in the lower half of the oven.
- **To test when a fruit cake is cooked — a metal skewer** inserted in the centre of the cake should come out clean.
- **Leave large, rich fruit cakes to go cold in the tin** before turning out.
- **Pour 1/2 cup of brandy or rum** over a fruit cake when cooled to improve the flavour.
- **To store a cake**, leave the baking paper on the cake and wrap securely in foil, then brown paper or calico.
- **Store cakes in a cool dark place**. Heavy fruit cakes improve on keeping.
- **Mature heavy fruit cakes for up to 4 weeks** before cutting to avoid crumbling and to improve the flavour. Cut with a sharp or serrated-edged knife.

BOILED FRUIT CAKE

500 g mixed fruit
water
250 g butter
1 1/2 cups sugar
3 eggs, beaten

3 cups Edmonds *standard plain flour*
4 teaspoons Edmonds *baking powder*
1/2 teaspoon almond essence
1/2 teaspoon vanilla essence

Put mixed fruit in a saucepan. Add just enough water to cover fruit. Cover and bring to the boil. Remove from heat. Stir in butter and sugar, stirring constantly until butter has melted. Allow to cool. Beat in eggs. Sift flour and baking powder into fruit mixture, stirring to combine. Stir in almond and vanilla essences. Line a 23 cm square cake tin with two layers of brown paper followed by one layer of baking paper. Spoon mixture into cake tin. Bake at 160°C for 1 to 1 1/2 hours or until an inserted skewer comes out clean when tested. Leave in tin until cold.

Top: Anzac Biscuits (pg 37) and Hokey Pokey Biscuits (pg 41),
Bottom: Carrot Cake (pg 48)

CATHEDRAL LOAF

125 g glacé pineapple rings
3 glacé pears
½ cup glacé green cherries
½ cup glacé red cherries
125 g glacé apricots
125 g blanched almonds
250 g whole brazil nuts
½ cup crystallised ginger

3 eggs
½ cup caster sugar
1 teaspoon vanilla essence
2 tablespoons brandy
¾ cup Edmonds *standard plain flour*
½ teaspoon Edmonds *baking powder*
1 teaspoon ground nutmeg
¼ teaspoon salt

Chop pineapple rings and pears into six pieces. Halve green and red cherries. Chop apricots into quarters. Put chopped fruits, almonds, brazil nuts and ginger into a bowl. Mix to combine. In a separate bowl beat eggs, sugar, vanilla and brandy together. Sift flour, baking powder, nutmeg and salt together. Fold sifted ingredients into egg mixture. Pour onto fruit and nuts, mixing thoroughly. Line a 23 cm loaf tin with two layers of brown paper followed by one layer of baking paper. Pour mixture into loaf tin. Bake at 150°C for 2 hours or until an inserted skewer comes out clean when tested. Allow to cool in tin. Remove paper and wrap in foil to store. Leave for two days before cutting. To serve, use a very sharp knife to cut into thin slices.

FRUIT CAKE

675 g mixed fruit
¼ cup mixed peel
2 to 3 tablespoons Edmonds *high grade flour*
225 g butter
1 cup brown sugar
2 tablespoons golden syrup

1 tablespoon marmalade
5 eggs
3 cups Edmonds *high grade flour*
1 teaspoon Edmonds *baking powder*
pinch of salt
1 teaspoon mixed spice
½ teaspoon ground nutmeg

Combine mixed fruit and peel in a bowl. Dust with the first measure of flour. Cream butter, sugar and golden syrup until light and fluffy. Stir in marmalade. In a separate bowl beat eggs until thick. Sift the second measure of flour, baking powder, salt, mixed spice and nutmeg together. Add flour and egg alternately to creamed mixture. Add prepared fruit and mix well. Line a deep, 20 cm square cake tin with two layers of brown paper followed by one layer of baking paper. Spoon mixture into cake tin, smoothing the surface. Bake at 150°C for 2 to 2½ hours or until an inserted skewer comes out clean. Leave in tin until cold.

GINGER ALE FRUIT CAKE

1¼ cups sultanas
1¼ cups dates
1¼ cups currants
1¼ cups raisins
¼ cup mixed peel
300 ml ginger ale
225 g butter, softened

1 cup sugar
4 eggs
2 cups Edmonds standard plain flour
1 teaspoon Edmonds baking powder
¼ teaspoon grated lemon rind
½ teaspoon vanilla essence
½ teaspoon almond essence

Combine sultanas, dates, currants, raisins and peel with the ginger ale in a large bowl. Leave in a warm place overnight. The next day, cream the butter and sugar until light and fluffy. Add the eggs one at a time, beating well after each addition. Sift flour and baking powder together. Add to creamed mixture, stirring well. Add soaked fruit mixture, lemon rind, vanilla and almond essences. Stir well. Line a 23 cm round cake tin with two layers of brown paper followed by one layer of baking paper. Spoon mixture into tin. Bake at 140°C for 3 hours or until an inserted skewer comes out clean. Leave in tin until cold.

RICH CHRISTMAS CAKE

1st EDITION RECIPE

1¾ cups orange juice
¾ cup dark rum or brandy
2 tablespoons grated orange rind
500 g currants
500 g raisins
2 cups sultanas
2 cups chopped dates
150 g crystallised ginger, chopped
150 g packet mixed peel
150 g packet glacé cherries, halved
½ teaspoon vanilla essence
¼ teaspoon almond essence

2 teaspoons grated lemon rind
1 cup blanched almonds
2½ cups Edmonds high grade flour
½ teaspoon Edmonds baking soda
1 teaspoon cinnamon
1 teaspoon mixed spice
½ teaspoon ground nutmeg
250 g butter
1½ cups brown sugar
2 tablespoons treacle
5 eggs

In a saucepan, bring to the boil orange juice, rum and orange rind. Remove from heat and add dried fruit. Cover and leave fruit to soak overnight. Stir essences, lemon rind and almonds into saucepan. Sift flour, soda and spices into a bowl. Cream butter, sugar and treacle until light and fluffy. Add eggs one at a time, beating well after each addition. Fold in sifted ingredients alternately with fruit mixture. Line a deep, square 23 cm tin with two layers of brown paper followed by one layer of baking paper. Spoon mixture into tin. Bake at 150°C for 4 hours or until an inserted skewer comes out clean when tested. Leave in tin until cold. Wrap in foil. Store in a cool place.

SIMNEL CAKE

500 g marzipan
icing sugar
250 g butter
1 cup sugar
4 eggs
2^1/$_2$ cups Edmonds *standard plain flour*

1 teaspoon Edmonds *baking powder*
1^1/$_2$ cups sultanas
1^1/$_2$ cups currants
^{1}/$_2$ cup mixed peel
^{1}/$_2$ cup glacé cherries, chopped

Cut marzipan into thirds. Using two of the marzipan pieces, roll out two rounds to fit a 22 cm round cake tin on greaseproof paper dusted with icing sugar. Cream butter and sugar until light and fluffy. Beat in eggs one at a time, beating well after each addition. Sift flour and baking powder together. Mix in sultanas, currants, peel and cherries. Fold into creamed mixture. Spoon half the mixture into the greased and lined cake tin, spreading the mixture evenly. Cover with one of the marzipan rounds, then spread remaining cake mixture on top and smooth. Bake at 150°C for 2 hours. Reduce heat to 130°C and bake for a further ^{1}/$_2$ to 1 hour or until an inserted skewer comes out clean. While the cake is cooking, use the remaining marzipan to make 11 balls. Place the remaining marzipan round on top of the hot cake and decorate with the 11 balls. Return the cake to the oven for about 15 minutes until the marzipan is lightly browned. Leave to cool in tin.

SULTANA CAKE

2 cups sultanas
250 g butter, chopped in small
  pieces
2 cups sugar
3 eggs, beaten

^{1}/$_2$ teaspoon lemon essence or
  almond essence
3 cups Edmonds *standard plain flour*
1^1/$_2$ teaspoons Edmonds *baking
  powder*

Put sultanas in a saucepan. Cover with water. Bring to the boil then simmer for 15 minutes. Drain thoroughly. Add butter. In a bowl beat sugar into eggs until well combined. Add sultana mixture and essence. Sift flour and baking powder together. Mix sifted ingredients into fruit mixture. Spoon mixture into a greased and lined 20 cm square cake tin. Bake at 160°C for 1 to 1^1/$_4$ hours or until cake springs back when lightly touched. Leave in tin for 10 minutes before turning out onto a wire rack.

TENNIS CAKE

175 g butter
1^1/$_2$ cups sugar
^{1}/$_2$ teaspoon vanilla essence
^{1}/$_2$ teaspoon almond essence
2 cups Edmonds *standard plain flour*
^{1}/$_4$ teaspoon cinnamon
1 teaspoon Edmonds *baking powder*

4 eggs, beaten
^{3}/$_4$ cup raisins
^{1}/$_2$ cup glacé cherries, chopped
2 tablespoons angelica, chopped
1 teaspoon grated lemon rind
2 tablespoons lemon juice

Cream butter and sugar until light and fluffy. Add vanilla and almond essences. Sift flour, cinnamon and baking powder together. To creamed mixture add eggs alternately with sifted dry ingredients. Mix in raisins, cherries, angelica, lemon rind and juice. Spoon mixture into a greased and lined 22 cm round cake tin. Bake at 160°C for 1^1/$_2$ to 2 hours or until cake springs back when lightly touched. Leave in tin for 10 minutes before turning out onto a wire rack.

Line your cake tin with baking paper to prevent cake sticking.

ALBERT SQUARES

125 g butter
³/₄ cup sugar
2 eggs
2 teaspoons golden syrup
¹/₂ teaspoon vanilla essence

1 cup currants
2 cups Edmonds *standard plain flour*
2 teaspoons Edmonds *baking powder*
pinch of salt
¹/₂ cup milk

ICING
1¹/₂ cups icing sugar
¹/₂ teaspoon vanilla essence

water to mix
3 tablespoons coconut
lemon rind, finely grated (optional)

Cream butter and sugar until light and fluffy. Add eggs one at a time, beating well after each addition. Beat in syrup and vanilla. Fold in currants. Sift flour, baking powder and salt together. Fold sifted ingredients into creamed mixture alternately with milk. Spread into a greased 20 × 30 cm sponge roll tin. Bake at 180°C for 30 minutes or until centre springs back when lightly touched. When cold ice and cut into squares.
Makes 24.

ICING
Mix icing sugar, vanilla and sufficient water to make a spreading consistency. Ice and sprinkle with coconut and lemon rind.

APPLE SHORTCAKE SQUARES

3 apples, peeled and sliced
1 tablespoon sugar
1 to 2 tablespoons water
2 cups Edmonds *standard plain flour*
1 teaspoon Edmonds *baking powder*

125 g butter
¹/₄ cup sugar
1 egg, beaten
1 to 2 tablespoons milk
icing sugar

Put apples, first measure of sugar and water in saucepan and cook slowly until apples are soft. Sift flour and baking powder into a bowl. Cut in butter until it resembles coarse breadcrumbs. Mix in first measure of sugar and the egg. Add sufficient milk to form a firm dough. Knead until smooth. Divide dough in half and roll out each piece to fit a 22 cm square cake tin. Place one piece of dough in tin and spread apple over it. Lightly press remaining dough on top. Bake at 180°C for 25 minutes. When cold sprinkle with sifted icing sugar and cut into squares.
Makes 16.

Low-fat milk can be used for baking.

CARAMEL DATE FINGERS

FILLING

1 cup dates, chopped
1 cup water
1 tablespoon brown sugar

1 teaspoon butter
2 teaspoons cocoa
$^1/_4$ teaspoon vanilla essence

BASE

125 g butter
$^1/_2$ cup sugar
1 egg

$1^3/_4$ cups Edmonds *standard plain flour*
1 teaspoon Edmonds *baking powder*

FILLING

Put dates in a saucepan. Add water, sugar, butter and cocoa. Cook gently over a low heat until a paste-like consistency is obtained. Add vanilla and cool.

BASE

Cream butter and sugar until light and fluffy. Add egg and beat well. Sift flour and baking powder together. Mix into creamed mixture. Press out half the mixture to fit the base of a 20 cm square tin. Spread with date mixture. On a piece of waxed paper pat or roll out remaining dough to a 20 cm square. Place on top of date filling. Bake at 180°C for 30 minutes or until lightly browned. Cut into fingers. Other dried fruits such as prunes, apricots and raisins, alone or mixed, can replace dates.
Makes 15.

CHINESE CHEWS

2 eggs
1 cup brown sugar
75 g butter, melted
1 teaspoon vanilla essence
$1^1/_2$ cups Edmonds *standard plain flour*
1 teaspoon Edmonds *baking powder*

pinch of salt
$^1/_2$ cup rolled oats
$^3/_4$ cup chopped dates
$^3/_4$ cup chopped walnuts
$^3/_4$ cup crystallised ginger

Beat eggs and sugar until well mixed. Add butter and vanilla. Into a large bowl sift flour, baking powder and salt. Stir in rolled oats. Pour egg mixture into the sifted dry ingredients. Add dates, walnuts and ginger. Mix well. Spread mixture into a lightly greased 23 cm square cake tin. Bake at 180°C for 30 to 35 minutes or until cooked. Cut into squares while still hot.
Makes 30.

CHOCOLATE BROWNIE

175 g butter
250 g cooking chocolate
$1^1/_2$ cups Edmonds *standard plain flour*
1 cup sugar

2 teaspoons vanilla essence
3 eggs, beaten
Chocolate Icing (page 77)
1 cup walnuts, chopped (optional)

In a medium-sized saucepan, melt butter and chocolate over a low heat. Remove saucepan from the heat and add flour, sugar, vanilla and eggs. Stir until well combined. Pour mixture into a greased and lined 20 × 30 cm sponge roll tin. Bake at 180°C for 30 minutes. Leave in tin for 10 minutes before turning out onto a wire rack. When cold ice with Chocolate Icing and sprinkle with chopped walnuts. Cut into squares.
Makes 20.

CHOCOLATE FRUIT FINGERS

1½ cups Edmonds *standard plain flour*
1 teaspoon Edmonds *baking powder*
125 g butter
¼ cup brown sugar
1 tablespoon cocoa

1 cup chopped dates
1 cup chopped walnuts
1 egg, beaten
Chocolate Icing (page 82)
extra walnuts

Sift flour and baking powder into a bowl. Cut in butter until it resembles coarse breadcrumbs. Add sugar, cocoa, dates and walnuts. Mix egg into dry ingredients. Spread mixture into a greased and lined 20 × 30 cm sponge roll tin. Bake at 190°C for 20 to 25 minutes. When cold ice with Chocolate Icing and sprinkle with chopped walnuts. Cut into fingers.
Makes 25.

CHOCOLATE NUT BARS

125 g butter, softened
1 cup sugar
1 egg
¼ teaspoon vanilla essence
1¼ cups Edmonds *standard plain flour*
1 teaspoon Edmonds *baking powder*

2 tablespoons cocoa
1¼ cups cornflakes
¾ cup coconut
¼ cup chopped walnuts
Chocolate Icing (page 82)

Cream butter and sugar until light and fluffy. Add egg and vanilla, beating well. Sift flour, baking powder and cocoa together. Mix into creamed mixture. Add cornflakes, coconut and walnuts, mixing well. Press mixture into a greased 20 × 30 cm sponge roll tin. Bake at 180°C for 30 minutes. When cold ice with Chocolate Icing and cut into bars.
Makes 30.

COCONUT CHOCOLATE BROWNIES

125 g butter
¼ cup cocoa
1 cup sugar
2 eggs
1 teaspoon vanilla essence

½ cup coconut
½ cup Edmonds *standard plain flour*
½ teaspoon Edmonds *baking powder*
icing sugar

Melt butter in a medium saucepan. Add cocoa. Stir over a low heat for 1 to 2 minutes. Remove from heat. Stir in sugar. Add eggs one at a time, beating well after each addition. Beat in vanilla and coconut. Sift flour and baking powder. Stir into mixture. Pour into a greased and lined shallow 20 cm square cake tin. Bake at 180°C for 30 to 35 minutes. Leave in tin for 5 minutes before turning out onto a wire rack. Cut into bars when cold. Dust tops with icing sugar.
Makes 16.

Soften butter in the microwave oven for easy creaming.

COCONUT DREAM

125 g butter, softened
1/2 cup brown sugar

1 1/2 cups Edmonds *standard plain flour*
1 teaspoon Edmonds *baking powder*

TOPPING
2 eggs
1 cup brown sugar
4 teaspoons Edmonds *standard plain flour*

1/2 teaspoon Edmonds *baking powder*
1 teaspoon vanilla essence
1 1/2 cups coconut
1 cup chopped nuts

Cream butter and sugar until light and fluffy. Sift flour and baking powder together. Mix into creamed mixture. Press into a greased 20 × 30 cm sponge roll tin. Bake at 200°C for 8 minutes. Pour topping mixture over cooked base. Bake at 160°C for 40 to 45 minutes or until brown. Cut into squares.
Makes 24.

TOPPING
Beat eggs. Add sugar and beat until thick. Mix flour and baking powder and fold into egg mixture. Stir in vanilla, coconut and nuts.

GINGER CRUNCH

125 g butter, softened
1/2 cup sugar
1 1/2 cups Edmonds *standard plain flour*

1 teaspoon Edmonds *baking powder*
1 teaspoon ground ginger

GINGER ICING
75 g butter
3/4 cup icing sugar

2 tablespoons golden syrup
3 teaspoons ground ginger

Cream butter and sugar until light and fluffy. Sift flour, baking powder and ginger together. Mix into creamed mixture. Turn dough out onto a lightly floured board. Knead well. Press dough into a greased 20 × 30 cm sponge roll tin. Bake at 190°C for 20 to 25 minutes or until light brown. Pour hot Ginger Icing over base while hot and cut into squares before it gets cold.
Makes 24.

GINGER ICING
In a small saucepan combine butter, icing sugar, golden syrup and ginger. Heat until butter is melted, stirring constantly.

JAM SLICE

200 g Sweet Shortcrust Pastry or
  1 sheet Edmonds *Sweet Short Pastry*
1/2 cup raspberry jam

2 eggs, beaten
5 tablespoons sugar
2 cups coconut

On a lightly floured board roll out pastry or use ready rolled sheet and use to line the base of a 20 × 30 cm sponge roll tin. Spread jam evenly over pastry. Beat eggs and sugar until thick and add coconut. Spread evenly over jam. Bake at 190°C for 30 minutes or until golden.
Makes 24.

Preheat a measuring spoon in hot water for easy measuring of golden syrup.

MERINGUES

2 egg whites
$^1/_2$ cup caster sugar

whipped cream

Beat egg whites until stiff but not dry. Add half the sugar and beat well. Repeat with remaining sugar. Pipe or spoon small amounts of meringue onto a greased oven tray. Bake at 120°C for 1 to 1$^1/_2$ hours or until the meringues are dry but not brown. Cool and when required to serve, sandwich meringues together in twos with whipped cream.
Makes 12.

MUESLI SLICE

50 g butter
$^1/_2$ cup brown sugar
2 eggs
$^3/_4$ cup Edmonds *standard plain flour*

$^1/_2$ teaspoon Edmonds *baking powder*
1 cup muesli
2 teaspoons grated lemon rind
$^1/_2$ cup chopped mixed peel
Chocolate Icing (page 82)

Cream butter and sugar until light and fluffy. Add eggs one at a time, beating well after each addition. Sift flour and baking powder together. Fold sifted ingredients, muesli, lemon rind and peel into creamed mixture, mixing well. Spread mixture into a greased shallow 20 cm square cake tin. Bake at 180°C for 25 minutes or until golden. When cold ice with Chocolate Icing and cut into slices.
Makes 16.

MUNCHKIN BARS

1 cup brown sugar
100 g butter
$^1/_2$ cup apricot jam
$^1/_4$ cup golden syrup
3 cups rolled oats
1 cup pumpkin kernels

1 teaspoon mixed spice
$^1/_2$ cup sesame seeds
$^1/_2$ cup coconut
1 teaspoon vanilla essence
1 cup sultanas (optional)

In a saucepan, melt together the sugar, butter, apricot jam and golden syrup. Combine the rest of the ingredients in a large bowl. Mix well. Pour in melted mixture. Mix together. Press mixture firmly into a greased 20 × 30 cm sponge roll tin. Bake at 180°C for 25 minutes or until golden. Cool slightly and cut into bars.
Makes 18.

Store unfilled meringues in an airtight container.

OATY DATE BARS

FILLING
1 1/2 cups chopped dates
3 tablespoons water

2 tablespoons lemon juice

BASE
125 g butter
3/4 cup raw sugar
1 egg
1 tablespoon golden syrup
1 teaspoon vanilla essence

1 cup Edmonds *wholemeal flour*
1 teaspoon Edmonds *baking powder*
1/4 teaspoon salt
1 cup rolled oats
1 cup coconut
Lemon Icing (page 82)

FILLING
Put dates, water and lemon juice in a small saucepan. Cook over a low heat until dates are soft. Cool.

BASE
Cream butter and sugar together until light and fluffy. Add egg and golden syrup. Beat well. Add vanilla, wholemeal flour, baking powder, salt, oats and coconut to creamed mixture. Mix well. Divide dough into two equal portions. Press out one portion thinly over the base of a greased 20 × 30 cm sponge roll tin. Spread cold filling over this. Dot small pieces of dough over filling and carefully spread it together to form a top layer. Bake at 180°C for 25 to 30 minutes or until golden brown. When cold ice with Lemon Icing. Cut into fingers.
Makes 36.

REFRIGERATED APRICOT AND LEMON SLICE

125 g butter
1/2 cup sweetened condensed milk
250 g packet malt biscuits, crushed
1 cup dried apricots, finely chopped

1 teaspoon grated lemon rind
1 cup coconut
Lemon Icing (page 82)
2 tablespoons coconut (optional)

In a small saucepan, add the butter and condensed milk. Stir over a gentle heat until butter has melted. In a bowl combine biscuit crumbs, apricots, lemon rind, first measure of coconut and mix well. Stir in butter mixture until well combined. Press into a greased 20 × 30 cm sponge roll tin. Refrigerate for 1 hour. Ice with Lemon Icing and sprinkle with second measure of coconut. Cut into squares when cold.
Makes 24.

HINTS ON SPONGE MAKING

- **Always have the eggs at room temperature** for maximum volume.
- **Sift the dry ingredients together** three times for better volume.
- **Eggs and sugar are beaten sufficiently** when the mixture is thick enough to draw a figure eight with the mixture falling off the ends of the beater in an unbroken trail.
- **Fold in dry ingredients** very gently with a metal spoon. Use an up, down and over movement — don't stir.
- **Speed is essential** from the moment the dry ingredients are added until the time the sponge is put into the oven.
- **For even layers when making a sponge sandwich**, weigh the mixture in each tin before baking.
- **Grease and flour the cake tins very lightly**, otherwise the sponge may peel away on the bottom.
- **To test when a sponge is done** — the sponge will spring back when lightly touched with a finger.
- **A sponge shrinks slightly from the sides of the tin** when cooked.
- **Cool sponges** in sandwich tins for 5 minutes before turning out onto a wire rack.
- **Serve sponges** with whipped cream and fresh fruit, or dust with sifted icing sugar if wished.

CHOCOLATE LOG

3 eggs
¹/₂ cup sugar
¹/₂ teaspoon vanilla essence
25 g butter, melted
1 tablespoon water
2 tablespoons cocoa

¹/₄ cup Edmonds *standard plain flour*
1 teaspoon Edmonds *baking powder*
icing sugar
raspberry jam
Chocolate Butter Icing (page 81)
whipped cream

Beat eggs, sugar and vanilla until thick. Add butter and water. Sift cocoa, flour and baking powder together. Fold into egg mixture. Pour mixture into a greased and lined 20 × 30 cm sponge roll tin. Bake at 190°C for 10 to 12 minutes or until cake springs back when lightly touched. When cooked turn onto baking paper sprinkled with sifted icing sugar. Spread with jam and roll from the short side immediately, using the paper to help. Leave the roll wrapped in the paper until cold, then unroll and fill with whipped cream. Reroll and ice with Chocolate Butter Icing and pipe with a shell pattern icing tube to resemble a log.

CINNAMON CREAM OYSTERS OR FINGERS

2 eggs
1/4 cup sugar
2 teaspoons golden syrup
6 tablespoons Edmonds standard plain
  flour
1 teaspoon Edmonds baking powder

1/2 teaspoon Edmonds baking soda
1 teaspoon cinnamon
1/2 teaspoon ground ginger
whipped cream

Beat eggs and sugar until thick. Add golden syrup and beat well. Sift flour, baking powder, baking soda, cinnamon and ginger together. Fold dry ingredients into egg mixture. Spoon small amounts of mixture into greased sponge oyster or finger tins. Bake at 200°C for 10 to 12 minutes or until the surface springs back when lightly touched. When cold cut oysters open with a sharp knife and fill with whipped cream.
Makes 16.

EDMONDS FIELDER'S CLASSIC SPONGE

3 eggs
pinch of salt
1/2 cup caster sugar
1/2 cup Edmonds Fielder's Cornflour

1 teaspoon Edmonds standard plain
  flour
1 teaspoon Edmonds baking powder

Separate eggs. Beat the egg whites and salt until stiff. Add sugar gradually and beat until stiff and sugar has dissolved. Add egg yolks. Beat until well blended. Sift together cornflour, flour and baking powder and fold into the mixture. Pour into two 20 cm greased and lined sandwich tins. Bake at 190°C for 15 to 20 minutes or until cake springs back when lightly touched. Leave in tin for 10 minutes before turning out onto a wire rack.

LAMINGTONS

200 g sponge block or sponge cake (page 72)
Chocolate Icing   coconut

CHOCOLATE ICING
2 tablespoons cocoa
6 tablespoons boiling water
25 g butter, melted

2 1/4 cups icing sugar
1/4 teaspoon vanilla essence

Make or purchase sponge the day before required. Cut sponge into 4 cm squares. Dip each square in the Chocolate Icing. Roll in coconut. Leave to dry.
Makes 20.

CHOCOLATE ICING
Dissolve cocoa in boiling water and combine with the butter. Sift icing sugar into a bowl. Add cocoa mixture. Add vanilla and stir until well combined.

LIGHT-AS-AIR SPONGE

3 eggs, separated
³/₄ cup caster sugar
³/₄ cup Edmonds Fielder's cornflour
1 tablespoon Edmonds standard plain
   flour

1 teaspoon Edmonds baking powder
2 teaspoons golden syrup
1 tablespoon boiling water

Beat egg whites until stiff. Beat in sugar then yolks. Sift cornflour, flour and baking powder into egg mixture. Dissolve golden syrup in boiling water. Add to egg mixture, stirring in gently with a metal spoon. Pour into two greased and lined 20 cm sandwich tins. Bake at 190°C for 20 minutes or until cake springs back when lightly touched. Leave in tins for 5 minutes before turning out onto a wire rack.

SPONGE CAKE

3 eggs
pinch of salt
³/₄ cup caster sugar

1 cup Edmonds standard plain flour
1 teaspoon Edmonds baking powder
50 g butter, melted

Beat eggs and salt. Add sugar and beat until thick. Sift flour and baking powder together. Add to egg mixture. Fold in butter. Pour into a greased and lined deep 20 cm round cake tin. Bake at 190°C for 25 to 30 minutes or until cake springs back when lightly touched. Leave in tin for 10 minutes before turning out onto a wire rack.

SPONGE DROPS

2 eggs
¹/₂ cup caster sugar
few drops vanilla essence

¹/₄ cup Edmonds standard plain flour
1 teaspoon Edmonds baking powder
whipped cream

Beat eggs, sugar and vanilla until very thick. Sift flour and baking powder together. Fold into egg mixture. Drop small spoonsful onto greased oven trays. Bake at 190°C for 7 to 10 minutes or until light golden. Sandwich together in twos with whipped cream several hours before using.

SPONGE ROLL

3 eggs
pinch of salt
1/2 cup caster sugar
1/2 teaspoon vanilla essence
5 tablespoons Edmonds standard plain
   flour

1 teaspoon Edmonds baking powder
25 g butter, melted
caster or icing sugar
jam or honey
whipped cream

Beat eggs and salt. Add sugar and vanilla and beat until thick. Sift flour and baking powder together. Fold lightly into egg mixture. Fold in butter. Pour into a greased 20 × 30 cm sponge roll tin. Bake at 200°C for 8 to 10 minutes or until lightly browned and cake springs back when lightly touched. Turn out onto a cloth or greaseproof paper sprinkled with caster or icing sugar. Trim edges. Spread with jam or honey and cream. Roll from short side.

SMALL SWISS ROLLS
Roll up sponge roll from long side. Cut into three.

SPONGE SANDWICH
Cook sponge roll mixture in two greased and floured 20 cm sandwich tins at 190°C for 15 to 20 minutes. Sandwich together with jam and cream.

THREE-MINUTE SPONGE

1 cup Edmonds *standard plain flour*
3/4 cup sugar
3 eggs
3 tablespoons melted butter

2 tablespoons milk
2 teaspoons Edmonds *baking powder*
raspberry jam
whipped cream

Put flour, sugar, eggs, butter and milk into an electric mixer bowl. Beat on high speed for 3 minutes. Stir in baking powder. Pour into two greased and lined 20 cm sponge sandwich tins. Bake at 190°C for 15 to 20 minutes or until cake springs back when lightly touched. Leave in tin for 5 minutes before turning out onto a wire rack. When cold sandwich together with jam and whipped cream.

LEMON SPONGE
Add 2 teaspoons grated lemon rind to above mixture.

ORANGE SPONGE
Add 1 tablespoon grated orange rind to above mixture.

Top: Little Fruit Flans (pg 208) and Chocolate Eclairs (pg 86),
Bottom: Vol au Vents (pg 89)

AFGHANS

1 packet Edmonds *Chocolate Cake Mix*
50 g butter, melted
2 eggs

2 cups cornflakes
3 tablespoons water
Chocolate Icing Mix (from pack)
walnuts (optional)

Combine all ingredients except Chocolate Icing Mix and walnuts to form a stiff dough. Drop tablespoonsful onto a greased oven tray. Bake at 180°C for 15 minutes. When cold ice with Chocolate Icing made up from the instructions on the pack and decorate with a walnut if wished.
Makes 30.

BANANA CAKE

1 packet Edmonds *Butter Cake Mix*
½ cup water
1 tablespoon milk

2 eggs
50 g butter, softened
2 ripe bananas, mashed

Put cake mix, water, milk, eggs and butter into an electric mixer bowl. Mix at low speed until the ingredients are combined. Beat for 2 minutes at medium speed. Scrape down sides of bowl occasionally. Fold in bananas. Pour mixture into a greased and lined 20 cm cake tin. Bake at 180°C for 35 to 40 minutes or until cake springs back when lightly touched. Leave in tin for 10 minutes before turning out onto a wire rack.

BLACK AND TAN SQUARE

1 packet Edmonds *Chocolate Cake Mix*
¼ cup water

2 eggs
50 g butter, melted

FILLING
½ cup sweetened condensed milk
25 g butter

1 tablespoon golden syrup

Put cake mix, water, eggs and butter into an electric mixer bowl. Mix at low speed until the ingredients are combined. Beat for 2 minutes at medium speed. Scrape down sides of bowl occasionally. Stir in melted butter. Spread two-thirds of mixture into a greased and lined 20 × 30 cm sponge roll tin. Spread filling over. Top with remaining mixture. Bake at 180°C for 20 minutes or until cooked. Cut into squares. Top with chocolate icing from pack if desired.
Makes 16.

FILLING
Combine all ingredients in a saucepan and heat until butter has melted.

*Over-ripe bananas can be mashed then frozen
until ready to use for banana cake, muffins or loaves.*

DATE CARAMEL BARS

1 cup chopped dates
50 g butter
1/4 cup water

1 packet Edmonds *Chocolate Cake Mix*
2 eggs, beaten

ICING
1 cup brown sugar
25 g butter

2 tablespoons milk
1 cup icing sugar

Put dates, butter and water in a medium saucepan. Gently heat until butter has melted. Cool. Add cake mix and eggs to dates, beating well to combine. Pour mixture into a greased 20 × 30 cm sponge roll tin. Bake at 180°C for 20 minutes or until cake springs back when lightly touched. Leave to cool then spread with icing. When icing is almost set cut into bars with a hot knife. Set aside until cold. Makes 16.

ICING
Put brown sugar, butter and milk in a saucepan. Cook over a gentle heat, stirring constantly until sugar has dissolved. Remove from heat and sift in icing sugar, mixing to a smooth paste. If necessary, add more milk to a give a spreading consistency.

FRUITY CITRUS CAKE

1 packet Edmonds *Butter Cake Mix*
2 eggs
1/2 cup water

50 g butter, softened
2 teaspoons grated lemon rind
1 cup raisins
icing sugar

Put cake mix, eggs, water and butter into an electric mixer bowl. Mix at low speed until the ingredients are combined. Beat for 2 minutes at medium speed. Scrape down sides of bowl occasionally. Fold in lemon rind and raisins. Pour into a greased and lined 20 cm cake tin. Bake at 180°C for 35 to 40 minutes or until cake springs back when lightly touched. Leave in tin for 10 minutes before turning out onto a wire rack. When cold dust with icing sugar.

No. 6 eggs are used in recipes in this book.

GOLDEN LEMON COCONUT CAKE

1 packet Edmonds *Butter Cake Mix*
2 eggs

$^1/_2$ cup water
50 g butter, softened
1 cup coconut

LEMON CREAM ICING
1 cup icing sugar
1 to 2 tablespoons lemon juice

75 g butter, softened
1 teaspoon grated lemon rind

Put cake mix, eggs, water and butter into an electric mixer bowl. Mix at low speed until the ingredients are combined. Beat for 2 minutes at medium speed. Scrape down sides of bowl occasionally. Fold coconut through mixture and pour into a greased and lined 20 × 30 cm sponge roll tin. Bake at 180°C for 35 to 40 minutes or until cake springs back when lightly touched. Leave in tin for 10 minutes before turning out onto a wire rack. When cold ice with Lemon Cream Icing and sprinkle grated lemon rind on top.

LEMON CREAM ICING
Beat sugar, lemon juice and butter together until light and creamy.

JAFFA CUPCAKES

1 packet Edmonds *Chocolate Cake Mix*
1 tablespoon grated orange rind
$^2/_3$ cup water

2 eggs
50 g butter, softened
Chocolate Icing Mix (from pack)

Put cake mix, orange rind, water, eggs and butter into an electric mixer bowl. Mix at low speed until all ingredients are moistened. Beat at medium speed for 2 minutes. Scrape down sides of bowl occasionally. Divide mixture evenly between 16 paper patty cases. Bake at 180°C for 12 to 15 minutes or until cakes spring back when lightly touched. When cold decorate with Chocolate Icing.
Makes 16.

MOCHA TORTE

1 packet Edmonds *Chocolate
   Cake Mix*
2 eggs
²/₃ cup water

50 g butter, softened
¹/₂ cup chopped walnuts,
   approximately
8 walnut halves

ICING
50 g butter, softened
1¹/₄ cups icing sugar, sifted

2 teaspoons instant coffee powder
2 teaspoons hot water

Put cake mix, eggs, water and butter into an electric mixer bowl. Mix at low speed until the ingredients are combined. Beat for 2 minutes at medium speed. Scrape down sides of bowl occasionally. Pour mixture into two greased and lined 20 cm sponge sandwich tins. Bake at 180°C for 25 minutes or until cake springs back when lightly touched. Leave in tin for 10 minutes before turning out onto a wire rack. When cold, sandwich together with one-quarter of the icing, then spread remaining icing over top and sides of cake. Press chopped walnuts onto sides of cake. Decorate with walnut halves.

ICING
Beat all ingredients together until smooth. Add more water if necessary to form a spreadable icing.

MUFFIN CAKE

1 packet Edmonds *Muffin Mix*
2 teaspoons mixed spice
1 egg
1 cup water

3 tablespoons oil
¹/₂ cup cornflakes
1 green apple (diced)
1 cup sultanas

Put muffin mix in a bowl. Stir in mixed spice. Add egg, water and oil. Beat with a wooden spoon until ingredients are just combined, then add apple and sultanas and mix. Spoon mixture into a greased and lined 20 cm ring tin. Sprinkle cornflakes over. Bake at 180°C for 40 minutes or until cake springs back when lightly touched. Leave in tin for 10 minutes before turning out onto a wire rack.

STRAWBERRY BUTTERFLY CAKES

1 packet Edmonds *Butter Cake Mix*
¹/₂ cup water
2 eggs
50 g butter, softened

1 cup whipped cream
2 strawberries
icing sugar

Put cake mix, water, eggs and butter into an electric mixer bowl. Mix at low speed until all ingredients are moistened. Beat at medium speed for 2 minutes. Scrape down sides of bowl occasionally. Divide mixture evenly between 16 paper patty cases. Bake at 190°C for 12 minutes or until cakes spring back when lightly touched. When cold cut a circle from the top. Cut each slice in half. Spoon whipped cream into the cavity. Arrange 'wings' on top of cream. Cut each strawberry into eighths lengthwise. Place slivers of strawberry between the wings. Dust with icing sugar.
Makes 16.

ALMOND ICING

2 cups icing sugar
5 × 70 g packets ground almonds
1 cup caster sugar

2 eggs, beaten
few drops almond essence

Sift icing sugar into a bowl. Add ground almonds and caster sugar. Mix well. Bind to a firm consistency with beaten eggs and essence. Knead.

TO ICE CAKE:
Brush cake with lightly beaten egg white. Roll Almond Icing out to fit cake. Place icing on cake and leave for 2 to 3 days to dry before icing with Royal Icing (page 83).

BUTTER FILLING

1 tablespoon butter, softened
6 tablespoons icing sugar, sifted

1 tablespoon Edmonds custard
   powder

Beat all ingredients together until smooth.

BUTTER ICING

100 g butter, softened
1/4 teaspoon vanilla essence

2 cups icing sugar, sifted
1 to 2 tablespoons hot water

Cream butter until light and fluffy. Add vanilla. Gradually beat in icing sugar, beating until smooth. Add sufficient water to give a spreading consistency.

CHOCOLATE BUTTER ICING
Sift two tablespoons cocoa with the icing sugar in above recipe.

CARAMEL ICING

1 cup brown sugar
25 g butter

2 tablespoons milk, approximately
1 cup icing sugar

Put brown sugar, butter and milk in a saucepan. Cook over a gentle heat, stirring constantly until sugar has dissolved. Remove from heat and sift in icing sugar, mixing to a smooth paste. If necessary, add more milk to a give a spreading consistency.

CREAM CHANTILLY

1 cup whipped cream
1/4 teaspoon vanilla essence

1 tablespoon icing sugar

Combine all ingredients. Mix lightly.
Makes 1 cup.

Cakes need not be iced. Dust lightly with icing sugar for a change.

CREAM CHEESE ICING

2 tablespoons butter, softened
1/4 cup cream cheese

1 cup icing sugar
1/2 teaspoon grated lemon rind

Beat butter and cream cheese until creamy. Mix in icing sugar and lemon rind, beating well to combine.

CRUMBLE TOPPING FOR CAKES

1/2 cup brown sugar
1/2 cup Edmonds standard plain flour
1/4 cup coconut

1/4 cup chopped nuts
100 g butter

In a bowl combine sugar, flour, coconut and nuts. Cut in butter until it resembles coarse breadcrumbs. Sprinkle over cakes before baking.

WHITE ICING

2 cups icing sugar
1/4 teaspoon butter, softened

2 tablespoons water, approximately
1/4 teaspoon vanilla essence

Sift icing sugar into a bowl. Add butter. Add sufficient water to mix to a spreadable consistency. Flavour with vanilla essence.

CHOCOLATE ICING
Sift 1 tablespoon cocoa with the icing sugar.

COFFEE ICING
Dissolve 2 teaspoons instant coffee in 1 tablespoon hot water. Mix into icing sugar.

LEMON ICING
Replace vanilla with 1 teaspoon grated lemon rind. Replace water with lemon juice. Add a few drops of yellow food colouring if wished.

ORANGE ICING
Replace vanilla with 2 teaspoons grated orange rind. Replace water with orange juice. Add a few drops of yellow and red food colouring if wished.

MELTED CHOCOLATE ICING

200 g cooking chocolate
25 g butter

1/2 cup cream

Break chocolate into top of a double boiler or a small bowl. Add butter and cream. Set over hot water and heat, stirring constantly, until it has melted and thickened slightly. Set aside until cool. Beat until thick before using. Suitable for decorating cakes, slices and also for piping.

Crumble toppings save time and add interest to cakes.

MOCK CREAM

100 g butter, softened
1 cup icing sugar
1 tablespoon milk

$^{1}/_{4}$ teaspoon vanilla essence or
1 teaspoon grated lemon rind

Cream butter and sugar until light and fluffy. Add milk and vanilla. Beat until thick and pale like cream.

PINEAPPLE FILLING

$^{1}/_{2}$ cup water
1 teaspoon gelatine

2 tablespoons sugar
1 cup crushed pineapple

Put water in a saucepan. Sprinkle gelatine over and leave to swell for 5 minutes. Gently heat the gelatine mixture, stirring until gelatine has dissolved. Stir in sugar, stirring until dissolved. Add pineapple. Bring to the boil. Allow to boil for 3 minutes. Remove from heat. Leave until cold then chill until set.

ROYAL ICING

4 egg whites
1 kg icing sugar, sifted

1 tablespoon lemon juice
few drops glycerine

Beat egg whites until soft peaks form. Gradually add icing sugar, beating to combine. Stir in lemon juice and glycerine. Keep covered with a damp cloth until ready to use. This quantity is sufficient to ice and decorate a 20 cm square fruit cake.

If you want to save time Edmonds make a range of ready-rolled puff, flaky and short pastries available in the freezer section of most supermarkets.

HINTS FOR PASTRY MAKING

- **Equipment and ingredients** — chill butter, water and mixing bowl before using.
- **Too much water** causes tough pastry and shrinkage.
- **Short pastry** — use lemon juice for a tender crust. Replace 1 tablespoon cold water with 1 teaspoon lemon juice and 2 teaspoons of cold water.
- **To prevent pastry from stretching and shrinking** — roll pastry away from you with light strokes. Do not turn pastry over when rolling. Lift pastry over the rolling pin into tins.
- **Bake pastry in a hot oven**. The richer the pastry, the higher the oven temperature.

CHEESE PASTRY

1½ cups Edmonds *standard plain flour*
1 teaspoon Edmonds *baking powder*
¼ teaspoon salt
pinch of cayenne pepper
75 g butter
³/₄ cup grated tasty cheese
3 tablespoons milk, approximately

Sift flour, baking powder, salt and cayenne together. Cut in the butter until it resembles fine breadcrumbs. Add grated cheese. Bind to a soft, but not a sticky dough with the milk. On a lightly floured surface roll out dough to 5 mm thickness and use as required for savoury pies, tarts, quiches and cheese straws.
Makes 350 g pastry.

CHOUX PASTRY

100 g butter
1 cup water
1 cup Edmonds *standard plain flour*
3 eggs

Combine butter and water in a saucepan. Bring to a rolling boil. Remove from heat and quickly add flour. Beat with a wooden spoon until mixture leaves the sides of the saucepan. Allow to cool for 5 minutes. Add eggs one at a time, beating well after each addition, until mixture is glossy. Use as required for éclairs and cream puffs.
Makes 500 g dough.

FLAKY PASTRY

2 cups Edmonds *high grade flour*
$^1/_4$ *teaspoon salt*
200 g butter

6 tablespoons cold water,
approximately

Sift flour and salt into a bowl. Cut one-quarter of the butter into the flour until it resembles fine breadcrumbs. Add sufficient water to mix to a stiff dough. On a lightly floured board roll out dough to a rectangle 0.5–1 cm thick. With the short end of the rectangle facing you, dot two-thirds of the pastry with a third of the remaining butter to within 1 cm of the dough edge. Fold the unbuttered pastry into the middle of the pastry. Fold the buttered section over to the folded edge. Seal the edges with a rolling pin and mark the dough with the rolling pin to form corrugations. Give the pastry a quarter turn. Roll into a rectangle. Repeat twice until all the butter is used. Chill pastry for 5 minutes between rollings if possible. Use as required for savoury pies and vol au vents.
Makes 500 g pastry.

PUFF PASTRY
Increase butter to 250 g. Roll and fold the pastry 6 times.

SHORT PASTRY

2 cups Edmonds *standard plain flour*
$^1/_4$ *teaspoon salt*

125 g butter
cold water

Sift flour and salt together. Cut in the butter until it resembles fine breadcrumbs. Mix to a stiff dough with a little water. Roll out very lightly and do not handle more than is necessary. Use as required for sweet or savoury pies and tarts, and quiches. Makes 375 g pastry.

WHOLEMEAL PASTRY
Replace flour with Edmonds wholemeal flour and add 1 teaspoon Edmonds baking powder.

FOOD PROCESSOR PASTRY
Have butter and water very cold. Dice butter. Put flour in food processor. Add butter. Pulse until it resembles fine breadcrumbs. Add water by drops and pulse until mixture forms small balls. Do not overmix. Turn out onto a lightly floured surface. Knead lightly. Wrap and chill for at least 15 minutes.

SUET PASTRY

2 cups Edmonds *standard plain flour*
$^1/_2$ *teaspoon salt*

1 cup suet
$^1/_2$ cup water, approximately

Sift flour and salt into a bowl. Stir in suet. Mix to a smooth soft dough with water. Knead a little. On a lightly floured board roll out two-thirds of dough and use to line a six-cup-capacity pudding basin. Use remaining one-third for top crust. Use for savoury puddings.

Try not to stretch pastry when rolling and handling. It will shrink on
cooking. If time permits, rest pastry before baking.

SWEET SHORTCRUST PASTRY

1 cup Edmonds *standard plain flour*
75 g butter
¼ cup sugar

1 egg yolk
1 tablespoon water

Sift flour. Cut in butter until it resembles fine breadcrumbs. Stir in sugar. Add egg yolk and water. Mix to a stiff dough. Chill for 30 minutes before using. Use as required for sweet pies and tarts.
Makes about 400 g pastry.

SPICE PASTRY
Add 2 teaspoons mixed spice to flour.

NUT PASTRY
Add ½ cup chopped walnuts or nuts of your choice, before mixing to a stiff dough.

CHOCOLATE ÉCLAIRS

100 g butter
1 cup water
1 cup Edmonds *standard plain flour*

3 eggs
whipped cream
Chocolate Icing (page 82)

Combine butter and water in a saucepan. Bring to a rolling boil. Remove from heat and quickly add flour. Beat with a wooden spoon until mixture leaves the sides of the saucepan. Allow to cool for 5 minutes. Add eggs one at a time, beating well after each addition, until mixture is glossy. Pipe 7 cm strips of the mixture onto greased oven trays. Bake at 200°C for 30 minutes or until éclairs are puffy and golden, then lower heat to 120°C and continue baking for about 15 minutes until dry. Cool thoroughly. Using a sharp knife, cut slits into the sides of each eclair. Fill with whipped cream and ice tops with Chocolate Icing.
Makes 30.

CREAM PUFFS
Pipe or spoon small teaspoonsful of Chocalate Éclair mixture onto greased oven trays. Bake as above. Cool thoroughly. Fill with whipped cream and ice tops with Chocolate Icing or dust with sifted icing sugar.

CHRISTMAS MINCE PIES

400 g Sweet Shortcrust Pastry or 2 sheets
    Edmonds *Sweet Short Pastry*
1 cup Christmas Mincemeat (see page 87)

1 egg, beaten
icing sugar

On a lightly floured board roll out pastry to 3 mm thickness or use ready rolled sheets. Cut out rounds using a 7 cm cutter, and use to line about 16 patty tins. Using a 6 cm round biscuit cutter, cut out tops from the remaining pastry. Spoon teaspoonsful of mincemeat into each base. Brush the edges of the bases with some of the egg. Place tops over the filling, pressing slightly around the edges to seal the pies. Glaze with the remaining beaten egg. Bake at 180°C for 15 minutes or until lightly browned. To serve, heat at 140°C for 15 minutes or until warm. Dust with sifted icing sugar.
Makes 16.

CHRISTMAS MINCEMEAT

2 medium apples, unpeeled,
   quartered and cored
275 g packet vegetable shortening or
   melted butter
1$^1/_4$ cups currants
1$^1/_4$ cups sultanas
1$^1/_4$ cups raisins

1$^1/_4$ cups mixed peel
$^1/_4$ cup blanched almonds
1 cup brown sugar
$^1/_4$ teaspoon salt
$^1/_2$ teaspoon ground nutmeg
2 tablespoons brandy or whisky or
   lemon juice

Mince or finely chop apples, suet, currants, sultanas, raisins, peel and almonds. Add sugar, salt, nutmeg and brandy. Mix well. Spoon mixture into clean jars and seal. If using fruit juice, refrigerate.
Makes 6 cups.

COCONUT MACAROONS

125 g Flaky Pastry or 1 sheet Edmonds
   Flaky Puff Pastry
3 tablespoons raspberry jam
2 egg whites

$^1/_2$ cup sugar
$^1/_2$ cup coconut
$^1/_4$ to $^1/_2$ teaspoon almond essence

On a lightly floured board roll out pastry to 3 mm thickness or use ready rolled sheet. Cut out rounds using a 6 cm cutter and line patty tins. Spoon a little jam into each pastry base. In a small bowl beat egg whites until soft peaks form. Add sugar, coconut and almond essence. Fold into egg white mixture. Spoon meringue over prepared bases. Bake at 180°C for 35 minutes or until cooked.
Makes 16.

CUSTARD SQUARES

PASTRY
175 g Flaky Pastry or 2 sheets Edmonds Flaky Puff Pastry

CUSTARD
4 tablespoons Edmonds custard powder
3 tablespoons icing sugar
2 cups milk

50 g butter
1 egg, beaten
icing sugar

Cut pastry in half, giving two rectangles. On a lightly floured board, roll each piece to 3 mm thickness and similar size or use ready rolled sheets. Prick well all over, place on two oven trays and bake at 215°C for 10 to 12 minutes or until lightly golden. Cool pastry sheets and sandwich together with cold custard. Dust with sifted icing sugar.
Makes 20.

CUSTARD
In a saucepan, mix custard powder, sugar and $^1/_4$ cup milk to a smooth paste. Add the remaining milk, butter and egg. Cook until mixture is very thick, stirring all the time. Cover with a damp paper towel or plastic wrap pressed onto the custard surface to prevent a skin forming. Leave until cold.

FRUIT SQUARES

200 g Flaky Pastry or 2 sheets
  Edmonds *Flaky Puff Pastry*

icing sugar

FRUIT FILLING
50 g butter, melted
1 medium Granny Smith apple,
  peeled, cored and grated
¹/₄ cup raisins
¹/₄ cup sultanas
¹/₄ cup currants

1 tablespoon lemon juice
¹/₄ teaspoon grated lemon rind
1 teaspoon cinnamon
¹/₄ cup brown sugar
1 teaspoon mixed spice

Divide pastry in half. On a lightly floured board roll out one-half to 2 mm thickness, forming a large rectangle approximately 20 × 30 cm or use ready rolled sheet. Spread fruit filling over pastry, leaving a 1 cm border around the edge for sealing. Moisten the edges with water. Roll out remaining pastry to the same thickness and shape or use second ready rolled sheet. Place on top of fruit filling. Press edges together. Prick pastry top with a fork. Bake at 200°C for 30 to 35 minutes or until golden. Cut while hot and sprinkle with sifted icing sugar.
Makes 24.

FRUIT FILLING
In a bowl combine all ingredients.

NEENISH TARTS

125 g butter, softened
1/2 cup sugar
1 egg
2 cups Edmonds standard plain flour or
   use 1 kg Edmonds Sweet Short Pastry

1 teaspoon Edmonds baking powder
pinch of salt
White Icing (page 82)
Chocolate Icing (page 82)

FILLING
1/2 cup icing sugar
100 g butter, softened

1/2 cup sweetened condensed milk
2 tablespoons lemon juice

Cream butter and sugar until light and fluffy. Add egg and beat well. Sift flour, baking powder and salt together. Mix into creamed mixture, stirring well. Turn mixture out onto a lightly floured board and knead well. Chill pastry for 15 minutes. Roll out pastry to 2 mm thickness or use ready rolled sheets. Cut out rounds using a 7 cm cutter and line patty tins. Prick bases. Bake at 180°C for 12 minutes or until cooked. Cool pastry cases and fill with filling. Allow filling to set in the fridge. Ice one half of each tart with White Icing and the other half with Chocolate Icing. Makes 30.

FILLING
Sift icing sugar into a bowl. Add butter, condensed milk and lemon juice. Beat until smooth.

VOL AU VENTS

200 g Flaky Pastry or 2 sheets
   Edmonds Flaky Puff Pastry

1 egg yolk
1 tablespoon water

FILLING
2 tablespoons butter
1 tablespoon finely chopped onion
2 tablespoons Edmonds standard plain
   flour

3/4 cup milk
salt
pepper

On a lightly floured board roll out pastry to 1.5 cm thickness or use ready rolled sheets. Cut out 5 cm rounds. Place on an oven tray. Using a smaller cutter, press halfway through the centre of each pastry round. This forms the lid. Combine egg yolk and water. Carefully brush egg mixture over the top of each pastry round, taking care it does not run down the sides, as this will prevent the pastry from rising. Bake at 220°C for 15 minutes or until golden and well risen. Transfer to a wire rack. When cool, carefully cut round the lid and ease the pastry away. Scrape any uncooked pastry away and discard. Spoon in filling. Replace pastry lid on top of filling. Serve hot.
Makes about 9.

FILLING
Melt butter in a saucepan. Add onion and cook until clear. Stir in flour and cook until frothy. Gradually add milk, stirring constantly until mixture boils and thickens. Remove from the heat. Season with salt and pepper to taste.

ADD ANY OF THE FOLLOWING TO THE SAUCE
grated cheese and chopped ham
canned smoked fish, drained and
   flaked
canned asparagus and hard-boiled eggs

grated cheese and cooked chopped
   mushroom
corned beef and mustard
canned shrimps, drained and chopped

CHICKEN STOCK

1 chicken carcass or bones
1 onion, peeled
1 carrot, peeled
1 stalk celery
1 bay leaf

sprig parsley
sprig thyme
6 white peppercorns
1½ litres cold water

Put chicken, onion, carrot and celery into a large saucepan. Tie bay leaf, parsley and thyme together to make a bouquet garni. Add bouquet garni, peppercorns and water to pan. Bring to the boil and simmer gently for 2 hours. Strain through a fine mesh sieve. Cool the liquid then refrigerate until chilled. Remove any fat from surface. Use as required. This stock can be frozen.
Makes about 4 cups.

FISH STOCK

1 fish head
other fish trimmings — bones and
  skin
4 cups cold water
2 slices lemon

1 bay leaf
sprig thyme
sprig parsley
1 teaspoon white peppercorns

Wash fish head then put into a saucepan with fish trimmings. Add water and lemon. Tie the bay leaf, thyme and parsley together to make a bouquet garni. Add to the saucepan with the peppercorns. Bring to the boil, skim if necessary. Simmer gently for 20 minutes. Strain through a fine mesh sieve.
Makes about 4 cups.

MEAT STOCK

1 kg uncooked beef bones, fat
  removed
2 litres cold water
250 g vegetables — e.g. leeks,
  carrots, celery

6 black peppercorns
1 bay leaf
sprig parsley
sprig thyme

Put bones and water into a large saucepan and bring to the boil. If the scum is dirty, drain water off. Wash bones, re-cover with cold water and reboil. Add prepared whole vegetables and peppercorns. Tie bay leaf, parsley and thyme together to make a bouquet garni. Add to pan. Simmer gently for 6 hours. Strain through a fine mesh sieve. Cool the liquid then refrigerate. Remove any fat from surface. Use as required. This stock can be frozen.
Makes about 4 cups.

FOR BROWN MEAT STOCK
Brown the bones well, either in a roasting dish in the oven or in a heavy-based saucepan. Drain off any fat then place bones into a large saucepan. Wash out any sediment from original roasting dish or pan with some of the measured water and use in stock. Proceed as above. A few soft tomatoes and mushrooms can be added when starting to cook the brown stock to give a richer flavour.

CREAM SOUP BASE

2 tablespoons butter
1 onion, finely chopped
2 tablespoons Edmonds *standard plain*
  flour
1½ cups milk

½ cup water
salt
pepper
prepared vegetables (see below)

Melt butter in a saucepan. Add onion. Cook until onion is clear. Stir in the flour and cook until frothy. Gradually add milk and water, stirring constantly. Bring to the boil stirring constantly, and cook for 2 to 3 minutes. Stir prepared vegetables into soup base. Mix well. Season to taste. Reheat to almost boiling.
Serves 4.

CREAM OF FRESH ASPARAGUS SOUP
Add 2 cups of cooked, puréed fresh asparagus and ¼ teaspoon sugar.

CREAM OF CANNED ASPARAGUS SOUP
Add a 340 g can of asparagus, drained and puréed. Garnish with paprika.

CREAM OF CARROT SOUP
Slice and cook 3 carrots and 1 stalk celery. Purée the vegetables together. Add to cream base with ¼ teaspoon chicken stock powder and ¼ teaspoon dried thyme. Garnish with chopped parsley or celery leaves.

CREAM OF CAULIFLOWER SOUP
Add 2 cups cooked, puréed cauliflower and ¼ teaspoon ground nutmeg or mace.

CREAM OF CELERY SOUP
Increase flour to 3 tablespoons. Add 2 cups of cooked, puréed celery and 1½ teaspoons chicken stock powder.

FRENCH ONION SOUP

3 tablespoons butter
6 medium onions, thinly sliced
1 teaspoon sugar
4 cups liquid beef stock

salt
black pepper
¼ cup dry sherry
4 to 6 slices cheese on toast

Melt the butter in a saucepan. Add onions and sugar. Cook slowly for 15 minutes or until onion is golden. Add beef stock. Bring to the boil then simmer for 15 minutes. Season with salt and pepper to taste. Just before serving add sherry. Grill cheese on toast. Cut into triangles or squares and place on soup.
Serves 4–6.

KUMARA SOUP

25 g butter
1 large kumara, chopped
1 onion, chopped
1 large potato, chopped
1 1/2 teaspoons hot curry powder

3 cups liquid chicken stock
1 cup milk
salt
chopped chives

Melt the butter in a saucepan. Add kumara, onion, potato and curry powder. Cook until onion is clear. Stir in stock and bring to the boil. Simmer gently until vegetables are tender. Purée in a food processor or blender until smooth. Add the milk and salt. Reheat until almost boiling. Serve garnished with chives.
Serves 6–8.

LEEK AND POTATO SOUP

5 medium potatoes, chopped
2 teaspoons oil or butter
2 small leeks, thinly sliced
1 clove garlic, crushed
200 g bacon pieces, finely chopped
6 cups liquid chicken stock
1 bay leaf

2 sprigs parsley
1 cup milk
1/4 cup chopped parsley
salt
white pepper
grated cheese

Cook potatoes in boiling salted water until tender. Drain and mash. Set aside. Heat the oil in a large saucepan. Add leeks, garlic and bacon. Cook without colouring until leeks are tender. Pour in stock. Add bay leaf and parsley sprigs. Bring to the boil. Reduce heat and simmer for 20 minutes. Remove bay leaf and parsley sprigs. Add mashed potato. Simmer for 15 minutes. Stir in the milk and chopped parsley. Season with salt and pepper to taste. Serve garnished with cheese.
Serves 4–5.

MINESTRONE

1/2 cup haricot beans
1/4 cup oil
2 tablespoons butter
2 onions, finely chopped
2 carrots, chopped
2 stalks celery, sliced
2 courgettes, sliced
1 potato, peeled and diced

1 cup shredded cabbage
100 g chopped green beans
2 × 400 g cans tomatoes in juice,
  chopped
5 cups liquid beef stock
salt
black pepper
grated parmesan cheese

Cover beans with cold water and soak overnight. Drain and set aside. Heat oil and butter in a large saucepan. Add onions and cook until pale golden. Add carrots, celery, courgettes, potato, cabbage and beans. Cook, stirring frequently, for about 8 minutes. Stir in undrained tomatoes, stock, soaked drained beans, salt and pepper to taste. Bring to the boil, reduce heat, cover and simmer gently for 1 1/2 to 2 hours or until soup is thick. Serve garnished with parmesan cheese.
Serves 8.

Use stale bread to make croûtons or Melba toast. Store in an airtight
container. Serve with soups, pâtés or salads.

MUSHROOM SOUP

3 tablespoons butter
1 onion, chopped
500 g mushrooms, sliced
3 tablespoons Edmonds standard plain
   flour
2 cups milk

1 cup liquid chicken stock
$1/2$ teaspoon salt
white pepper
1 teaspoon lemon juice
chopped parsley or chives

Melt butter in a saucepan. Add onion and mushrooms. Cook until onion is clear. Stir in the flour. Cook, stirring, for 1 minute. Gradually add milk and stock, stirring constantly. Bring to the boil. Cook for 5 minutes or until soup thickens slightly. Add salt, pepper and lemon juice. Serve garnished with parsley.
Serves 4–5.

MUSSEL SOUP

250 g white fish fillets
4 cups water
400 g can tomatoes in juice
2 tablespoons butter
1 teaspoon curry powder
2 tablespoons Edmonds standard plain
   flour
$1/4$ cup dry white wine

2 teaspoons chicken stock powder
2 tablespoons tomato paste
$1/4$ teaspoon basil
16 to 20 fresh cleaned mussels in
   shell
salt
black pepper
chopped parsley

Put fish and water into a large saucepan. Bring to the boil then simmer for 15 minutes. Remove fish from pan and flake. Reserve all the liquid. Drain and chop tomatoes, reserving juice. In another saucepan melt the butter. Add curry powder and cook for 30 seconds. Stir in flour and cook until frothy. Gradually add reserved liquid, wine, reserved tomato juice and chicken stock powder. Bring to the boil, stirring constantly until mixture thickens slightly. Add tomato paste, basil and chopped tomatoes. Bring to the boil. Add mussels, simmer for 10 minutes or until mussels open. Discard any which do not open. Stir in the flaked fish, salt and pepper to taste. Serve garnished with parsley.
Serves 4–6.

OLD-FASHIONED VEGETABLE SOUP

1 kg beef bones, fat removed
3 litres water
$1/2$ cup red lentils
$1/2$ cup pearl barley
$1/2$ cup split peas

3 cups chopped vegetables — e.g.
   carrots, potatoes, parsnips
salt
black pepper

Put bones, water, lentils, barley and split peas in a large saucepan. Bring to the boil and simmer for 2 to 3 hours until meat is falling off the bones. Remove bones, fat and gristle from the soup. Add vegetables. Cook for 30 to 45 minutes. Season with salt and pepper to taste.
Serves 8–10.

A smoother-textured soup can be made by using a blender.

OYSTER SOUP

25 g butter
1/4 cup Edmonds standard plain flour
3 cups liquid fish stock
1 cup milk
salt

white pepper
pinch of ground nutmeg or mace
1 1/2 dozen raw oysters, chopped
2 tablespoons lemon juice
chopped parsley or chives

Melt the butter in a saucepan. Stir in flour and cook until frothy. Gradually add stock and milk, stirring constantly. Continue stirring and bring to the boil. Cook for 5 minutes or until mixture thickens slightly. Season with salt, pepper and nutmeg to taste. Stir in oysters and lemon juice. Serve garnished with parsley.
Serves 4.

PEA AND HAM SOUP

500 g bacon or ham bones
250 g split peas
1 medium onion, finely chopped

1 teaspoon salt
1.5 litres water
pepper

Put all ingredients in a large saucepan. Simmer slowly for 2 to 3 hours until peas are soft. For a very creamy soup remove bones and purée soup in a blender or push through a sieve. Cut meat from bones and return to soup.
Serves 6.

PUMPKIN SOUP

1 tablespoon oil
1 onion, chopped
750 g pumpkin, peeled and chopped
1 large potato, peeled and chopped
4 cups liquid chicken stock

salt
black pepper
nutmeg

Heat oil in a saucepan. Add onion and cook until clear. Add pumpkin, potato and stock. Cover, bring to the boil and cook until vegetables are soft. Purée vegetable mixture in a blender or push through a sieve. Season with salt, pepper and nutmeg to taste. For extra flavour, a ham hock or bacon bones can be added when cooking the pumpkin.
Serves 6.

Gently reheat cream soups to prevent curdling.

SEAFOOD SOUP

4 cups liquid chicken stock
few sprigs parsley
1 bay leaf
6 black peppercorns
2 tablespoons butter
2 leeks, thinly sliced
3 carrots, thinly sliced

1 turnip, thinly sliced
2 stalks celery, thinly sliced
500 g white fish fillets, cut into large
   chunks
salt
white pepper

Bring stock, parsley, bay leaf and peppercorns to the boil and simmer for 10 minutes. While stock is simmering, melt butter in another saucepan. Add leeks, carrots, turnip and celery. Gently cook without colouring until vegetables are glossy and just tender. Place fish on top of vegetables. Pour stock through a sieve onto fish and vegetables. Reheat until fish is opaque and season with salt and pepper to taste.
Serves 6.

SPICY LENTIL SOUP

2 teaspoons butter
2 teaspoons oil
1 clove garlic, crushed
1 carrot, finely chopped
1 onion, finely chopped
1 stalk celery, finely chopped
1 teaspoon curry powder

1 cup brown lentils
250 g bacon bones
400 g can tomatoes in juice, chopped
4 cups liquid beef stock
salt
black pepper
2 tablespoons chopped parsley

Heat butter and oil in a large saucepan. Add garlic, carrot, onion and celery. Cook until onion is clear. Stir in curry powder. Cook, stirring constantly, for 30 seconds. Add lentils, bacon bones, tomatoes and juice, and stock. Cover. Bring to the boil, then reduce heat and simmer covered for $1^{1}/_{2}$ hours or until lentils are cooked. Remove and discard bacon bones. Season with salt and pepper to taste. Serve garnished with parsley.
Serves 4–5.

SPINACH SOUP

50 g butter
1 onion, chopped
1 clove garlic, crushed
500 g spinach, washed, stems
   removed
2 cups liquid chicken stock

$^{1}/_{2}$ teaspoon salt
black pepper
$^{1}/_{2}$ teaspoon sugar
pinch of nutmeg
sour cream or unsweetened natural
   yoghurt

Melt the butter in a saucepan. Add onion and garlic, and cook until onion is clear. Add spinach, stock, salt and pepper to taste. Bring to the boil, cover and leave to simmer for 10 to 15 minutes or until spinach is limp, but still very green. Add sugar. Purée in a blender until smooth. Add nutmeg. Serve garnished with a swirl of sour cream.
Serves 4–5.

TOMATO SOUP

1st EDITION RECIPE

2 teaspoons butter or oil
1 onion, finely chopped
1 stalk celery, chopped
6 medium tomatoes
$\frac{1}{2}$ teaspoon salt
black pepper

$\frac{1}{4}$ cup tomato paste
2 cups liquid chicken stock
pinch of chilli powder or cayenne
  pepper
sour cream

Heat butter in a medium saucepan. Add onion and celery and cook until onion is clear. Blanch the tomatoes by placing in boiling water for 30 seconds then plunging into cold water. Remove skins. Chop the flesh. Stir the tomatoes, salt, pepper, tomato paste and stock into the onion and celery. Add the chilli powder. Bring almost to the boil. Purée in blender. Serve garnished with a swirl of sour cream. Serves 4–5.

Top: Mussel Soup (pg 93), Centre: Minestrone (pg 92),
Bottom: Pumpkin Soup (pg 94)

CROÛTONS

slices stale toast bread

Cut bread into small dice. Place on an oven tray and bake at 190°C for 10 minutes or until evenly browned on all sides. Shake tray occasionally during cooking. Croûtons may be toasted or fried instead of baked. Serve in the soup or on a side plate.

MELBA TOAST

1 loaf unsliced white bread

Remove crusts. Cut bread into 5 mm thick slices. Then cut into triangles. Grill on both sides until crisp and golden. Use a sharp knife to split each piece in half and grill the uncooked side until golden. Cool. Store in an airtight container.

TASTY CROÛTES

1 loaf French bread   *onion stock powder*
mayonnaise

Cut bread into 2 cm thick slices. Spread thinly with mayonnaise. Sprinkle with a pinch of onion stock powder. Grill until golden. Serve with soup.

BACON AND EGG PIE

2 sheets Edmonds *Flaky Puff Pastry*
   (or 500 g homemade Flaky Pastry,
   thinly rolled into 2 equal sheets —
   see page 85)
1 onion, chopped
1 cup chopped bacon

¹/₂ cup mixed vegetables
2 tablespoons spicy chutney
6 eggs
salt and pepper
milk

Use 1 sheet of pastry to line a greased 20 cm square shallow cake tin. Sprinkle onion, bacon and mixed vegetables evenly over pastry. Dot the chutney on top. Break eggs evenly over, pricking the yolks so they run slightly. Season with salt and pepper to taste. Carefully lift second sheet of pastry over filling. Brush top with milk. Bake at 200°C for 40 minutes or until well risen and golden. To serve, cut into squares. Serve hot or cold.
Serves 6.

BASIC QUICHE

200 g Short Pastry or 1 sheet Edmonds *Savoury Short Pastry*

FILLING
1 tablespoon butter
3 rashers bacon, chopped
1 onion, chopped
2 tablespoons Edmonds *standard plain*
   flour

1 cup milk
2 eggs
¹/₂ cup grated tasty cheese
salt
pepper

On a lightly floured board roll out pastry or use ready rolled sheet. Use to line a 20 cm flan ring or quiche dish. If using flan ring, place ring on an oven tray before lining with pastry. Trim excess pastry off and discard. Bake blind at 200°C for 12 minutes. Remove baking blind material. Return to the oven for 1 minute to dry pastry out. Remove from oven. Pour filling into pastry base. Return to oven and bake for a further 30 minutes or until filling is golden and set. Serve hot or cold.
Serves 4–6.

FILLING
Melt butter in a saucepan. Add bacon and onion. Cook until onion is clear. Stir in flour and cook until frothy. Gradually add milk, stirring constantly until mixture boils and thickens. Remove pan from heat. Lightly beat eggs with a fork. Add eggs and cheese to saucepan. Stir to combine. Season with salt and pepper to taste.

BOILED EGGS

Gently lower required number of eggs into a saucepan of simmering water. Adjust heat to maintain water at a simmering point. Cook according to the degree of firmness required and size of eggs.

soft-boiled   3 to 4 minutes
firm white, soft yolk   4 to 7 minutes
hard-boiled   8 minutes

Place hard-boiled eggs in cold water when cooked. This helps prevent the formation of a greyish-green ring between the yolk and white.

CURRIED EGGS

25 g butter   3/4 cup milk
1 small onion, finely chopped   salt
1 teaspoon curry powder   4 hard-boiled eggs
1 tablespoon Edmonds standard plain
    flour

Melt the butter in a saucepan. Add onion and cook until onion is clear. Stir in curry powder and cook for 30 seconds. Stir in flour and cook until frothy. Gradually add milk, stirring constantly until the mixture boils and thickens. Boil for 1 minute. Remove from heat. Season with salt to taste. Shell the eggs and cut in half lengthwise. Arrange in a serving dish. Pour the hot curry sauce over eggs.
Serves 4.

SALMON CURRIED EGGS
Add a 185 g can drained and flaked salmon to sauce and pour sauce over eggs, then spoon buttered crumbs on top.

EGG NOG

1 egg   1 teaspoon sugar
1 cup milk   1/4 teaspoon ground nutmeg

Put egg, milk and sugar into a blender. Process until combined. Pour mixture into a glass. Serve garnished with nutmeg. Alternatively, beat egg, milk and sugar together until well combined.
Serves 1.

EGGS BENEDICT

3 English muffins   salt
1 tablespoon butter   pepper
6 slices ham   1/2 cup Hollandaise Sauce (page 192)
6 eggs

Split the muffins and toast them. Keep warm. Melt the butter in a frying pan. Add ham and cook until golden on both sides. While ham is cooking, poach the eggs. Place a slice of ham on each muffin. Place poached eggs on top of ham. Season with salt and pepper to taste. Top with Hollandaise Sauce.
Serves 6.

MERINGUES

2 egg whites
½ cup caster sugar

whipped cream

Beat egg whites until stiff but not dry. Add half the sugar and beat well. Repeat with remaining sugar. Pipe or spoon small amounts of meringue onto a greased oven tray. Bake at 120°C for 1 to 1½ hours or until the meringues are dry but not brown. Cool and when required to serve, sandwich meringues together in twos with whipped cream.
Makes 12.

OMELET

2 eggs
1 tablespoon milk
salt

pepper
2 teaspoons butter
parsley

Lightly beat egg and milk together. Season with salt and pepper to taste. Heat an omelet pan. Add the butter. When butter is foaming, not brown, pour in the egg mixture. Cook over moderate heat, lifting mixture with a spatula so uncooked egg runs underneath. Cook until egg is set and golden. Loosen from pan with spatula. Fold in half. Turn out onto a hot serving dish. Garnish with parsley.

POACHED EGGS

Half to three-quarters fill a frying pan with water. Add approximately 1 tablespoon of DYC vinegar and bring to the boil. Break an egg into a saucer and slip it carefully into the pan. Cover and simmer gently until white is just set. Serve on hot buttered toast. Alternatively, an egg poacher can be used. Heat the water in the poaching pan. Lightly grease the poaching cups. Break the eggs into the cups. Cover and cook until the egg white is firm. Turn out onto buttered toast.

PUFFY OMELET

2 eggs
1 tablespoon water
salt

pepper
2 teaspoons butter
parsley

Separate the eggs. Combine yolks and water. Season with salt and pepper to taste. In a separate bowl beat egg whites until stiff but not dry. Carefully fold egg whites into yolk mixture. Heat an omelet pan. Add butter and heat until foaming but not brown. Pour mixture into pan. Leave until set and golden on the bottom. Place under hot grill until set. Fold over and garnish with parsley. Before folding omelet over you can fill with any of the following:

grated cheese
sweetcorn and bacon
chopped cooked spinach
Serves 1.

smoked fish
cooked chicken livers

SWEET OMELET
Fill with 1 tablespoon of jam and fold over. Dust with icing sugar before serving.

QUICK QUICHE

2 cups milk
1 cup Edmonds *Pancake and Pikelet
   Mix*
4 eggs
$^{1}/_{4}$ cup chopped parsley
1 cup grated tasty cheese

1 tablespoon butter
1 onion, finely chopped
$^{1}/_{2}$ cup chopped bacon
salt
pepper

Combine milk, pancake mix, eggs and parsley in a bowl. Stir in the cheese. Melt butter in a saucepan. Add onion and bacon. Cook until onion is clear. Season with salt and pepper to taste. Spoon mixture into a greased 20 cm quiche dish. Pour pancake mixture over. Bake at 190°C for 40 minutes or until set and golden. Serve hot or cold. The same fillings can be added to this quiche as to the basic quiche on page 100.
Serves 4–6.

SCOTCH EGGS

400 g sausagemeat
$^{1}/_{4}$ cup finely chopped onion
1 tablespoon tomato sauce

4 hard-boiled eggs
toasted breadcrumbs
oil for deep-frying

Put sausagemeat, onion and tomato sauce in a bowl. Mix to combine. Shell the eggs. Divide sausagemeat mixture evenly into four. With wet hands, mould sausagemeat mixture around each egg. Roll in breadcrumbs. Deep-fry in hot oil for 8 minutes or until golden. Drain on absorbent paper. To serve, cut in half length-wise. Serve hot or cold.
Serves 4.

SCRAMBLED EGG

1 egg
1 tablespoon milk
salt
pepper

1 teaspoon butter
chopped parsley
1 slice buttered toast

Lightly beat egg. Add milk, salt and pepper to taste. Melt butter in a small frying pan. Pour in egg mixture and cook over a low heat until set. Using a wooden spoon, gently push the mixture around the outside of the pan to the centre to allow the mixture to cook evenly. Scrambled eggs should have large clots of cooked egg so do not stir vigorously. Stir in parsley and serve on hot buttered toast. If eggs are overcooked they will become tough with a watery liquid separating out.
Serves 1.

VARIATIONS
Any of the following can be added:
Add finely sliced mushrooms to uncooked egg mixture.
Fold in cooked chopped bacon after eggs are cooked.
Fold in chopped smoked salmon after eggs are cooked.

USING THE WHITES AND YOLKS OF EGGS

Often when cooking there are leftover egg yolks or egg whites. These suggestions are ways to use them up.

EGG YOLKS
Cheese Straws or biscuits
coating for cutlets etc.
custard filling (for cakes)
Salad Dressing
boiled custard
steamed custard
Baked Custard

EGG WHITES
2 egg whites can replace
  1 egg in a recipe
Pavlova
Meringues
Royal Icing
clearing soup stock
Pineapple Snow
Lemon Sponge

After beating eggs, rinse utensils and bowls immediately under cold water
for easier cleaning.

PASTA

TO COOK PASTA
- For every 250 g of *Diamond* pasta use 2 litres of water and 2 teaspoons salt.
- Add pasta slowly to boiling, salted water.
- Cook in rapidly boiling water with the lid off.
- Drain well and toss through a tablespoon of oil to prevent the pasta sticking together.

DIAMOND PASTA — APPROXIMATE COOKING TIMES

spaghetti	7–10 minutes
spaghetti, wholemeal	8–10 minutes
vermicelli	4–6 minutes
egg noodles	6–8 minutes
spinach and garlic fettucine	7–10 minutes
macaroni	6–9 minutes
lisci	6–9 minutes
farfalle — bows	7–9 minutes
spirals	6–9 minutes
sea shells	6–9 minutes
salad pasta — vegetelli or spirals	6–9 minutes
lasagne	5–8 minutes
penne	12–14 minutes

- Pasta is cooked when it is firm to the bite. This is called 'al dente'.

BASIL AND GARLIC SAUCE (PESTO) FOR PASTA

1 tablespoon oil
2 tablespoons pine nuts
3 cloves garlic, chopped
2 cups fresh basil leaves

¹/₄ cup oil
salt
black pepper
200 g Diamond *pasta, cooked*

Heat first measure of oil in a small frying pan. Add pine nuts and cook, stirring frequently until golden. Drain on absorbent paper. Put garlic, basil and pine nuts into bowl of food processor or blender. Process until finely chopped. Continue processing while adding second measure of oil in a thin, steady stream. Process for a few seconds to just combine. Season with salt and pepper to taste. Serve over hot pasta.
Serves 4.

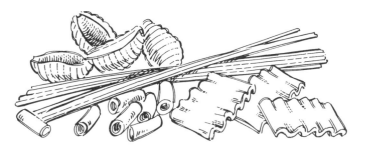

BOLOGNESE SAUCE WITH SPAGHETTI

2 tablespoons oil
1 large onion, finely chopped
500 g lean beef mince
1/4 cup tomato paste
400 g can tomatoes in juice
1 teaspoon basil

1 teaspoon oregano
4 cups water
salt
black pepper
250 g Diamond spaghetti, cooked
grated parmesan cheese

Heat oil in a large frying pan. Add onion and cook until golden, stirring constantly. Stir in meat and quickly brown. Add tomato paste. Push tomatoes and juice through sieve. Add to pan. Stir in basil, oregano and water. Bring to the boil, reduce heat and cook uncovered for 45 minutes or until mixture is a thick sauce consistency. Season with salt and pepper to taste. Serve over hot pasta garnished with parmesan cheese.
Serves 4–6.

LASAGNE

MEAT SAUCE
2 tablespoons oil
1 onion, chopped
3 cloves garlic, crushed
500 g lean beef mince
100 g mushrooms, sliced
2 × 400 g cans tomatoes in juice,
    chopped

1 cup tomato purée
1 teaspoon oregano
1/2 teaspoon basil
1 teaspoon sugar
salt
pepper

CHEESE SAUCE
50 g butter
3 tablespoons Edmonds standard plain
    flour
1 1/2 cups milk

3/4 cup grated cheese
salt
pepper
2 tablespoons grated parmesan
    cheese

250 g Diamond wide lasagne, cooked

MEAT SAUCE
Heat oil in a large frying pan. Add onion and garlic. Cook until onion is golden. Increase heat. Add meat and brown well. Add mushrooms, tomatoes in juice, tomato purée, oregano, basil and sugar. Stir. Bring to the boil then reduce heat and simmer gently for 40 minutes or until meat mixture has thickened slightly, stirring occasionally. Season with salt and pepper to taste. Set aside until cool.

CHEESE SAUCE
Melt butter in a saucepan. Add flour and cook until frothy. Gradually add milk, stirring constantly until mixture boils and thickens. Remove from heat. Stir in cheese. Season with salt and pepper to taste. Cover with a lid or plastic wrap to prevent a skin forming. Set aside until cool.

Place half the lasagne in a greased ovenproof dish. Spread with half the meat mixture and half the cheese sauce. Repeat the layers. Top with parmesan cheese. Cook at 180°C for 20 minutes or until golden and heated through.
Serves 4–6.

MACARONI CHEESE

2 tablespoons butter
1 small onion, finely chopped
2 tablespoons Edmonds standard plain
  flour
$^{1}/_{2}$ teaspoon dry mustard
2 cups milk

salt
pepper
2 cups grated tasty cheese
2 cups Diamond macaroni elbows,
  cooked

Melt butter in a saucepan. Add onion and cook until clear. Stir in flour and cook until frothy. Add mustard. Gradually add milk, stirring constantly until sauce boils and thickens. Remove from heat. Season with salt and pepper to taste. Stir in half the cheese. Add macaroni, stirring to combine. Pour mixture into an oven-proof dish. Sprinkle over the remaining cheese. Cook at 190°C for 20 minutes or until golden and heated through. Chopped cooked bacon or ham can be added to the sauce if wished.
Serves 4–6.

SEAFOOD SAUCE (MARINARA) FOR PASTA

$^{1}/_{2}$ cup dry white wine
1 small onion, chopped
12 fresh mussels, scrubbed and
  debearded
250 g white fish fillets — e.g.
  gurnard, tarakihi, snapper
1 teaspoon oil

1 clove garlic, chopped
400 g can tomatoes in juice
$^{1}/_{2}$ cup chopped parsley
100 g cooked shrimps
250 g Diamond pasta, cooked — e.g.
  fettucine, spaghetti

Put wine, onion and mussels into a large frying pan. Cover and cook until mussels open. Remove mussels from shell. Discard any which do not open. Add fish to pan and gently cook for 10 minutes or until fish flakes easily. Carefully lift fish from pan, reserving all liquid. Continue cooking the liquid until it has reduced by half. In a separate saucepan, heat oil and garlic and cook until golden. Stir in tomatoes in juice and parsley. Bring to the boil. Add reserved fish liquid. Mash tomatoes slightly. Reduce heat and cook uncovered until sauce thickens slightly. Stir in mussels, shrimps and fish. Gently heat through. Serve over hot pasta.
Serves 4–6.

A small amount of oil mixed through cooked drained pasta prevents the pasta sticking together.

SPAGHETTI AND MEATBALLS

SAUCE

1 tablespoon oil	$^1/_4$ cup tomato paste
1 clove garlic, crushed	salt
1 onion, chopped	pepper
400 g can tomatoes in juice	

MEATBALLS

500 g lean beef mince	1 clove garlic, crushed
2 tablespoons tomato sauce	1 teaspoon curry powder
1 onion, finely chopped	$^1/_2$ cup soft breadcrumbs

500 g packet Diamond spaghetti, cooked

SAUCE
Heat oil in a saucepan. Add garlic and onion. Cook until golden. Purée tomatoes in juice. Add to pan. Bring to the boil. Stir in tomato paste. Reduce heat and simmer for 10 to 15 minutes or until thickened to a sauce consistency. Season with salt and pepper to taste and keep warm until meatballs are ready.

MEATBALLS
Put mince, tomato sauce, onion, garlic, curry powder and breadcrumbs in a bowl. Mix thoroughly. Measure tablespoonsful of mixture and shape into balls. Place on an oven tray or in a shallow ovenproof dish. Cook at 200°C for 8 to 10 minutes or until cooked through.
To serve, add hot meatballs to the prepared sauce and coat. Spoon on top of spaghetti.
Serves 4–6.

SPAGHETTI CARBONARA
(HAM AND MUSHROOM SAUCE)

2 tablespoons oil	1 egg yolk
2 ham steaks, chopped	pepper
1 onion, chopped	250 g Diamond spaghetti, cooked (or
200 g mushrooms, sliced	other pasta, e.g. fettucine, spirals,
250 g pot sour cream	seashells or egg noodles)
	1 tablespoon chopped parsley

Heat oil in a frying pan or saucepan. Add ham and onion. Cook until onion is clear and ham slightly browned. Stir in mushrooms and cook for a further 2 minutes. Remove from heat. In a bowl beat sour cream and egg yolk together. Add this to ham mixture. Return pan to a low heat and cook, stirring constantly until sauce thickens slightly. Do not allow to boil. Season with pepper to taste. Add hot pasta. Stir to combine. Garnish with parsley.
Serves 4–6.

SPINACH AND BACON WITH PASTA

1 tablespoon butter
1 onion, chopped
1 clove garlic, crushed
4 rashers bacon, chopped

2 to 3 bunches spinach, chopped
250 g Diamond *pasta, cooked* — *e.g.*
   fettucine, spirals

Melt butter in a large frying pan. Add onion, garlic and bacon. Cook until onion is clear and bacon is cooked. Stir in spinach and cook for a further 2 minutes or until spinach is a rich, dark green colour, stirring constantly. Serve over hot pasta. Serves 4.

TOMATO SAUCE

2 tablespoons oil
1 onion, chopped
1 clove garlic, crushed
2 rashers bacon, chopped
1 stalks celery, chopped
1 tablespoon Edmonds *standard plain flour*
³/₄ cup tomato purée

1 cup liquid beef stock, boiling
¹/₂ teaspoon sugar
salt
pepper
250 g Diamond *pasta, cooked* —
   e.g. spaghetti, lisci
chopped parsley or basil

Heat oil in a saucepan. Add onion, garlic, bacon and celery. Cook until golden. Stir in flour and cook until frothy. Mix in tomato purée. Remove from heat and cool slightly. Gradually add stock, stirring constantly. Add sugar. Return to heat and cook, stirring, until mixture boils. Reduce heat and simmer gently for 45 minutes or until of sauce consistency. Season with salt and pepper to taste. Serve over hot pasta. Garnish with parsley.
Serves 4.

TUNA SAUCE

2 tablespoons butter
1 small onion, chopped
2 × 185 g cans tuna, flaked
250 g pot sour cream
1¹/₄ red pepper, chopped

salt
pepper
250 g Diamond *pasta, cooked* —
   e.g. vermicelli, lisci

Heat butter in a saucepan. Add onion and cook until clear. Add tuna and sour cream. Heat gently. Do not allow to boil. Stir in red pepper. Season with salt and pepper to taste. Serve over hot pasta.
Serves 4–6.

VEGETARIAN LASAGNE

25 g butter
1 onion, chopped
2 cloves garlic, crushed
1 small leek, sliced
2 stalks celery, sliced
2 carrots, sliced
2 courgettes, sliced
2 tablespoons Edmonds standard plain
   flour
1 bunch spinach

milk
$^1/_2$ cup grated cheese
salt
pepper
250 g packet Diamond lasagne,
   cooked
200 g pot natural unsweetened
   yoghurt
2 eggs
1 cup grated tasty cheese

Melt butter in a large saucepan. Add onion, garlic and leek. Cook until onion is clear. Add celery, carrots and courgettes. Cover and cook without allowing to colour until celery and carrot are just tender. Add flour and cook until frothy. Remove from heat. Wash spinach thoroughly and, with only the water clinging to the leaves, cook until tender. Drain, reserving all the liquid. Measure liquid and make up to 1 cup with milk. Return flour and vegetables to the heat, gradually add the liquid, stirring constantly until mixture boils and thickens. Remove from heat. Add first measure of cheese. Season with salt and pepper to taste. Set aside. Place one-third of lasagne at the bottom of a greased ovenproof dish. Spread with half the vegetable mixture. Repeat layers, finishing with a layer of lasagne. In a bowl lightly beat yoghurt and eggs until combined. Spread this on top of lasagne. Sprinkle second measure of cheese on top. Cook at 180°C for 20 minutes or until golden and heated through.
Serves 4–6.

RICE

- 1/3 cup uncooked rice will give 1 cup cooked rice.
- Long grain rice is usually used for savoury dishes.
- Short grain rice is used to make puddings.

TO COOK WHITE RICE
- Wash long grain rice if wished.
- Add rice to a large quantity of boiling water.
- Cook uncovered until rice is tender, approximately 10 to 15 minutes.
- When cooked, rinse rice under hot water. Drain well.

RICE CAN ALSO BE COOKED BY
- Oven cooking — Place rice in a casserole dish. Add 2 cups of boiling water for each cup of rice. Cover and cook at 180°C for 35 to 40 minutes.
- Pan steaming — Place rice in a saucepan. Add 2 cups of cold water for each cup of rice. Bring to the boil. When holes appear on the surface of the rice, turn down to a low heat and cover with a lid. Steam cook for 15 to 20 minutes or until water is absorbed and rice cooked.

TO COOK BROWN RICE
- Cook in boiling water for about 40 minutes or until tender.

TO DRY COOKED RICE FOR FRYING
- Spread rice out on a teatowel on an oven tray, tray or roasting dish. Leave uncovered to dry overnight.

ALMOND RICE

25 g butter
1 large onion, chopped
1 clove garlic, crushed
2 tablespoons raisins
1½ cups liquid chicken stock

salt
pepper
1 cup long grain rice
½ cup sliced almonds, toasted

Melt butter in a saucepan. Add onion and garlic and cook until onion is clear. Stir in raisins, stock and salt and pepper to taste. Cover and bring to the boil. Add rice, reduce heat and cook over a low heat for 15 to 20 minutes or until rice is tender and liquid absorbed. Stir. Add most of the almonds, reserving 1 tablespoon for garnish. Spoon rice into serving dish. Garnish with reserved almonds.
Serves 4–6.

COCONUT CHILLI RICE

1 cup long grain rice
375 ml can coconut cream

1 chilli, seeded and chopped, or
1 teaspoon prepared chopped chilli

Put rice in a medium saucepan. Add coconut cream and chilli. Cover and bring to the boil. Reduce heat and slowly cook until rice is tender and all the liquid has been absorbed, stirring occasionally.
Serves 4.

FRIED RICE

2 cups cooked long grain rice
2 eggs
1 teaspoon soy sauce
3 tablespoons oil
6 rashers bacon, chopped

1 clove garlic, crushed
2 teaspoons grated root ginger
6 spring onions, chopped
1 tablespoon soy sauce

Spread rice out on trays and leave to dry. Lightly beat eggs and first measure of soy sauce. Heat 1 tablespoon of the measured oil in a wok. Pour in half egg mixture and cook until golden on both sides. Repeat with remaining egg. Cut egg into 1 cm wide strips. Set aside. Heat another tablespoon of oil and cook bacon until crisp. Remove from wok. Cook garlic, ginger and spring onions over a low heat. Add remaining oil, heat. Add rice and stir-fry for 5 minutes. Return strips of egg and bacon to wok. Stir-fry to heat through. Add second measure of soy sauce. Stir to mix in.
Serves 4–6.

LEMON RICE

1 cup long grain rice
1 cup water
25 g butter
1 tablespoon grated lemon rind

2 tablespoons lemon juice
salt
pepper

Put rice, water, butter, lemon rind and juice into a medium saucepan. Cover and bring to the boil. Turn the heat off but leave the pan on the element until rice is cooked and all liquid is absorbed. Stir. If using gas, allow mixture to cook over a low heat for about 7 minutes before turning heat off. Season with salt and pepper to taste. Serve immediately.
Serves 4.

PILAF

25 g butter
1 large onion, chopped
1 cup long grain rice
2 cups liquid chicken stock

salt
pepper
25 g butter
2 tablespoons chopped chives

Melt first measure of butter in an ovenproof casserole dish. Add onion and cook until clear. Stir in rice and cook for 2 minutes, stirring constantly. Pour in stock. Season with salt and pepper to taste. Bring to the boil. Cover and bake at 220°C for 20 minutes or until rice is tender. The rice should be quite dry. Just before serving, stir in second measure of butter and chives.
Serves 4.

SAVOURY BROWN RICE CASSEROLE

1 cup brown rice
3 rashers bacon, chopped
1 green pepper, chopped
1 red pepper, chopped
4 tomatoes, blanched and chopped
2 cups liquid chicken stock

1 large onion, chopped
2 cloves garlic, crushed
1 teaspoon salt
pepper
25 g butter

Put rice, bacon, half the green and red peppers, tomatoes, stock, onion, garlic, salt and pepper into an ovenproof casserole dish. Cover with a tight-fitting lid or foil. Cook at 180°C for 1½ hours or until rice is tender. Stir halfway through cooking. Just before serving, stir in butter and remaining red and green peppers.
Serves 4–6.

*Long grain rice is usually used for savoury dishes
and short grain rice for rice puddings.*

TOMATO RICE CASSEROLE

1 cup long grain rice
1 large onion, chopped
2 cloves garlic, crushed
1 teaspoon salt
400 g can tomatoes in juice, chopped

135 g can tomato paste
1 teaspoon curry powder
$1/4$ teaspoon sugar
25 g butter, cubed

Put rice, onion, garlic, salt, tomatoes in juice, tomato paste, curry powder and sugar into an ovenproof dish. Add butter to dish. Stir to combine. Cover with a tight-fitting lid or foil. Cook at 180°C for 40 minutes, stirring occasionally.
Serves 6.

TUNA RICE BAKE

2 tablespoons butter
1 clove garlic, crushed
1 onion, sliced
2 stalks celery, sliced
1 tablespoon Edmonds standard plain
   flour
1 cup milk

2 eggs
$1/4$ cup grated cheese
425 g can tuna, drained and flaked
salt
pepper
2 cups cooked long grain rice
chopped parsley

Melt butter in a saucepan. Add garlic, onion and celery. Cook until onion is clear. Stir in flour and cook until frothy. Gradually add milk, stirring constantly until mixture boils and thickens. Remove from heat. Add eggs and cheese, beating until well combined. Stir in tuna. Season with salt and pepper to taste. Combine tuna sauce and rice. Pour mixture into a greased ovenproof dish. Cook at 180°C for 20 minutes or until golden. Garnish with parsley. Serve hot or cold.
Serves 4–6.

Cook rice in stock for added flavour.

BEEF MEATBALLS

1 onion, finely chopped
375 g lean beef mince
³/₄ cup soft breadcrumbs
2 teaspoons chopped fresh herbs or
  1 teaspoon dried herbs

2 tablespoons tomato sauce
1¹/₂ tablespoons oil
1 packet Beef Rice Risotto

Combine onion, mince, breadcrumbs, herbs and tomato sauce. Measure table-spoonsful of mixture and shape into balls about the size of a walnut. Heat the oil in a large frying pan. Add meatballs and cook until browned all over. Shake the pan as meatballs are cooking. Remove from pan. Set aside. Add contents of rice sachet to pan. Cook according to packet directions. Place the meatballs on top of rice when the added water comes to the boil. Cover and simmer over a low heat for 15 minutes. Remove lid and cook for a further 5 minutes or until rice is tender.
Serves 4.

LEEK AND SAUSAGE RISOTTO

1 tablespoon oil
1 tablespoon basil
3 cloves garlic, crushed
1 packet Chicken Rice Risotto

3 cups leeks, finely chopped
2 to 3 cooked sausages, sliced
2¹/₂ cups hot water

Sauté in oil, basil, garlic and contents of the rice sachet until the rice is lightly browned. Add the leeks, sausages and hot water. Stir in the flavour sachet. Cover and simmer over a low heat for 15 minutes. Remove lid and cook for 5 minutes or until the rice is tender. Serve immediately.
Serves 4.

VARIATION
For a spicier Rice Risotto use a spicy sausage (like chorizo) or salami.

YOGHURT LAMB RICE

350 g lamb leg steaks
1¹/₂ teaspoons curry powder
1 teaspoon coriander
4 tablespoons natural low fat yoghurt

1 teaspoon oil
1 packet Creamy Tandoori Rice Risotto
Fresh coriander or parsley, finely
  chopped

Slice the lamb into strips. In a bowl mix together lamb, curry powder, coriander and yoghurt. Stir well and marinate for 1 hour. Cook the Rice Risotto according to packet directions. While the rice is cooking, heat the oil in a frying pan and sauté lamb strips briefly (3–4 minutes) until just cooked through but still pink and juicy. Remove from pan and keep warm. To serve, transfer the rice to a heated dish and top with lamb. Garnish with coriander and serve immediately.
Serves 4.

Top: Tuna Rice Bake (pg 109),
Bottom: Coconut Chilli Rice (pg 111)

SEAFOOD

FISH TYPES

whole fish — snapper, sole, flounder, blue and red cod, John Dory, hapuka, hake, hoki, ling, tarakihi, trevally.

medium-firm fish — blue cod, John Dory, hapuka, gurnard, kahawai, ling, moki, orange roughy, snapper, tarakihi, trevally.

soft-textured fish — red cod, flounder, gemfish, hake, hoki, sole.

fish steaks — salmon, hapuka.

BUYING FISH

Look for fish that has:
— no smell of ammonia or strong odour.
— translucent, firm flesh.
— scales that are intact.
— gills that are bright red.
— bulging, bright eyes.
— no blood in the body cavity.

COOKING FISH

POACHING (BOILING)

Weigh fish and calculate cooking time. Wrap fish in foil or place on a steaming rack. Place fish in a saucepan with sufficient water to just cover. Cover and simmer gently until fish is tender. Drain and serve with sauce of your choice. Suitable for all fish types.

STEAMING

Place fish in a lightly greased steamer and cook until done. Suitable for all fish types.

GRILLING

Heat the grill. Lightly grease the grilling rack. Remove head, fins and tail from whole fish. Cut slashes in the flesh of thick fish to allow heat to penetrate. Brush with melted butter or oil. During cooking time brush again with melted butter or oil. Suitable for all fish types.

BAKING

Remove fins from fish. Weigh fish and calculate the cooking time. Stuff fish cavity if wished. Close opening with small skewers laced together with fine string or sew opening together with a needle and coarse thread. Place fish in a greased baking dish or roasting pan. Brush with melted butter or oil and bake at 180°C until cooked. Suitable for all fish types.

FRYING

Wipe fish and cut into serving-sized pieces if wished.
Pan frying — dust with seasoned flour.
Shallow or deep frying — dip in egg and coat in breadcrumbs. Alternatively dust with seasoned flour and coat with batter.

Fry in hot oil until golden and cooked. Drain fish on absorbent paper. Suitable for all fish types.

COOKING TIMES FOR FISH

Cooking times are a guide only and are dependent of the size and thickness of the fish.

poached or steamed whole — 10–15 minutes per 500 g
                          fillets —   4–6 minutes per 500 g
grilling   whole — 10–13 minutes per 500 g
                          fillets —   4–8 minutes per 500 g
baking   whole — 30 minutes per 500 g
                          fillets — 10–15 minutes per 500 g
microwaving   whole or fillets — 1 minute per 100g on full power
                              5 minutes per 500g on full power

TO TEST FOR DONENESS

Fish is cooked when the flesh flakes easily, or when the flesh separates from the bones, or when a creamy white juice comes from the flesh.

BARBECUED FISH

2 kg whole fish — e.g. snapper,
  tarakihi, trevally, trout
1 onion, sliced
1 lemon, sliced
sprig thyme

sprig parsley
2 tablespoons melted butter
salt
black pepper

Clean and scale fish. Remove fins. Make three or four slashes on each side of fish. Place onion, lemon, thyme and parsley in cuts and gut cavity. Brush with melted butter. Season with salt and pepper to taste. Wrap securely in non-stick foil. Barbecue over moderate heat for 15 minutes each side or until fish flakes easily. Trout may take longer depending on the condition of fish.
Serves 6.

BEER BATTER

$^1\!/_2$ cup Edmonds standard plain flour
$^1\!/_2$ teaspoon salt

$^1\!/_4$ cup beer, approximately

Sift flour and salt into bowl. Add measure of beer without a head. Mix to a smooth batter.
Makes about 1 cup.

CRISP BATTER

$^1\!/_4$ cup Edmonds Fielder's cornflour
$^1\!/_2$ cup Edmonds standard plain flour
1 teaspoon Edmonds baking powder

$^1\!/_4$ teaspoon salt
$^1\!/_2$ cup milk
oil for deep-frying

Sift cornflour, flour, baking powder and salt into bowl. Gradually add milk, mixing until smooth. Dip the items to be cooked in the batter, ensuring they are well coated. Deep-fry in hot oil until golden. Drain on absorbent paper before serving.
Makes about 1 cup.

When buying fish, check for any smell of ammonia.
This indicates that it is not fresh.

CRISPY CHINESE BATTER

Edmonds Fielder's *cornflour*   *1 egg white*

Coat the items to be cooked with cornflour. Lightly beat the egg white with a fork. Dip the coated items in egg white then deep-fry. Drain on absorbent paper.

FISH CAKES

250 g cooked fish
2 cups cold mashed potatoes
1 small onion, finely chopped
1/4 teaspoon mixed herbs
1 teaspoon salt
black pepper

1 tablespoon chopped parsley
1 egg
1 tablespoon water
1 to 1 1/2 cups toasted breadcrumbs
oil for shallow frying

Flake fish. Place in bowl with potato, onion, herbs, salt, pepper to taste and parsley. Mix well to combine. Turn onto lightly floured surface and divide mixture into eight even-sized portions. Shape into rounds. Lightly beat egg and water together. Dip each fish cake in egg mixture. Coat with breadcrumbs. Heat oil in large frying pan. Add fish cakes and cook until golden on both sides. Drain on absorbent paper. Serves 4.

FISH PIE SUPREME

25 g butter
1 tablespoon milk
3 cups cooked mashed potatoes
3/4 teaspoon salt
black pepper
1 tablespoon butter
1 tablespoon Edmonds standard plain flour

1 cup milk
500 g smoked fish, flaked or 425 g can tuna drained and flaked
1 tablespoon chopped parsley
2 hard-boiled eggs, chopped

Mix first measure of butter and milk into the potatoes, beating with a fork to combine. Season with salt and pepper to taste. Line a 20 cm pie dish with half the potatoes. Set remaining potatoes aside. Heat second measure of butter in a saucepan. Stir in flour and cook until frothy. Gradually add second measure of milk, stirring constantly until sauce boils and thickens. Remove from heat. Add fish, parsley and eggs. Pour this mixture into the lined pie dish. Cover with remaining potato. Cook at 190°C for 20 minutes or until pale golden. Serves 4–6.

FISH WITH PARSLEY SAUCE

3 to 4 firm white fish fillets — e.g.
  gurnard, tarakihi, snapper
1 cup milk
1 tablespoon butter
1 tablespoon Edmonds standard plain flour
1 tablespoon chopped parsley
1/2 teaspoon salt
white pepper

Wipe fish. Place in a large frying pan with lid. Add milk. Cover and bring to the boil. Reduce heat and simmer gently for 15 minutes or until fish flakes easily. Carefully lift fish from pan and keep warm. Pour poaching milk from pan into jug. Add butter to pan and melt. Stir in flour and cook until frothy. Gradually add poaching milk, stirring constantly until mixture boils and thickens. Add parsley. Season with salt and pepper to taste. Pour sauce over fish.
Serves 4.

SMOKED FISH WITH PARSLEY SAUCE
Smoked red cod etc. could be used in the foregoing recipe. Cut fish into serving-sized pieces. Poach in milk and follow instructions as above.

FRIED OYSTERS

1 1/2 dozen oysters
1/4 cup Edmonds standard plain flour
1/2 teaspoon salt
black pepper
1 egg
3/4 cup soft breadcrumbs
oil for shallow frying
lemon wedges

Drain oysters. Debeard if necessary. Combine flour, salt and pepper to taste. Lightly beat egg. Coat each oyster with seasoned flour, then dip in egg and coat with breadcrumbs. Heat oil in a large frying pan. Add oysters and cook until golden. Drain on absorbent paper. Serve with lemon. Oysters can also be dipped in batter and deep-fried.
Serves 4.

KEDGEREE

250 g smoked fish
50 g butter
1 small onion finely chopped
1 cup cooked long grain rice
2 hard-boiled eggs
salt
black pepper
1 tablespoon chopped parsley

Flake fish. Melt butter in a saucepan. Add onion and cook until clear. Add rice and fish and heat through. Halve eggs and remove yolks and set aside. Chop egg white. Add to saucepan. Season with salt and pepper to taste. When kedgeree is very hot transfer to serving dish. Garnish with parsley and sieved reserved egg yolks.
Serves 3–4.

Fish is cooked when the flesh is white and flakes easily.
It should still be moist.

LATTICE PIE

2 tablespoons butter
1 small onion, chopped
$^1/_2$ teaspoon curry powder
2 tablespoons Edmonds *standard plain*
   flour
$^3/_4$ cup milk

310 g can smoked fish, drained and
   flaked
black pepper
2 sheets pre-rolled flaky pastry
1 egg yolk

Melt butter in a saucepan. Add onion and cook until clear. Stir in curry powder. Cook for 30 seconds. Stir in flour and cook until frothy. Gradually add milk, stirring constantly until mixture boils and thickens. Remove from heat. Add fish and pepper to taste. Stir then set aside until cool. Place a sheet of pastry on oven tray. Spread fish mixture over pastry, leaving a 2 cm edge all the way round. Dampen this edge lightly with water. Carefully fold second sheet of pastry in half. From centre fold make 1.5 cm wide cuts to within 2 cm of edge. Open pastry out and carefully lift over filling. Press edges firmly together. Lightly beat egg yolk and brush top surface of pastry with this mixture, making sure egg does not drip down sides as this will prevent pastry from rising. Cook at 220°C for 20 minutes or until golden and well risen.
Serves 4–6.

LUNCHEON SALMON MOULD

1 tablespoon gelatine
$^1/_2$ cup water
2 × 210 g cans salmon
2 teaspoons chicken stock powder
$^1/_2$ teaspoon dry mustard

2 tablespoons DYC *malt vinegar*
2 spring onions, finely chopped
$^1/_2$ cup Mayonnaise (page 190)
cucumber slices

Combine gelatine and water. Leave to swell for 10 minutes. Drain and flake salmon, reserving liquid. Dissolve gelatine over hot water. Add stock powder, mustard, vinegar, salmon, spring onions and mayonnaise. Mix well to combine. Pour mixture into wet fish mould or other mould, smoothing top surface. Chill until firm. Unmould onto serving plate. Garnish with cucumber. Serve with salad and Melba Toast.
Serves 6.

MARINATED RAW FISH

500 g firm white fish fillets — e.g.
   snapper, John Dory, tarakihi,
   gurnard
1 teaspoon salt
$^1/_4$ cup lemon juice

1 medium onion, finely chopped
$^1/_2$ cup coconut milk
2 tomatoes, diced
$^1/_2$ cup chopped cucumber

Cut fish into bite-sized pieces. Sprinkle with salt then lemon juice. Cover and chill for 2 hours or until fish whitens, stirring occasionally. Drain. Stir in onion and coconut milk. Sprinkle tomatoes and cucumber over. Serve chilled.
Serves 4–6.

To remove gelatine moulds from the container, quickly dip base of the
container into hot water before inverting onto a serving plate.

MUSSELS

Scrub mussels well, removing and discarding the beards. Place mussels in large saucepan or frying pan. Add cold water to 2.5 cm depth. Cover saucepan or frying pan and bring to the boil. Cook for 8 minutes or until majority of mussels are open. Discard any that do not open. Before serving, release mussels from the shells.

MUSSELS IN TOMATO SAUCE

1 onion, chopped
1 cup water
36 mussels, cleaned
1 tablespoon butter
1 clove garlic, crushed

1 tablespoon Edmonds *standard plain flour*
300 g can tomato purée
pepper
1 tablespoon chopped parsley

Put half the onion in a large frying pan. Add water and bring to the boil. Add mussels. Cover and cook for 8 minutes or until mussels open. Remove from heat. Drain, reserving $^3/_4$ cup of cooking liquid. Discard any mussels which do not open. Arrange mussels in half-shell on a large serving platter. Set aside. Melt butter in a saucepan. Add remaining onion and garlic. Cook until onion is clear. Stir in flour and cook until frothy. Gradually add tomato purée and reserved cooking liquid. Bring to the boil. Boil for 1 minute. Season with pepper to taste. Pour sauce over mussels. Garnish with chopped parsley. Serve with crusty French bread.
Serves 4–6.

PAN-FRIED FISH

$^1/_2$ cup Edmonds *standard plain flour,*
    approximately
1 teaspoon grated lemon rind
salt
pepper
1 egg
2 tablespoons water

$2^1/_2$ cups soft breadcrumbs,
    approximately
2 tablespoons butter
2 tablespoons oil
4 fillets firm white fish — e.g.
    tarakihi, snapper, gurnard
lemon slices

Combine flour, lemon rind, salt and pepper to taste. Lightly beat egg and water together. Coat fish with seasoned flour. Dip into egg mixture and breadcrumbs. Heat butter and oil in a frying pan. Place fish in pan and cook for 5 minutes on each side or until golden. Garnish with lemon.
Serves 4.

SALMON RISSOLES

210 g can salmon
1 cup mashed potato
1 small onion, finely chopped
$^1/_2$ cup Edmonds *standard plain flour*
2 teaspoons Edmonds *baking powder*

salt
black pepper
$^1/_4$ cup chopped parsley
oil for shallow frying

Press cloves of garlic with the flat of the knife to remove skin.

Drain and flake salmon, reserving liquid. Combine salmon, reserved liquid, potato and onion. Sieve flour and baking powder together into salmon mixture. Season with salt and pepper to taste. Add parsley. Mix well to combine. Divide mixture into eight even-sized portions. Shape into rounds. Heat oil in a large frying pan. Add rissoles and cook until golden on both sides. Drain on absorbent paper.
Serves 4.

SALMON STEAKS WITH MUSTARD AND DILL

4 salmon steaks
oil
$1/2$ cup Mayonnaise (page 190)

$1/2$ teaspoon chopped fresh dill
$1/2$ teaspoon prepared mustard

Brush salmon steaks with oil. Grill for 10 minutes or until salmon is cooked through, turning once during cooking. While salmon is cooking, combine mayonnaise, dill and mustard. Carefully remove skin and bones from salmon. Place salmon onto serving plates. Serve with mustard and dill mayonnaise.
Serves 4.

SAVOURY FISH STEAKS

4 fish steaks — e.g. hapuka, tuna,
    kingfish
4 tomatoes, blanched and sliced
4 teaspoons DYC malt vinegar

1 cup soft breadcrumbs
2 teaspoons finely chopped onion
2 tablespoons melted butter

Wash and pat fish steaks dry. Place in an ovenproof dish. Arrange tomato slices on top. Sprinkle with vinegar. In a bowl combine breadcrumbs, onion and butter. Spoon this mixture on top of tomatoes. Cook at 200°C for 20 minutes or until fish is cooked through.
Serves 4.

SCALLOPED OYSTERS

$1^1/2$ dozen oysters
1 tablespoon butter
1 tablespoon Edmonds standard plain
    flour
1 cup milk
salt

white pepper
2 tablespoons lemon juice
pinch of nutmeg
$1/2$ cup soft breadcrumbs
1 tablespoon melted butter

Drain oysters. Debeard if necessary. Melt butter in a saucepan. Stir in flour and cook until frothy. Gradually add milk, stirring constantly. Bring to the boil. Cook, stirring until mixture boils and thickens. Season with salt and pepper to taste. Stir in lemon juice and nutmeg. Remove from heat. Add oysters. Transfer mixture to ovenproof serving dish. Combine breadcrumbs and melted butter. Sprinkle this over oyster mixture. Grill until golden.
Serves 2–3.

SCALLOPS MORNAY

2 dozen scallops
2 tablespoons butter
2 tablespoons Edmonds standard plain
  flour
1¹/₂ cups milk

¹/₂ cup grated tasty cheese
salt
pepper
2 cups hot mashed potato
chopped parsley or paprika

Remove any feed tubes from scallops. Set aside. Melt butter in a saucepan. Stir in flour and cook until frothy. Gradually add milk, stirring constantly until mixture boils. Add scallops to sauce. Continue cooking for 5 minutes, stirring occasionally. Remove from heat and stir in half the cheese. Season with salt and pepper to taste. Decorate edge of scallop shells or ovenproof dish with mashed potato. Spoon scallop mixture into serving shells or dish to be used. Sprinkle remaining cheese on top. Grill until golden. Garnish with parsley.
Serves 4–6.

SEAFOOD COCKTAIL

2 cups mixed seafood — shrimps,
  crab, prawns, oysters, crayfish
1 cup cream
¹/₄ cup tomato sauce

2 teaspoons lemon juice
white pepper
1 cup shredded lettuce
paprika or chopped parsley

Combine seafood. Chill while preparing sauce. Put cream in a bowl and beat until thickened slightly, about the consistency of egg white. Beat in tomato sauce, lemon juice and pepper. Place a small amount of lettuce into individual serving dishes. Divide seafood mixture evenly among the prepared dishes. Spoon cream mixture over seafood. Garnish with paprika. Replace cream with natural unsweetened yoghurt and ¹/₂ teaspoon sugar if wished.
Serves 4–5.

SOUSED FISH

1 to 1.5 kg whole fish — e.g.
  snapper, trevally, trout, salmon
water
1 onion, sliced
6 black peppercorns
1 teaspoon salt

sprig parsley
sprig thyme
1 bay leaf
1¹/₂ cups DYC white vinegar
parsley
lemon slices

Clean fish. Cut into steaks. Put fish steaks into a large casserole dish. Cover with water. Add onion, peppercorns, salt, parsley, thyme, bay leaf and vinegar. Cover and cook at 150°C for 1¹/₂ hours. Leave to cool slightly. Chill until completely cold. Garnish with parsley and lemon.
Serves 6.

Overcooking fish causes it to dry out.

SQUID RINGS

500 g squid rings
2 cloves garlic, crushed
1 egg
1 tablespoon Edmonds Fielder's
   cornflour

1 tablespoon milk
1 cup toasted breadcrumbs,
   approximately
oil for deep-frying

Put squid and garlic in a bowl. Leave for 15 minutes. Beat egg, cornflour and milk together. Dip squid rings into egg mixture. Coat with breadcrumbs. Deep-fry in hot oil for 2 minutes or until golden. Do not overcook as this will toughen the squid. Serve with a dipping sauce.
Serves 4.

SWEET AND SOUR FISH

375 g firm white fish fillets — e.g.
   snapper, trevally, tarakihi, orange
   roughy
salt
white pepper
1 tablespoon oil
1 onion, sliced
1/2 green pepper, sliced

225 g can pineapple chunks
2 tablespoons Edmonds Fielder's
   cornflour
1 teaspoon grated root ginger
1 tablespoon brown sugar
1 tablespoon soy sauce
3 tablespoons DYC spiced vinegar
1/2 cup chopped cucumber

Cut fish into serving-sized pieces. Arrange in an ovenproof dish. Sprinkle with a little salt and pepper to taste. Heat oil in saucepan. Add onion and green pepper. Cook until onion is clear. Remove from heat. Drain pineapple, reserving juice. In a bowl mix cornflour, ginger, sugar, soy sauce, reserved pineapple juice and vinegar. Add this mixture to pan. Bring to the boil, stirring constantly until mixture thickens. Pour sauce over fish. Cover and cook at 180°C for 25 minutes or until fish is cooked. Stir in pineapple chunks and cucumber.
Serves 4–5.

WHITEBAIT FRITTERS

1 cup Edmonds standard plain flour
1/2 teaspoon Edmonds baking powder
1/2 teaspoon salt
1 egg
1/2 cup milk, approximately

125 g whitebait or strips of firm
   white fish — e.g. lemon fish,
   trevally, orange roughy
oil for shallow frying
lemon wedges

Sift flour, baking powder and salt into bowl. Add egg and sufficient milk to mix to a smooth batter. Drain whitebait well. Stir in whitebait or fish. Coat well with egg mixture. Heat oil in a large frying pan. Add fritters and cook until golden on both sides. Drain on absorbent paper. Serve with lemon.
Serves 4–6.

Drain fried food on stale bread slices instead of absorbent paper.

MEAT

CUTS OF MEAT AND THEIR COOKING METHODS

BEEF

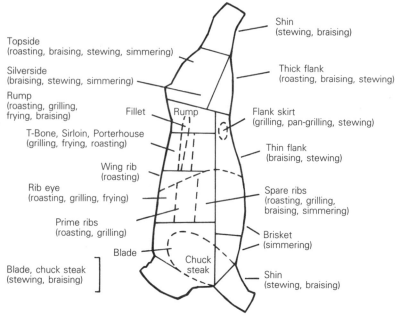

Shin
(stewing, braising)

Topside
(roasting, braising, stewing, simmering)

Silverside
(braising, stewing, simmering)

Rump
(roasting, grilling,
frying, braising)

Fillet

Rump

T-Bone, Sirloin, Porterhouse
(grilling, frying, roasting)

Wing rib
(roasting)

Rib eye
(roasting, grilling, frying)

Prime ribs
(roasting, grilling)

Blade

Chuck
steak

Blade, chuck steak
(stewing, braising)

Thick flank
(roasting, braising, stewing)

Flank skirt
(grilling, pan-grilling, stewing)

Thin flank
(braising, stewing)

Spare ribs
(roasting, grilling,
braising, simmering)

Brisket
(simmering)

Shin
(stewing, braising)

LAMB

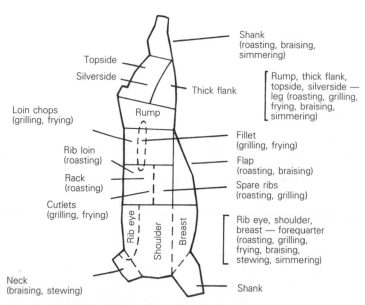

Topside

Silverside

Thick flank

Rump

Loin chops
(grilling, frying)

Rib loin
(roasting)

Rack
(roasting)

Cutlets
(grilling, frying)

Rib eye

Shoulder

Breast

Neck
(braising, stewing)

Shank
(roasting, braising,
simmering)

Rump, thick flank,
topside, silverside —
leg (roasting, grilling,
frying, braising,
simmering)

Fillet
(grilling, frying)

Flap
(roasting, braising)

Spare ribs
(roasting, grilling)

Rib eye, shoulder,
breast — forequarter
(roasting, grilling,
frying, braising,
stewing, simmering)

Shank

Partially freeze meat before cutting thinly for stir-frying.

COOKING MEAT

GUIDE TO ROASTING MEAT AT 160°C–180°C

Meat		Minutes per 500 g	Internal Temp °C
Beef	rare	20–30	60–65
	medium	25–35	70–73
	well done	40–45	75–78
Lamb	medium rare	20–30	70–73
	medium	25–30	75–78
	well done	35–40	79–82
Mutton	well done	35–45	79–82
Pork	medium	25–35	71
	well done	40–45	76
Veal	well done	35–40	75–78

APPROXIMATE TIMES FOR GRILLING MEAT

Beef steaks: 2–2.5 cm thick

rare	3–4 minutes each side
medium	5–6 minutes each side
well done	6 minutes each side, then reduce heat and cook to your liking

Lamb and mutton chops:

medium	5–6 minutes each side
well done	7–8 minutes each side

Pork steaks and chops

medium	4–6 minutes each side
well done	7–8 minutes each side

Grilling times depend on the thickness of the meat and its temperature immediately before cooking. All meats should ideally be at room temperature before grilling.

TO SIMMER MEAT

Calculate the cooking time, allowing 30 to 40 minutes per 500 g.
- Fresh meat (mutton, etc). Place meat in a saucepan with sufficient hot water to cover. Bring to the boil. Add 1 teaspoon salt. Cover and simmer gently until the meat is tender. Garnish with vegetables and serve with Parsley Sauce.
- Salt meat (corned beef, etc). Place meat in cold water with a little vinegar, 1 onion and a few pickling spices. Cover. Bring to the boil then simmer gently until the meat is tender. Corned beef is improved by the addition of 1 tablespoon golden syrup (or a little sugar) to the water.

GRAVY

1 tablespoon fat in roasting dish
1½ to 3 tablespoons Edmonds
  standard plain flour

1 cup water, liquid stock or vegetable
  water
salt
pepper

Pour off fat from roasting dish, leaving 1 tablespoon. Sprinkle flour into pan. Use 1½ tablespoons for thin gravy and up to 3 tablespoons for thick gravy. Lightly brown the flour over a medium heat. Add the water slowly, stirring constantly. Stir until boiling. Season with salt and pepper to taste. Pour into a warmed gravy boat or jug.

Use tongs to turn meat. Piercing with a fork allows juices to escape.

CARVING
- Leave the roast in a warm place for 10–15 minutes before carving. This allows the meat to 'set' and makes it easier to carve.
- Use a really sharp carving knife. Hold the meat with a carving fork.
- Cut across the fibres and the meat will appear to be more tender.
- The following diagrams show how to carve joints.

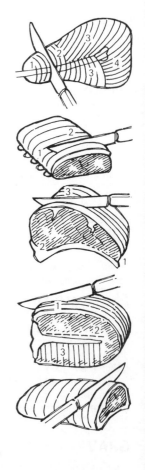

LEG OF LAMB, MUTTON OR PORK
- Make a cut straight down to the bone at (1). Then cut slightly slanting slices at (2), then (3), and finish at (4). Be careful that the slices are always across the grain of the meat.

BRISKET OF BEEF
Cut slices downwards along the lines (1) and (2), and cut down close to the bone.

RIBS OF BEEF
Run the knife along the bone from (1) to (2) to loosen the meat. Then slice downwards along the lines (3).

BEEF SIRLOIN
Cut downwards along the dotted line (1) and then loosen the slices from the bone at (2). Cut the lower part along the lines (3).

LOIN OR NECK
Cut down along the lines, cutting off one chop at a time. The bones should be jointed before cooking.

TRADITIONAL MEAT ACCOMPANIMENTS

Roast beef	horseradish sauce, mustard, Yorkshire Pudding, brown gravy
Corned beef	Mustard Sauce
Roast lamb	Mint Sauce or Jelly, gravy
Boiled mutton	caper, Onion or Parsley Sauce
Roast pork	Apple Sauce or rings, pineapple, gravy
Roast veal	Sausagemeat Stuffing or balls, sausages and bacon rolls, gravy

Overcooked meats become dry, stringy and tough. Calculate the cooking time before cooking meat.

APRICOT-STUFFED FOREQUARTER

1 kg boned lamb forequarter
¹/₂ cup chopped dried apricots
³/₄ cup soft breadcrumbs

¹/₂ teaspoon grated root ginger
black pepper

Open meat out and place on a flat surface, skin side down. Combine apricots, breadcrumbs, ginger and pepper to taste. Spread this over the flesh of the meat then roll up like a sponge roll. Secure with string. Place in a roasting pan or oven bag. Cook at 160°C for 1¹/₂ hours or until juices run clear when tested with a skewer. Serve hot or cold.
Serves 8.

BEEF CASSEROLE

1 kg chuck or blade steak
¹/₄ cup Edmonds standard plain flour
2 tablespoons oil
1 large onion, chopped
4 cups liquid beef stock
2 carrots, sliced

salt
black pepper
1 bay leaf
sprig thyme
sprig parsley

Trim fat from meat and cut into 2.5 cm cubes. Heat oil in a heavy-based fryingpan. Add onion and cook until golden. Using a slotted spoon, remove onion and place in a casserole dish. Coat meat in flour. Add one-quarter of meat and quickly brown on all sides. Remove from pan. Repeat with remaining meat, one-quarter at a time. Place meat in dish with onions. Gradually add stock to saucepan, stirring. Bring to the boil. Add carrots. Season with salt and pepper to taste. Make a bouquet garni with bay leaf, thyme and parsley. Add bouquet garni and liquid to casserole dish. Cover and cook at 160°C for 1¹/₂ hours or until meat is tender. Remove bouquet garni before serving. Serve with dumplings.
Serves 6–8.

BEEF AND MUSHROOM CASSEROLE
Replace half the beef stock with red wine. Add ¹/₄ cup tomato purée and 1 cup sliced mushrooms.

BEEF AND MUSTARD CASSEROLE
At end of cooking time, stir in 1 tablespoon whole grain mustard.

BEEF AND PEPPER CASSEROLE
Add 1 chopped red or green pepper when cooking the onions.

When roast vegetables are cooked around the meat, always drain on
paper towels to remove excess fat before serving.

BEEF OLIVES

1 cup soft breadcrumbs
½ cup chopped prunes
1 small onion, finely chopped
½ teaspoon grated lemon rind
½ teaspoon thyme
6 pieces (600 g) beef schnitzel

2 tablespoons oil
2 tablespoons Edmonds standard
   plain flour
1½ cups liquid beef stock
2 tablespoons soy sauce

Combine breadcrumbs, prunes, onion, lemon rind and thyme. Lay pieces of schnitzel out flat. Divide breadcrumb mixture evenly among pieces of meat. Spread each piece of meat with breadcrumb mixture then roll up like a sponge roll. Secure with toothpicks. Heat oil in a frying pan. Add beef olives and brown on all sides. Transfer to a casserole dish. Stir flour into frying pan and cook for 1 minute. Gradually add stock, stirring constantly. Bring to the boil. Add soy sauce. Pour this over beef olives. Cook at 160°C for 45 minutes or until meat is tender. Remove toothpicks before serving. Serves 4.

PORK OLIVES
Use pork schnitzel in place of beef in the foregoing recipe. It may be necessary to double the number of schnitzel as pork pieces are usually smaller in size.

BEEF POT ROAST

1 tablespoon oil
1 kg piece beef topside, trimmed
32 g packet onion soup mix
1 cup liquid beef stock
1 bay leaf

1 tablespoon Edmonds Fielder's
   cornflour
1 tablespoon water
1 teaspoon wholegrain mustard

Heat the oil in a large saucepan. Add the meat and brown well on all sides. Remove meat from pan and pour off fat. Return meat to pan. In a bowl, combine soup mix and stock. Pour this over the meat. Add bay leaf. Cover, bring to the boil, reduce heat and simmer gently for 3 hours or until meat is tender. Check liquid level from time to time, adding a little water if necessary. Remove bay leaf. In a bowl, combine cornflour and water, mixing until smooth. Remove meat from pan. Add cornflour mixture to the pan. Bring to the boil, stirring constantly until mixture thickens. Add mustard. Serve with sliced meat. If wished, potato and carrot can be added to the pan 30 minutes before end of cooking time. Serves 8.

CORNED BEEF

1 kg corned silverside
1 bay leaf
sprig parsley
4 black peppercorns

1 tablespoon golden syrup
1 thinly peeled strip orange rind
1 tablespoon DYC malt vinegar

Put silverside in a saucepan. Add bay leaf, parsley, peppercorns, golden syrup, orange rind and vinegar. Barely cover with water. Cover and bring to the boil then simmer gently for 1 hour or until meat is tender. Drain. Some of the cooking liquid can be used in a sauce to serve with the meat. If desired, serve hot or cold with White Sauce, Mustard Sauce or Plum Sauce. Serves 8–10.

To save time, use a pressure cooker to cook fillings for meat pies.

CURRIED SAUSAGES

2 teaspoons oil
8 sausages
1 onion, chopped
1 teaspoon hot curry powder

1 tablespoon Edmonds *standard plain flour*
$^3/_4$ cup liquid beef stock
1 tablespoon relish or chutney

Heat oil in a frying pan. Cook sausages for 10 minutes or until golden on all sides and cooked through. Remove sausages from pan and pour off all but 2 tablespoons of fat. And onion and cook until clear. Stir in curry powder and cook for 30 seconds. Stir in flour and cook for 30 seconds. Gradually add stock, stirring constantly until mixture boils. Reduce heat and add relish and sausages. Cook for a further 5 minutes to heat through. Slice sausages and serve with rice.
Serves 4–6.

HAMBURGER STEAKS

500 g lean beef mince
32 g packet onion soup mix
$^1/_2$ cup soft breadcrumbs
$^1/_4$ cup tomato sauce

black pepper
1 egg, lightly beaten
oil for frying

Put mince into a bowl. Add soup mix, breadcrumbs, tomato sauce, pepper to taste and egg. Mix to combine. Shape mixture into 6 patties. Heat oil in a frying pan and cook patties over a low heat until browned and cooked through. Alternatively brush each meat patty with oil and grill until juices run clear when tested with a skewer.
Serves 6.

IRISH STEW

1 kg hogget shoulder chops, fat
  removed
6 potatoes, sliced
3 onions, sliced
3 carrots, sliced

2 cups liquid beef stock
salt
black pepper
1 tablespoon chopped parsley

Put chops, potatoes, onions, carrots and beef stock into a large saucepan. Cover, bring to the boil. Reduce heat and simmer for 1$^1/_2$ hours or until meat is tender. Season with salt and pepper to taste. Garnish with parsley.
Serves 4–6.

Always put cold fillings into meat pies to avoid a soggy pastry base.

LIVER AND BACON

500 g lamb's fry (liver)
1 tablespoon oil
1 onion, sliced
1½ tablespoons Edmonds standard
  plain flour

1 cup liquid beef stock
salt
black pepper
8 rashers bacon, rind removed
parsley

Remove skin then thinly slice the lamb's fry. Heat oil in a frying pan. Add lamb's fry in batches and quickly brown on all sides. Remove from pan. Add onion and cook until golden. Stir in flour and cook for 1 minute. Gradually add stock, stirring constantly. Bring to the boil. Season with salt and pepper to taste. Simmer for 5 minutes. Grill the bacon until crisp. Return lamb's fry to pan and continue simmering for about 5 minutes or until just cooked, but still slightly pink. Serve with bacon. Garnish with parsley.
Serves 6.

MEAT LOAF

500 g lean beef mince
500 g sausagemeat
1 onion, finely chopped
2 cloves garlic, crushed
1 egg
1 cup grated carrot

½ cup chopped parsley
2 teaspoons prepared mustard
2 teaspoons mixed herbs
1 teaspoon salt
black pepper

TOPPING
2 tablespoons rolled oats
1 tablespoon brown sugar

2 tablespoons tomato sauce
¼ cup chopped parsley

Combine mince, sausagemeat, onion, garlic, egg, carrot, parsley, mustard, herbs, salt and pepper to taste. Mix well. Press mixture into a 22 cm loaf tin. Spread with prepared topping. Cover with foil and cook at 190°C for 30 minutes. Remove foil and cook for a further 30 minutes or until juices run clear when tested with a skewer. Serve hot or cold.
Serves 8–10.

TOPPING
Combine all ingredients.

MINCE PIE

1 tablespoon oil
1 onion, finely chopped
2 cloves garlic, crushed
500 g lean beef mince
1½ tablespoons Edmonds standard
  plain flour
½ cup liquid beef stock
2 tablespoons tomato purée

salt
black pepper
400 g Flaky or Shortcrust Pastry
  or 2 sheets Edmonds Savoury
  Short Pastry for bottom & 1 sheet
  Edmonds Flaky Puff Pastry for top
1 egg yolk
1 tablespoon water

(continued on p. 135)

Heat oil in a frying pan. Add onion and garlic and cook until onion is golden, stirring constantly. Add mince and cook quickly until meat is browned and crumbly. Stir in flour and cook for 30 seconds. Gradually add stock. Bring to the boil, stirring constantly. Stir in tomato purée, salt and pepper to taste. Simmer gently for 10 minutes. Set aside to cool. Cut pastry in half or use ready rolled sheets. On a lightly floured board roll out one portion and line a 22 cm pie plate. Trim off excess. Wet edge of pastry. Spoon meat filling onto pastry. Roll remaining pastry to fit top of plate or use ready rolled sheet. Carefully place pastry over filling. Press edges firmly together. Decorate with any pastry trimmings. Combine egg yolk and water and brush over pastry. Make two holes in the centre of pastry. Bake at 200°C for 25 minutes or until golden.
Serves 6.

PORK FILLET, CHINESE STYLE

2 medium whole pork fillets
$1/4$ cup soy sauce
1 tablespoon liquid honey
1 tablespoon brown sugar
2 cloves garlic, crushed

1 spring onion, sliced
1 teaspoon grated root ginger
$1/2$ teaspoon cinnamon
1 teaspoon red food colouring
(optional)

Trim fat from meat. In a large bowl or shallow ovenproof dish, combine soy sauce, honey, sugar, garlic, spring onion, ginger, cinnamon and food colouring. Stir to combine. Add pork fillets, turning to coat. Leave to marinate for at least 1 hour, turning occasionally. Drain pork from marinade and place on a rack over roasting dish. Cook at 190°C for 20 minutes or until juices run clear when tested with a skewer. Baste with marinade during cooking time. Serve with stir-fried vegetables.
Serves 4–6.

SHEPHERD'S PIE

1 tablespoon oil
1 onion, chopped
500 g lean beef mince
2 tablespoons Edmonds standard
   plain flour
1 tablespoon tomato sauce
1 tablespoon chutney or relish

$3/4$ cup liquid beef stock
3 potatoes, chopped
1 tablespoon butter
1 tablespoon finely chopped onion
$1/2$ cup grated tasty cheese
salt
black pepper

Heat oil in a large frying pan. Add onion and cook until clear. Add mince and cook until well browned, stirring constantly. Stir in flour and cook for 1 minute. Add tomato sauce, chutney and stock. Bring to the boil, reduce heat and simmer for 5 minutes. Set aside. Cook potatoes in boiling, salted water until tender. Drain and heat for a few minutes to dry off excess moisture. Shake the pan frequently during this time. Mash potato. Add butter, onion and half the cheese, mixing until smooth and creamy. Season with salt and pepper to taste. Put mince into a pie dish. Top with potato mixture. Sprinkle with remaining cheese. Bake at 190°C for 20 minutes or until golden and heated through.
Serves 4.

Top: Italian Green Beans (pg 167), Centre: Marinated Chicken Wings (pg 147),
Bottom: Chicken Kebabs (pg 143)

STEAK AND KIDNEY PIE

400 g beef chuck or blade steak
100 g beef or lamb kidneys
2 tablespoons oil
1 onion, chopped
2 stalks celery, sliced
1 tablespoon Edmonds *standard plain flour*
1 cup liquid beef stock
¼ cup tomato purée
½ teaspoon mixed herbs
salt
black pepper
200 g flaky pastry or 2 sheets Edmonds *Flaky Puff Pastry*
1 egg yolk
1 tablespoon water

Trim fat from meat and cut into 2 cm cubes. Heat oil in a heavy-based frying pan. Add meat in batches and quickly brown on all sides. Using a slotted spoon, remove meat from pan and set aside. Add onion and celery and cook until onion is clear. Stir in flour and cook for 30 seconds. Gradually add stock, stirring constantly. Bring to the boil. Return meat to pan. Stir in tomato purée and herbs. Cover and cook gently for 1 hour or until meat is tender. Season with salt and pepper to taste. Using a slotted spoon, transfer meat and vegetables to a 20 cm pie plate or dish. Pour ¼ cup of the cooking liquid over the meat. Reserve remaining liquid. Allow to cool. On a lightly floured board roll out pastry to 3 cm larger than the pie plate or dish or use ready rolled sheets. Cut a 3 cm wide strip off the edge. Wet edge of pie plate with water and place the pastry strip all round. Cover with pastry round, pressing edges firmly together. Pierce holes in centre of pie. Decorate with any pastry trimmings. Beat egg yolk and water together. Brush over pastry. Bake at 220°C for 20 minutes or until golden and well risen. Reheat reserved cooking liquid and serve with the pie.
Serves 4–6.

STEAK AND KIDNEY PUDDING

2 cups Edmonds *standard plain flour*
2 teaspoons baking powder
½ teaspoon salt
1 cup suet
½ cup water, approximately

FILLING
600 g beef chuck or blade steak
150 g ox kidneys
2 tablespoons Edmonds *standard plain flour*
2 teaspoons baking powder
½ teaspoon salt
black pepper
1 onion, chopped
½ teaspoon mixed herbs
¼ cup tomato purée
¼ cup water

Sift flour, baking powder and salt into a bowl. Stir in the suet. Mix to a smooth soft dough with water. Knead a little. On a lightly floured board, roll out two-thirds of dough and use to line a six-cup-capacity pudding basin.

FILLING
Trim fat from meat and cut into 2 cm cubes. Combine flour, salt and pepper to taste. Coat meat in seasoned flour. Place meat and onion into the lined pudding basin. In a bowl combine herbs, tomato purée and water. Pour this over meat mixture. Roll remaining portion of pastry to fit top of basin. Press edges firmly together. Cover with pleated greased paper or foil. Steam for 4 hours, checking the water level occasionally. When cooking time has finished, carefully lift pudding from pan. Remove foil. To serve either unmould onto a serving plate, or serve from the basin. Serves 6–8.

STUFFED LAMB CUTLETS

6 large lamb or hogget cutlets,
    frenched
1 slice pressed ham
1/4 cup grated tasty cheese
1/4 cup Edmonds standard plain flour
1/2 teaspoon salt

black pepper
1 egg
2 tablespoons water
3/4 cup dry breadcrumbs
oil for frying

Cut meat horizontally almost through to bone. Open out. This should resemble butterfly wings. Cut ham into sixths. Place a piece of ham onto cut side of meat. Top with a small amount of cheese. Close meat again to completely encase filling. Combine flour, salt and pepper to taste. Dip lamb into the seasoned flour. Beat egg and water together. Dip lamb in egg then in breadcrumbs, shaking off the excess. Repeat with egg and breadcrumbs. Heat oil in a frying pan. Fry lamb for 5 minutes each side or until golden. Drain on absorbent paper. Serve hot.
Serves 3.

SWEET AND SOUR PORK

500 g pork pieces
2 tablespoons oil
2 small onions, quartered
2 cloves garlic, crushed
1/2 cup chicken liquid stock
225 g can pineapple pieces in syrup
1 tablespoon Edmonds Fielder's
    cornflour

1/4 cup tomato sauce
1/2 teaspoon grated root ginger
2 tablespoons DYC white vinegar
2 tablespoons brown sugar
1/2 cup chopped red pepper
1/2 cup chopped cucumber
1/2 cup baby sweetcorn
100 g mushrooms, quartered

Trim fat from pork and cut into 2 cm pieces. Heat oil in a saucepan or wok. Add onion and garlic and cook until onion is clear. Remove from pan. Add half the pork pieces and quickly brown on all sides. Remove from pan. Repeat with remaining meat. Return meat and onions to pan. Add stock and bring to the boil. Cover and cook gently for 30 minutes or until meat is tender. Drain pineapple, reserving juice. Combine juice and cornflour, mixing until smooth. Add pineapple pieces, tomato sauce, ginger, vinegar, sugar, pepper, cucumber, sweetcorn and mushrooms to pan. Cook for 5 minutes. Return to the boil. Stir in cornflour mixture and boil for 2 minutes or until mixture thickens slightly. Serve with rice or noodles.
Serves 4–6.

Brown meat in batches. Browning too much meat at a time causes the meat to simmer in its own juices.

WIENER SCHNITZEL

1 egg
1 tablespoon Edmonds Fielder's
  cornflour
6 pieces (600 g) beef or lamb schnitzel

1 cup dry breadcrumbs,
  approximately
oil for frying

Beat egg until combined. Beat in cornflour. Coat each piece of schnitzel with egg mixture, draining excess, then coat with breadcrumbs. Heat oil in a frying pan. Add schnitzel and cook until golden on both sides, turning once during cooking time. It may be necessary to cook in batches. If so, add a little oil each time you cook.
Serves 6.

DUMPLINGS

1½ cups Edmonds *standard plain flour*
2 teaspoons Edmonds *baking powder*
¼ teaspoon salt
½ teaspoon mixed herbs

1 tablespoon finely chopped onion
100 g butter
½ cup milk, approximately

Sift flour, baking powder and salt into a bowl. Stir in herbs and onion. Rub butter into dry ingredients until mixture resembles coarse breadcrumbs. Add enough milk to mix to a soft dough. Drop large spoonsful of dough on top of boiling stew. Cover and cook for 10 minutes or until dumplings are cooked through.
Serves 4–6.

YORKSHIRE PUDDING

1st EDITION RECIPE

1 cup Edmonds *standard plain flour*
½ teaspoon salt
2 eggs

½ cup milk
2 tablespoons water
2 tablespoons fat

Sift flour and salt into a bowl. Make a well in the centre. Add eggs. Lightly beat together then gradually add milk and water, mixing to a smooth batter. Chill for 1 hour. Stir again. Heat fat in a roasting dish until smoking hot. Quickly pour batter into roasting dish. Bake at 200°C for 30 minutes or until golden, well risen and crisp around the edges. Cut into squares and serve with roast beef.
Serves 6.

POULTRY

GUIDE TO NUMBER OF SERVINGS

	Size	Weight	Servings		Weight	Servings
chicken	No. 5	1.1 kg	2 to 3	turkey	2 to 3.5 kg	8–12
	No. 6	1.2 kg	3 to 4		4 to 5 kg	12–16
	No. 7	1.4 kg	4 to 5		5.5 to 6.5 kg	16–22
	No. 8	1.5 kg	4 to 6			
	No. 9	1.6 kg	5 to 6			

ROASTING TIMES (APPROXIMATE)

Poultry	Weight	Time	Oven Temp °C
chicken	per 500 g	25 minutes per 500 g plus 20 minutes	180°C
turkey	3 to 4 kg	3 to 3½ hours	160°C
	5 to 6 kg	4 to 5½ hours	
duck	2 to 3 kg	1 to 1½ hours	180°C

COOKING CHICKEN

PREPARATION FOR ROASTING
- Remove giblets from poultry.
- Stuff poultry just before cooking or cook stuffing separately.
- Unstuffed — Place fresh herbs and a lemon wedge or clove of garlic in body cavity. Calculate cooking time.
- Stuffed — Spoon the stuffing into the cavity of the bird and secure opening with skewers. Truss the chicken. Weigh the stuffed chicken and calculate cooking time.
- Brush the outside with butter, oil or marinade of your choice.
- Cook chicken, breast side down.
- Baste chicken during cooking.
- The oven temperature can be increased to 200° for the last 10 minutes of cooking to crisp the skin if wished.
- Chicken is cooked when the juice from the thickest part of the thigh, when pierced, runs clear.
- Leave the cooked chicken in a warm place to 'rest' for 5 to 10 minutes before carving. This stops the juices from running.
- Always reheat cooked poultry dishes thoroughly before serving.

TRUSSING
This keeps poultry in a good shape for roasting.
- Fold the neck skin under the body.
- Fold the tips of the wings back towards the backbone.
- Press the legs into the sides.
- Make a slit in the skin at the tail end and put the parson's nose through this.
- Take a piece of string and place below the breast bone at the neck end. Bring the string down over the wings, cross it underneath then take it up to tie the legs together.

CARVING

Remove the legs by cutting through the skin at (1) and, pressing outwards with the knife, pull off the leg. Do the same with the wing, cutting at (2). Then cut slices of the breast meat, cutting downwards at (3).

TRADITIONAL ACCOMPANIMENTS FOR ROAST POULTRY

CHICKEN	TURKEY	DUCK
forcemeat balls	forcemeat balls	sage and onion stuffing
chipolatas	chipolatas	Apple Sauce
bacon rolls	bacon rolls	thin gravy
thin gravy	bread sauce	
	cranberry sauce	
	giblet gravy	

- Forcemeat balls are made using any stuffing mixture rolled into balls rather than put inside the bird. They are roasted around the bird or fried separately.

STORING POULTRY

- Remove packaging and cover bird loosely with plastic wrap or waxed paper. Allow air to circulate.
- Store in the coolest part of the refrigerator for a maximum of 3 days.
- Frozen poultry must be completely thawed before cooking. Thaw in the refrigerator or use a microwave. Do not leave poultry on the kitchen bench to thaw. Use as soon as possible after thawing.

APRICOT CHICKEN

6 chicken pieces   *oil for frying*

SAUCE
425 g can apricot halves
1/2 teaspoon grated lemon or lime rind
2 tablespoons lemon or lime juice
1/2 teaspoon ground ginger
2 tablespoons Edmonds Fielder's
   cornflour

1 tablespoon DYC *spiced vinegar*
1/2 teaspoon sugar
salt
pepper

Remove skin and fat from chicken pieces. Heat oil in a frying pan and cook chicken for 10 minutes each side or until juices run clear when tested. Drain on absorbent paper. Pour apricot sauce over chicken.
Serves 4–6.

SAUCE
Purée apricots and juice in a food processor or blender. Put purée in a saucepan. Add lemon rind, juice, ginger and cornflour. Mix well. Gently heat, stirring constantly until mixture boils and thickens. Stir in vinegar, sugar, salt and pepper to taste.

BASIC BREAD STUFFING

3 cups soft breadcrumbs
1 onion, finely chopped
1 teaspoon sage
2 tablespoons melted butter

1 egg
salt
pepper

Combine breadcrumbs, onion, sage, butter and egg in a bowl. Season with salt and pepper to taste.
Makes about 1½ cups.

SAUSAGEMEAT STUFFING
Add 200 g sausagemeat to half a quantity of basic stuffing.

ORANGE AND ROSEMARY STUFFING
Add 2 tablespoons grated orange rind and 2 teaspoons rosemary.

APRICOT STUFFING
Add ½ cup chopped dried apricots which have been soaked in ¼ cup orange juice for 2 hours.

CHEESY SESAME-COATED CHICKEN

8 chicken drumsticks
2 tablespoons Edmonds standard plain flour
2 tablespoons grated parmesan cheese

1 teaspoon chicken stock powder
¼ teaspoon mixed herbs
2 tablespoons dry breadcrumbs
2 teaspoons sesame seeds
oil

Remove skin from chicken. Moisten chicken slightly with water. Combine flour, parmesan cheese, stock powder, herbs, breadcrumbs and sesame seeds. Put this mixture into a plastic bag. Add 2 drumsticks to bag and shake to coat. Repeat with remaining chicken, coating only 2 at a time. Place drumsticks in a lightly oiled baking dish. Allow to stand for 15 minutes. Cook at 200°C for 20 minutes or until juices run clear when tested. Serve hot or cold.
Serves 4–6.

CHICKEN AND APPLE HOT-POT

1 kg chicken pieces
¼ cup Edmonds standard plain flour, approximately
½ teaspoon salt
black pepper
2 tablespoons oil
3 rashers bacon, chopped

1 onion, chopped
1 clove garlic, crushed
2 tomatoes, blanched and chopped
1 cup apple and orange juice
2 cooking apples, peeled and sliced
chopped parsley

Remove skin and fat from chicken. Combine flour, salt and pepper. Coat chicken in seasoned flour. Heat oil in a large frying pan. Add chicken pieces and cook until golden on both sides. Remove chicken and set aside. Add bacon, onion and garlic. Cook until onion is clear. Stir in tomatoes and fruit juice. Return chicken to pan, reduce heat then add apple slices. Cover and simmer gently for 20 minutes or until juices run clear when tested. Garnish with parsley.
Serves 4–6.

Press cloves of garlic with the flat of the knife to remove skin.

CHICKEN AND ORANGE CASSEROLE

1 kg chicken pieces
1 tablespoon butter
1 onion, finely chopped
1 cup sliced celery
1/2 cup orange juice
1/2 cup liquid chicken stock
1/4 teaspoon cinnamon

1/8 teaspoon ground allspice
1 tablespoon grated orange rind
1 tablespoon Edmonds Fielder's
  cornflour
1 tablespoon DYC white vinegar
orange slices

Remove skin and fat from chicken. Melt butter in a large frying pan or flameproof casserole dish. Add chicken and quickly brown on all sides. Remove from pan and set aside. Add onion and celery. Cook until onion is clear. Add orange juice, stock, cinnamon, allspice and orange rind. Bring to the boil. Add chicken. Cover and bake at 180°C for 40 minutes or until juices run clear when tested. Alternatively, to continue cooking on top of stove, reduce heat, cover and simmer gently for 30 minutes. Mix cornflour and vinegar to a smooth paste. Add to chicken mixture. Stir until mixture thickens. Garnish with orange slices.
Serves 4–6.

CHICKEN CREOLE

No. 8 chicken
2 onions, chopped
1 green pepper, chopped
1 ham steak, chopped
140 g pot tomato paste

400 g can tomatoes in juice, chopped
1/4 teaspoon sweet basil
50 g salami, chopped
salt
black pepper

Remove neck and giblets from chicken. Place chicken in a large ovenproof dish. Add onions, green pepper, ham steak, tomato paste, tomatoes and juice. Cover and cook at 180°C for 1 1/2 hours or until juices run clear when tested. Add basil and salami. Stir in salt and pepper to taste. Serve with rice.
Serves 4–6.

CHICKEN CROQUETTES

1 cup cooked chicken
1 onion, finely chopped
1 clove garlic, crushed
2 tablespoons butter
2 tablespoons Edmonds standard plain
  flour
1/2 cup liquid chicken stock

1 teaspoon lemon juice
1 egg, separated
2 tablespoons chopped parsley
salt
black pepper
3/4 cup dry breadcrumbs, approximately
oil for deep frying

Mince or finely chop chicken. Add onion and garlic. Set aside. Melt butter in a saucepan. Stir in flour and cook until frothy. Gradually add stock, stirring constantly until mixture boils and thickens. Remove from heat. Add lemon juice, egg yolk, parsley, salt and pepper to taste. Stir in chicken mixture. Spread in an 18 × 20 cm tin or dish. Allow to stand until cold. Divide mixture into eight even-sized portions. On a lightly floured board, shape each portion into a cylinder. Lightly beat egg white. Dip each croquette in egg white then coat in breadcrumbs. Deep-fry in hot oil for 5 minutes or until golden. Drain on absorbent paper.
Serves 3–4.

Chicken is cooked when the juices run clear when a skewer is inserted into the thickest part of the meat.

CHICKEN CURRY

1 tablespoon oil
2 cloves garlic, crushed
1 onion, chopped
1 teaspoon grated root ginger

1 tablespoon curry powder
1 cup liquid chicken stock
4 chicken breasts

Heat oil in a large frying pan. Add garlic, onion and ginger. Cook until onion is clear. Stir in curry powder and cook for 30 seconds. Add stock and chicken. Cover and bring to the boil. Reduce heat and simmer for 30 minutes or until chicken is tender. Serve with rice.
Serves 4.

CHICKEN DELICIOUS

No. 8 chicken
2 teaspoons oil
2 cups apple juice
30 g packet cream of chicken soup
1 large onion, chopped
1 green pepper, sliced

2 tomatoes, blanched and chopped
2 rashers bacon, diced
1 tablespoon Edmonds Fielder's
  cornflour
1 tablespoon water

Rub the skin of the chicken with oil. Roast chicken at 180°C for 40 minutes. In a saucepan heat apple juice slightly. Add soup mix and dissolve. Pour this over chicken. Add onion, pepper, tomatoes and bacon. Return to oven and cook for a further 45 minutes or until juices run clear when tested. Baste occasionally during cooking time. Place chicken on a serving dish. Mix cornflour and water to a smooth paste. Bring the cooking liquid to the boil on top of stove. Add cornflour mixture and cook until sauce boils and thickens. Pour over chicken before serving.
Serves 4–6.

CHICKEN KEBABS

375 g boneless chicken pieces
3 tablespoons soy sauce
1 tablespoon chilli sauce
1 large red pepper

1 onion, diced large
2 courgettes, sliced
soaked bamboo skewers

Remove skin and fat from chicken. Cut the flesh into cubes. In a bowl combine soy and chilli sauces. Add the chicken and leave to marinate for about 30 minutes. Drain, reserving the marinade. Deseed the pepper and cut into large cubes. Thread chicken, pepper, onion and courgettes onto soaked skewers. Barbecue or grill until golden and cooked through, brushing with marinade during cooking.
Serves 4–6.

Soak bamboo skewers in cold water for 1/2 hour prior to using for kebabs or other barbecued foods.

CHICKEN LOAF

1 cup chopped cooked chicken
1 onion, roughly chopped
200 g sausagemeat
2 eggs
1 tablespoon tomato sauce

1/2 cup chopped parsley
salt
pepper
2 hard-boiled eggs

Remove chicken from bones. Put chicken and onion into the bowl of a food processor or through a mincer. Process or mince until finely chopped. Add sausagemeat. Pulse to combine. Add eggs, tomato sauce, parsley, salt and pepper to taste. Process to combine. Press half the mixture into an 18 cm loaf tin. Shell the hard-boiled eggs and place on top of chicken mixture. Cover with remaining chicken mixture. Cook at 190°C for 40 minutes or until juices run clear when tested. Serve hot or cold.
Serves 4–6.

CHICKEN MARYLAND

4 whole chicken legs
2 bananas, halved
pineapple slices, drained
1/2 cup Edmonds standard plain flour, approximately

2 eggs
1/2 cup water
3/4 cup dry breadcrumbs, approximately
oil for deep-frying

Coat chicken, bananas and pineapple in flour. Beat eggs and water together. Dip chicken, banana and pineapple in egg mixture. Coat with breadcrumbs. Deep-fry chicken in hot oil for 10 minutes or until juices run clear when tested. Do not have oil too hot as chicken will brown but not be cooked through. Drain on absorbent paper. Deep-fry bananas and pineapple until golden. Drain. Serve chicken with bananas and pineapple.
Serves 4.

CHICKEN PAPRIKA

4 chicken breasts
2 tablespoons oil
1 large onion, chopped
2 teaspoons paprika
1 tablespoon Edmonds standard plain flour

1/2 cup liquid chicken stock
250 g pot sour cream or 300 ml cream
1 tablespoon lemon juice
salt
black pepper

Remove skin and fat from chicken. Heat oil in a large frying pan. Add chicken and quickly brown on all sides. Remove from pan and set aside. Add onion and cook until clear. Stir in paprika and cook for 30 seconds. Stir in flour and cook, stirring, for 1 minute. Gradually add stock, stirring constantly. Bring to the boil. Return chicken to pan. Cover, reduce heat and simmer gently for 15 minutes. Stir in sour cream. Continue cooking gently for a further 10 minutes or until juices run clear when tested. Add lemon juice. Season with salt and pepper to taste. Serve with rice.
Serves 4.

No. 6 eggs are used in recipes in this book.

CHICKEN STIR-FRY WITH CASHEWS

2 single boneless chicken breasts
1 tablespoon Edmonds Fielder's
  cornflour
1 egg white
2 tablespoons oil
2 stalks celery, sliced
6 spring onions, sliced
100 g button mushrooms, quartered

2 teaspoons grated root ginger
1/2 cup liquid chicken stock
1/2 teaspoon sugar
2 teaspoons Edmonds Fielder's
  cornflour
1 tablespoon dry sherry
1/4 cup roasted cashew nuts

Remove skin and fat from chicken. Cut flesh into 2.5 cm cubes. Coat in first measure of cornflour then in lightly beaten egg white. Heat oil in a wok or large frying pan. Add chicken and cook until crisp and golden. Remove chicken from pan with a slotted spoon. Set aside. Add celery to pan and stir-fry until just tender. Add spring onions, mushrooms and ginger. Stir-fry until spring onions are bright green in colour. Blend stock, sugar, second measure of cornflour and sherry. Add to pan. Cook, stirring until mixture boils and thickens slightly. Add chicken and cashews. Stir to heat through.
Serves 4.

CHINESE LEMON CHICKEN

1/2 cup lemon juice
2 teaspoons grated lemon rind
2 teaspoons chicken stock powder
2 tablespoons Edmonds Fielder's
  cornflour
3 tablespoons brown sugar
2 teaspoons grated root ginger

1 1/2 cups water
4 single boneless chicken breasts
1/4 cup Edmonds Fielder's cornflour
1 egg white
oil for deep-frying
4 spring onions, chopped

Combine lemon juice, rind, stock powder, first measure of cornflour, sugar, ginger and water in a saucepan. Bring to the boil, stirring constantly until mixture boils and thickens. Remove from heat. Cover and keep warm. Remove skin from chicken and cut flesh into bite-sized pieces. Coat in second measure of cornflour. Lightly beat egg white. Dip a few pieces of chicken into egg white. Deep-fry until crisp and golden. Drain and keep warm. Continue doing this until all chicken has been cooked. Arrange chicken on serving plate. Pour hot sauce over chicken. Garnish with spring onions.
Serves 4–6.

CRUNCHY-COATED CHICKEN

3 cups cornflakes, crushed
1/2 cup coconut
2 tablespoons grated orange rind
2 teaspoons chicken stock powder
1 teaspoon ground nutmeg
1 teaspoon ground ginger
1 kg chicken pieces

1/4 cup Edmonds standard plain flour,
  approximately
1/2 teaspoon salt
black pepper
1 egg
2 tablespoons water

Combine cornflakes, coconut, orange rind, stock powder, nutmeg and ginger. Remove skin and fat from chicken. Combine flour, salt and pepper to taste. Coat chicken with seasoned flour. Lightly beat egg and water together. Dip chicken pieces into egg mixture. Coat in cornflake mixture. Place chicken on a rack in roasting dish. Cook at 180°C for 40 minutes or until juices run clear when tested.
Serves 4–6.

DUCK WITH ORANGE

2 kg duck
1 tablespoon melted butter
2 large oranges
2 tablespoons sugar
1 tablespoon DYC white vinegar
1 cup liquid chicken stock

1 tablespoon Edmonds Fielder's
  cornflour
2 tablespoons sherry
salt
pepper

Brush the duck with melted butter. Place on a rack in roasting dish. Cook at 180°C for 40 minutes. While duck is cooking, pare the rind from the oranges thinly. Cut the rind into thin strips. Juice the oranges. This should yield 1/2 cup juice. Put the orange strips and juice, sugar, vinegar and chicken stock into a saucepan. Cook until liquid has reduced by one-quarter. Mix cornflour and sherry together until smooth. Add to the saucepan. Stir until sauce boils and thickens. Remove from heat. Drain pan juices from the duck. Remove rack and place duck directly into the roasting dish. Pour sauce over duck. Cook for a further 30 minutes, basting frequently with orange sauce during cooking. Season with salt and pepper to taste. Serve with sauce.
Serves 4.

EASY CHICKEN

1 kg chicken pieces
3 tablespoons oil
1 tablespoon prepared mustard
1 teaspoon soy sauce
1 teaspoon grated root ginger
3 tablespoons red currant jelly

1 tablespoon Worcestershire sauce
1 cup orange juice
1 tablespoon DYC white vinegar
salt
black pepper

Remove skin and fat from chicken. Heat oil in a large frying pan. Add chicken pieces and cook until golden on both sides. Remove chicken and drain oil from pan. In a bowl, combine mustard, soy sauce, ginger, red currant jelly, Worcestershire sauce and orange juice. Add to pan and bring to the boil, stirring occasionally. Return chicken to pan. Cover, reduce heat and simmer for 20 minutes or until juices run clear when tested. Stir in vinegar. Season with salt and pepper to taste.
Serves 4–6.

FAMILY CHICKEN PIE

8 boneless chicken thighs
2 tablespoons oil
3 rashers bacon, chopped
100 g mushrooms
1 onion, chopped
1 clove garlic, crushed
2 tablespoons Edmonds *standard plain*
   flour
1 cup liquid chicken stock

$^1/_4$ teaspoon mixed herbs
$^1/_2$ cup milk
$^1/_2$ teaspoon salt
white pepper
1 cup drained canned corn kernels
200 g flaky pastry or 2 sheets
   Edmonds *Flaky Puff Pastry*
1 egg yolk

Remove skin from chicken. Cut flesh into 2.5 cm cubes. Heat oil in a large saucepan. Add bacon, mushrooms, onion and garlic. Cook until onion is clear. Stir in flour and cook until frothy. Gradually add stock and bring to the boil. Add chicken, herbs, milk, salt and pepper to taste. Reduce heat and cook gently for 20 minutes or until juices run clear when tested, stirring occasionally. Remove from heat and allow to cool. Stir in corn. Pour chicken mixture into a 20 cm pie dish. Brush edge of dish with water. On a lightly floured board roll out pastry to a circle large enough to fit top of pie dish or use ready rolled sheets. Carefully place pastry over filling. Press edges firmly to seal, then trim. Decorate pie with pastry trimmings. Cut steam holes in centre of pastry top. Brush pastry with egg yolk. Bake at 220°C for 20 minutes or until pastry is golden and well risen.
Serves 6.

GARLIC LEMON CHICKEN

8 chicken drumsticks
1 tablespoon grated lemon rind
5 tablespoons lemon juice
2 cloves garlic, crushed

2 tablespoons soy sauce
1 teaspoon paprika
salt
black pepper

Remove skin from chicken. Combine lemon rind, juice, garlic, soy sauce and paprika. Brush each drumstick well with this mixture. Place on a large sheet of foil. Wrap foil tightly to enclose chicken. Place flat in a shallow dish. Cook at 180°C for 30 minutes or until juices run clear when tested. Season with salt and pepper to taste. Serve hot or cold.
Serves 4.

MARINATED CHICKEN WINGS

3 cloves garlic, crushed
3 tablespoons soy sauce
2 tablespoons liquid honey

1 tablespoon tomato sauce
2 teaspoons grated root ginger
500 g chicken wings

Combine garlic, soy sauce, honey, tomato sauce and ginger. Brush chicken wings well with this. Leave to marinate for 1 hour. Grill for 8–10 minutes or until golden, turning once during cooking time. Alternatively place wings in roasting dish. Cook at 200°C for 10 minutes or until crisp and golden. Serve hot or cold.
Serves 4–6.

Halve the stated amount of fresh herbs when substituting
with dried herbs in the recipe.

POT-ROAST CHICKEN

No. 9 boiling chicken
25 g butter
1 onion, sliced
sprig thyme
1 bay leaf

sprig parsley
$^1/_4$ cup water
salt
black pepper

Truss the chicken. Heat butter in a heavy-based casserole dish with well-fitting lid. Add chicken and brown lightly all over. Add onion, thyme, bay leaf, parsley and water. Cover and cook at 180°C for 1 hour. Turn chicken and cook for a further 40 minutes. Season with salt and pepper to taste. Cover and continue to cook for 30 minutes or until juices run clear when tested. Alternatively, the chicken can be cooked on top of the stove. Remove chicken and carve into serving portions.
Serves 4–6.

SESAME CHICKEN

4 boneless single chicken breasts
2 cloves garlic, crushed
$^1/_4$ cup Plum Sauce (page 240)

$^1/_4$ cup oil
5 tablespoons sesame seeds,
    approximately

Remove skin and fat from chicken. Combine garlic, plum sauce and oil. Brush the chicken with this mixture. Roll in sesame seeds. Place in a lightly oiled oven-proof dish. Cook at 180°C for 15 minutes or until golden and juices run clear when tested.
Serves 4.

SPICY CHICKEN

8 large chicken drumsticks
2 cloves garlic, crushed
2 teaspoons curry powder
$^1/_4$ teaspoon chilli powder

1 tablespoon coriander leaves
1 teaspoon grated lemon rind
200 g pot natural unsweetened
    yoghurt

Remove skin from chicken. Combine garlic, curry powder, chilli powder, coriander, lemon rind and yoghurt. Pour this mixture over chicken and leave to marinate for at least 1 hour. Grill chicken until browned and juices run clear when tested, turning occasionally during cooking.
Serves 4.

*Wash boards and knives that come into contact with raw poultry
in very hot soapy water.*

TARRAGON CHICKEN

4 single boneless chicken breasts
2 tablespoons oil
1 onion, chopped
1 clove garlic, crushed
1 tablespoon Edmonds standard plain
    flour
1/2 cup dry white wine

1/2 cup liquid chicken stock
1 tablespoon chopped fresh tarragon
    or 1 1/2 teaspoons dried tarragon
1/4 cup cream
1 egg yolk
salt
white pepper

Remove skin and fat from chicken. Heat oil in a large frying pan. Add onion and garlic. Cook until onion is clear. Stir in flour and cook until frothy. Gradually add wine and stock. Bring to the boil, stirring constantly. Add chicken and tarragon to the pan. Cover, reduce heat then simmer gently for 15 minutes or until juices run clear when tested. Remove chicken from pan and keep warm. Bring liquid back to the boil and continue boiling until liquid has reduced by a quarter. Remove from heat. Stir in cream and egg yolk. Season with salt and pepper to taste. Pour sauce over chicken.
Serves 4.

ANTIPASTO (Italy)

425 g can artichoke hearts
1/2 cup black olives
6 to 8 slices smoked beef or pork

250 g tasty cheese
cherry tomatoes
6 to 8 slices salami

Rinse artichoke hearts. Drain. Arrange artichokes, olives, beef, cheese, tomatoes and salami decoratively on a serving platter.
Serves 4–6.

BEEF STROGANOFF (Russia)

500 g rump steak
2 tablespoons butter
1 tablespoon oil
1 onion, sliced
150 g mushrooms, sliced

1/4 cup white wine
3/4 cup sour cream
1 tablespoon lemon juice
salt
pepper

Trim fat from meat. Cut meat into thin strips against the grain. Heat butter and oil in a frying pan. Add meat and quickly brown on both sides. Remove from pan and set aside. Add onion and mushrooms to pan. Cook until onion is clear. Return meat to pan. Add wine and sour cream. Reheat gently. Add lemon juice. Season with salt and pepper to taste. Serve with rice.
Serves 4–6.

BOEUF BOURGUIGNON (France)

750 g chuck steak
2 tablespoons Edmonds standard plain
   flour
salt
pepper
2 tablespoons oil
8 pickling onions
2 rashers bacon, chopped

2 cloves garlic, crushed
3/4 cup red wine
1/2 cup liquid beef stock
4 carrots, quartered lengthwise
sprig parsley
sprig thyme
bay leaf

Trim fat from meat. Cut meat into serving-sized pieces. Combine flour, salt and pepper. Coat meat in seasoned flour. Heat oil in a flameproof casserole dish. Add onions and bacon and cook until golden. Using a slotted spoon, remove from pan and set aside. Add half the meat and quickly brown on all sides. Repeat with remaining meat. Return onions and bacon to pan with garlic. Add wine and stock, stirring well. Add carrots. Make a bouquet garni from parsley, thyme and bay leaf. Add to casserole. Cover and cook at 180°C for 1 1/2 hours or until meat is tender. Serve with French bread and salad.
Serves 4–6.

Top: Greek Salad (pg 156), Centre: Veal Cordon Bleu (pg 160),
Bottom: Frittata (pg 155)

CHEESE FONDUE (Switzerland)

1 clove garlic, crushed
1 cup dry white wine
250 g gruyère cheese, grated
250 g cheddar cheese, grated

2 tablespoons Edmonds Fielder's
  cornflour
2 tablespoons water
crusty French bread or bread cubes

Put garlic and wine in a fondue pot or bowl over a pan of hot water. Heat the wine until almost boiling. Gradually add cheeses, whisking constantly until all the cheese has been added. In a bowl combine cornflour and water. Mix until smooth. Add to cheese mixture and continue to cook for 4 minutes or until mixture thickens, stirring continuously. Dip French bread or bread cubes into cheese mixture.
Serves 4–6.

CHICKEN CHOW MEIN (China)

2 boneless chicken breasts
2 teaspoons soy sauce
2 teaspoons dry sherry
2 teaspoons Edmonds Fielder's
  cornflour
1/2 teaspoon grated root ginger
2 tablespoons oil
1 onion, quartered

2 cloves garlic, crushed
1 cup broccoli florets
1/2 cup sliced celery
1 red pepper, sliced
1/2 cup liquid chicken stock
2 teaspoons Edmonds Fielder's
  cornflour
1 tablespoon soy sauce

Remove skin from chicken. Cut flesh into strips. Combine chicken, first measure of soy sauce, sherry, first measure of cornflour and root ginger. Set aside to marinate for 30 minutes. Heat oil in a wok. Add onion and garlic and cook until onion is clear. Stir in chicken and quickly stir-fry until meat is browned on all sides. Add broccoli, celery and pepper. Stir-fry until vegetables are bright in colour. In a bowl combine stock and second measure of cornflour. Add to wok. Cover and cook until mixture boils and thickens. Sprinkle with second measure of soy sauce. Toss. Serve with crispy noodles.
Serves 4.

CHICKEN ENCHILADAS (Mexico)

400 g can tomatoes in juice
113 g can jalapeño peppers
1 teaspoon ground coriander
1/2 teaspoon salt
250 g pot sour cream
2 tablespoons oil

2 cups chopped cooked chicken
1 small onion, finely chopped
3/4 teaspoon salt
12 cooked flour Tortillas (page 155)
3/4 cup grated tasty cheese

Put tomatoes in juice, jalapeño peppers, coriander and salt into a food processor or blender. Process until smooth. Add sour cream and process to combine. Set aside. Heat oil in a saucepan. Add chicken, onion and salt. Cook, stirring constantly, until onion is clear. Dip each tortilla in tomato mixture, draining excess off. Spread a little of the chicken mixture onto the tortilla. Roll up like a sponge roll. Place seam side down in ovenproof dish. Repeat with remaining tortillas and chicken. Pour remaining tomato mixture over. Sprinkle with cheese. Cover dish with lid or foil. Cook at 180°C for 30 minutes. Remove lid then grill until golden.
Serves 6.

Top: Cheese Fondue (pg 153), Bottom: Chicken Enchiladas (pg 153)
with Tomato Salsa (pg 159)

CHILLI CON CARNE (Mexico)

1 tablespoon oil
2 onions, chopped
1 clove garlic, crushed
1 green pepper, chopped
500 g lean beef mince
1½ teaspoons chilli powder

1 cup water
300 g can tomato paste
¼ teaspoon oregano
salt
465 g can red kidney beans

Heat oil in a large frying pan or saucepan. Add onions, garlic and green pepper. Cook until onion is clear. Stir in meat and cook until meat is browned. Add chilli powder, water, tomato paste, oregano and season with salt to taste. Bring to the boil, stirring constantly. Reduce heat and simmer gently for 30 minutes or until mixture is quite thick. Drain beans. Add to pan. Continue cooking for a further 10 minutes, stirring occasionally.
Serves 4–6.

COQ AU VIN (France)

25 g butter
2 rashers bacon, chopped
8 pieces chicken
12 pickling onions
100 g button mushrooms
2 tablespoons brandy
1½ cups red wine
2 cloves garlic, crushed
1 tablespoon tomato paste

1 bay leaf
sprig thyme
sprig parsley
salt
pepper
2 tablespoons Edmonds standard
  plain flour
25 g butter

Melt first measure of butter in a flameproof casserole dish or saucepan. Add bacon and cook for 4 minutes. Remove from pan. Remove skin from chicken. Add to pan and cook until browned on both sides. Remove from pan. Add onions and cook until golden. Return bacon and chicken to pan. Add mushrooms. Pour brandy over chicken. Stir in wine, garlic and tomato paste. Make a bouquet garni with bay leaf, thyme and parsley. Add to saucepan. Bring to the boil. Cover, reduce heat and simmer gently for 45 minutes or until chicken is tender. Season with salt and pepper to taste. Put flour and second measure of butter into a small bowl. Mix together to form a paste called *beurre manié*. Remove chicken from pan and keep warm. Bring cooking liquid to the boil and whisk in the *beurre manié* a little at a time, cooking gently until sauce is smooth and thickened slightly. Remove bouquet garni. Return chicken to the pan and serve.
Serves 4–6.

CRISPY FRIED NOODLES (China)

250 g Diamond *vermicelli noodles*   oil for deep-frying

Cook vermicelli according to packet directions. Drain well. Lay vermicelli out flat until cold. Heat oil in a wok or deep pan. Lower vermicelli into oil and cook until crisp and golden. Drain on absorbent paper.
Serves 4.

FLOUR TORTILLAS (Mexico)

2 cups Edmonds *standard plain flour*
½ teaspoon salt

5 tablespoons oil
½ cup warm water, approximately

Sift flour and salt into a bowl. Stir in oil. Add sufficient water to form a soft dough. Knead dough for 3 minutes or until smooth and elastic. Wrap in plastic wrap and leave at room temperature for 30 minutes. Lightly knead dough again. Divide dough evenly into 12. Roll each portion of dough into a ball. Cover. Take one portion of dough at a time and on a lightly floured board roll to a 20 cm circle, turning dough over frequently during this time. Repeat with remaining dough, stacking between sheets of waxed paper. Heat a heavy-based frying pan. Cook one tortilla for approximately 20 seconds or until golden. Turn and cook other side. If tortilla puffs up while second side is cooking, gently press it down with a fish slice or spatula. Transfer to plate. Cover with foil. Repeat with remaining tortillas. Use as required.
Makes 12.

FRITTATA (Italy)

50 g butter
2 onions, chopped
3 cups grated vegetables — e.g.
  courgettes, carrots, potatoes
4 eggs

2 tablespoons water
½ cup grated tasty cheese
salt
pepper
¼ cup grated parmesan cheese

Melt butter in a large heavy-based frying pan. Add onions and cook until clear. Add vegetables and cook, stirring for 10 minutes or until just tender. In a bowl beat together eggs, water, cheese and salt and pepper to taste. Pour this over vegetable mixture. Gently cook until egg mixture is set. Sprinkle with parmesan. Grill until golden. To serve, cut into wedges.
Serves 4–6.

GINGER BEEF STIR-FRY (China)

500 g skirt steak
1 tablespoon oil
1 tablespoon soy sauce
2 teaspoons grated root ginger
2 teaspoons soy sauce
2 tablespoons DYC *white vinegar*
2 teaspoons Edmonds Fielder's
  cornflour

½ teaspoon sugar
¼ cup liquid beef stock
2 tablespoons oil
1 green pepper, chopped
1 red pepper, chopped
4 spring onions, chopped

Cut meat into thin strips against the grain. Put meat, first measure of oil, first measure of soy sauce and ginger in a bowl. Leave to marinate for 30 minutes. In a separate bowl mix second measure of soy sauce, vinegar, cornflour, sugar and stock to a smooth paste. Heat half the second measure of oil in a wok. Add half the meat and quickly stir-fry until browned. Remove from wok. Repeat with remaining oil and meat, set aside. Add peppers and spring onions to wok. Stir-fry until vegetables are bright in colour. Add soy sauce mixture to wok and cook for 1 minute or until liquid boils and thickens. Return meat to pan, quickly heat through and serve.
Serves 6.

Partially freeze meat before cutting thinly for stir-frying.

GREEK SALAD (Greece)

1 lettuce
1 green pepper, sliced
1 small onion, sliced
3 tomatoes, quartered

$^1/_2$ cup sliced celery
$^1/_2$ diced cucumber
$^1/_2$ cup pitted black olives
100 g feta cheese, cubed

DRESSING
$^1/_4$ cup olive oil
1 clove garlic, crushed

2 tablespoons DYC spiced vinegar
$^1/_4$ teaspoon sugar

Tear lettuce into bite-sized pieces and place in a salad bowl. Add pepper, onion, tomatoes, celery and cucumber. Pour dressing over and toss to coat. Decorate with olives and feta cheese.
Serves 4.

DRESSING
Put all ingredients in a screw-top jar. Shake vigorously to combine just before using.

LAMB CURRY (India)

$1^1/_2$ tablespoons Edmonds standard
   plain flour
salt
pepper
750 g lamb pieces
oil
1 large onion, chopped
2 cloves garlic, crushed

1 tablespoon tomato paste
$1^1/_2$ teaspoons grated root ginger
1 teaspoon chopped fresh chilli
$1^1/_2$ teaspoons ground cumin
1 teaspoon ground coriander
1 teaspoon ground cardamom
$^1/_2$ cup liquid chicken stock

Combine flour, salt and pepper in a bowl. Coat meat in seasoned flour. Set aside. Heat oil in a large saucepan. Add onion and garlic and cook until onion is clear. Remove with slotted spoon. Add half of the meat to pan and quickly brown all over. Remove from pan and repeat with remaining meat. Return meat and onion mixture to saucepan. Add tomato paste, ginger, chilli, cumin, coriander, cardamom and stock, stirring well. Bring to the boil. Cover, reduce heat and simmer gently for 1 hour or until meat is tender. Serve with cucumber yoghurt sauce (raita) and poppadoms.
Serves 4.

CUCUMBER YOGHURT SAUCE (RAITA)

1 cucumber, seeded and chopped
1 teaspoon salt
1 teaspoon cumin seeds

2 spring onions, chopped
1 cup natural unsweetened yoghurt
1 tablespoon lemon juice

Put cucumber in a bowl. Sprinkle with salt. Set aside for 15 minutes. Rinse under cold water. Drain well. Put cumin seeds into a small saucepan. Cook over a low heat until golden. Combine cucumber, cumin seeds, spring onions, yoghurt and lemon juice.
Serves 6.

Brush avocados, apples and pears with lemon juice to prevent browning.

LAMB SATAY (Indonesia)

4 lamb leg steaks
1 tablespoon chopped fresh coriander
2 teaspoons oil

1 teaspoon sambal oelek or chilli
  paste
soaked bamboo skewers

SAUCE
1/4 cup soy sauce
1/4 cup chopped spring onions

1 teaspoon sambal oelek or chilli paste
2 tablespoons lemon or lime juice

Trim fat from meat. Cut meat into small cubes. Put meat into a bowl. Add coriander, oil and sambal oelek. Leave to marinate for 30 minutes. Thread meat onto soaked bamboo skewers. Grill for 8 minutes or until just cooked, turning occasionally during cooking time. Serve with sauce.
Serves 4.

SAUCE
Combine all ingredients.

MOUSSAKA (Greece)

2 tablespoons oil
2 onions, chopped
2 cloves garlic, crushed
3 cups cooked lean minced lamb
4 tomatoes, blanched and chopped
1/2 cup tomato purée
1/2 cup liquid chicken stock
salt
pepper
1 tablespoon salt
1 large eggplant, sliced

1/4 cup oil
2 egg yolks
1 tablespoon Edmonds standard plain
  flour
200 g pot natural unsweetened
  yoghurt
salt
pepper
1 tablespoon grated parmesan
  cheese

Heat first measure of oil in a saucepan. Add onion and garlic and cook until onion is clear. Stir in meat, tomatoes, tomato purée and stock. Bring to the boil. Season with salt and pepper to taste. Reduce heat, cover and simmer gently for 30 minutes. While meat is cooking, sprinkle salt over eggplant and set aside for 30 minutes. Rinse and pat dry. Heat second measure of oil in a frying pan. Fry eggplant until light brown and soft. Place one-third of the eggplant in an ovenproof dish. Spread with half of meat mixture. Top with another third of eggplant and repeat with meat, finishing with eggplant. In a bowl combine egg yolks, flour, yoghurt, salt and pepper to taste. Spread on top of eggplant. Top with parmesan cheese. Cook at 180°C for 40 minutes or until golden and crisp.
Serves 6.

Press cloves of garlic with the flat of the knife to remove skin.

NACHOS (Mexico)

200 g corn chips
1 cup grated tasty cheese

250 g pot sour cream

Put corn chips into a large ovenproof serving dish. Sprinkle with cheese. Bake at 200°C for 8 minutes or until all the cheese has melted. Spoon over sour cream. Serves 4–6.

REFRIED BEAN NACHOS
Top corn chips with hot refried beans, cheese and sour cream.

AVOCADO NACHOS
Top corn chips with grated cheese and sour cream. Bake as above and serve topped with Avocado Dip and Tomato Salsa.

PIZZA (Italy)

BASE
1 tablespoon Edmonds active yeast
½ teaspoon sugar
1 cup tepid water

1 teaspoon salt
3 cups Edmonds standard plain flour
1 tablespoon oil

TOMATO SAUCE
2 tablespoons olive oil
1 large onion, chopped
2 stalks celery, chopped
1 carrot, chopped
3 cloves garlic, crushed
6 tomatoes, blanched and chopped
1 bay leaf

1 teaspoon sugar
1 teaspoon basil
1 teaspoon oregano
1 teaspoon salt
1 tablespoon chopped parsley
½ cup liquid vegetable stock

TOPPING
1 cup grated tasty cheese
½ cup chopped ham

½ cup sliced mushrooms

Put yeast, sugar and water in a small bowl. Set aside for 15 minutes or until frothy. Sift salt and flour into another bowl. Add oil and yeast mixture. Mix well. Turn dough out onto lightly floured board and knead until smooth and elastic. Lightly oil bowl. Return dough to bowl. Cover with teatowel and set in warm place until double in size. Punch dough down in the centre then lightly knead again. Press into lightly oiled 25 cm pizza pan. Spread with prepared tomato sauce. Top with cheese, ham and mushrooms. Cook at 220°C for 15 minutes or until well risen and golden.
Serves 6.

TOMATO SAUCE
Heat oil in saucepan. Add onion, celery, carrot and garlic. Cook for 5 minutes. Add tomatoes and cook for a further 5 minutes. Stir in bay leaf, sugar, basil, oregano, salt, parsley and stock. Bring to the boil, reduce heat and simmer gently for 30 minutes or until sauce is quite thick, stirring frequently. Remove bay leaf. Purée tomato mixture.

TACOS (Mexico)

1 tablespoon oil
1 clove garlic, crushed
1 onion, chopped
500 g lean beef mince
$1/2$ to 1 teaspoon chilli powder
1 tablespoon Edmonds standard plain
   flour

$1/4$ cup tomato paste
$1/2$ cup liquid beef stock
salt
12 taco shells
1 cup grated cheese
2 cups shredded lettuce
prepared taco sauce

Heat oil in a frying pan. Add garlic and onion and cook until onion is clear. Add mince and cook until well browned. Stir in chilli powder and flour. Cook for 1 minute. Add tomato paste and stock. Bring to the boil, stirring constantly. Reduce heat then simmer gently until mixture thickens. Season with salt to taste. Spoon meat mixture into taco shells. Top with cheese, lettuce and prepared taco sauce. Serves 6.

TOMATO SALSA (Mexico)

1 large tomato, chopped
$1/4$ cup chopped fresh coriander or
   parsley

2 tablespoons finely chopped onion
1 tablespoon lime or lemon juice

Combine all ingredients in a bowl. Set aside for 1 hour before serving.

TOSTADAS (Mexico)

6 cooked flour Tortillas (page 149)
450 g can refried beans
2 small avocados, sliced
2 cups shredded lettuce

2 cooked chicken breasts
250 g pot sour cream
Tomato Salsa

DRESSING
2 tablespoons lemon or lime juice
$1/4$ teaspoon salt

$1/2$ teaspoon ground cumin
$1/4$ cup oil

Warm tortillas in oven or microwave. Heat refried beans in a saucepan. Spread a little onto each tortilla. Top with avocado slices, lettuce, slices of chicken and sour cream. Sprinkle with dressing. Serve with Tomato Salsa.
Serves 4.

DRESSING
Put all ingredients in a screw-top jar. Shake vigorously to combine just before using.

VEAL OR LAMB CORDON BLEU (Switzerland)

8 small pieces (600 g) beef or lamb
   schnitzel
2 large slices ham
4 slices cheese
$\frac{1}{4}$ cup Edmonds standard plain flour,
   approximately
salt

pepper
2 eggs
$\frac{1}{4}$ cup water
$1\frac{1}{2}$ cups dry breadcrumbs
50 g butter
2 tablespoons oil

Put a piece of plastic wrap over one schnitzel at a time. Using a rolling pin, roll the meat thinner. Repeat with remaining meat. Cut ham in half. On half the pieces of meat, place a piece of ham. Top with a slice of cheese. Place another piece of meat on top, pressing edges together. Combine flour, salt and pepper to taste. Coat schnitzels in seasoned flour. Beat eggs and water together. Dip schnitzels in this. Coat in breadcrumbs. Repeat with egg and breadcrumbs. Heat butter and oil together in a large frying pan. Add schnitzel and cook for 5 minutes each side or until golden.
Serves 4.

CHICKEN CORDON BLEU
Use single boneless chicken breasts instead of schnitzel. Roll thinly then proceed as for schnitzel.

BANANA SMOOTHIE

*1 cup chilled milk or natural
    unsweetened yoghurt
1 banana*

*1 tablespoon honey
ground nutmeg*

Put milk, banana and honey into a food processor or blender. Process until well combined and smooth. Serve in a chilled glass. Garnish with nutmeg.
Serves 2.

BREAKFAST TOPPINGS FOR ENGLISH MUFFINS

English muffins

Split the muffins and toast. Top with any of the following:
*banana and cooked bacon
ham and avocado*

*cooked bacon and peanut butter
jam and cheese*

FILLED CROISSANTS

*4 croissants
4 rashers bacon
1/2 avocado, sliced*

*1 teaspoon lemon juice
pepper*

Cut croissants in half horizontally, almost right through. Set on an oven tray and keep warm until ready to fill. Remove rind from bacon and cook until crisp. Keep warm. Brush each slice of avocado with a little lemon juice. Divide bacon and avocado among croissants. Season with pepper to taste. Serve warm.
Serves 4.

VARIATIONS
Any of the following can be used as a filling:
*ham and cheese
camembert*

*cooked bacon and mushroom
cream cheese and chives*

FRENCH TOAST

*2 eggs
2 tablespoons milk
salt*

*pepper
4 to 6 slices toast bread
butter*

Lightly beat eggs and milk together. Season with salt and pepper to taste. Cut slices of bread in half. Heat butter in a frying pan. Dip bread in egg. Place in frying pan and cook until golden on underside. Turn and cook the other side.
Serves 4.

GRILLED GRAPEFRUIT

grapefruit
brown sugar

cherries

Cut grapefruit in half. Carefully cut the flesh from the skin and cut between the membranes to loosen the segments. Sprinkle with brown sugar. Grill until sugar melts. Garnish with a cherry.

NATURAL MUESLI

3 cups rolled oats
1/2 cup Edmonds wheatgerm or
* bran flakes*
1/2 cup coconut
1 1/2 cups dried fruit — e.g. sultanas,
* raisins, apricots*

3/4 cup brown sugar
1 cup nuts — e.g. walnuts, almonds,
* cashews*

Mix all the ingredients together. Store in an airtight container.
Makes about 6 cups.

PORRIDGE

1 cup rolled oats
1/2 cup cold water

1/2 teaspoon salt
4 cups boiling water

Put the porridge, cold water and salt into a saucepan. Mix to a smooth paste. Gradually stir in boiling water. Boil for 3 to 5 minutes, stirring constantly.
Serves 4. (Microwave instructions are also included on most rolled oat packs).

VARIATIONS
Any of the following toppings can be added:
brown sugar and milk
bananas and cinnamon

fruit and yoghurt
strawberries and honey

TOASTED MUESLI

1/4 cup oil
1/4 cup brown sugar
1/4 cup honey
3 cups rolled oats
1/2 cup coconut
1/2 cup Edmonds wheatgerm

1/2 cup bran flakes
1/2 cup sesame seeds
1/2 cup sunflower seeds
1/2 cup chopped nuts
1/2 to 1 cup raisins or sultanas

Put oil, sugar and honey into a saucepan. Heat gently until sugar dissolves. In a bowl combine rolled oats, coconut, wheatgerm, bran flakes, sesame and sunflower seeds and nuts. Pour oil mixture over and mix thoroughly. Turn into a large roasting pan. Bake at 140–150°C for 30 to 40 minutes or until lightly browned. Stir occasionally. Leave to cool. Add raisins or sultanas. Store in an airtight container.
Makes about 6 cups.

Stale French sticks, cut in thick slices, make delicious French toast.

HINTS FOR VEGETABLES

- **Choose a variety of vegetables** each week for interesting meals and good nutrition.
- **Wash vegetables** before cutting to remove loose soil and pests.
- **Remove any green from potatoes** before cooking as this is poisonous.
- **Cook beetroot whole**, leaving 2 to 3 cm of beetroot tops on the beet to prevent loss of colour during cooking. Cut after cooking.
- **If vegetables are to be peeled, pare thinly** as precious vitamins and minerals are next to the skin.
- **Soaking prepared vegetables in water leaches out valuable nutrients.**
- **Use as little water as possible** when cooking vegetables to retain the nutrients.
- **Overcooking vegetables destroys valuable nutrients**. Cook for as short a time as possible.
- **Cover vegetables** when boiling or steaming to ensure quick cooking.
- **Store fresh vegetables in the refrigerator crisper.**
- **Store potatoes, onions and pumpkins in a cool, dark, dry place.**

METHODS OF COOKING

Cooking times, recommended methods and serving suggestions are included later in this section.

BOILING

Put prepared vegetables in a small amount of boiling water. Choose a saucepan large enough to fit vegetables easily. Root vegetables require more cooking water. Cover tightly and bring the water quickly back to boiling point. Cook vegetables over a moderate heat until tender yet firm when tested. Drain well. Serve immediately. Use the cooking water for sauces, soups, or gravy.

STEAMING

Put prepared vegetables in a steamer over rapidly boiling water. Cover tightly and adjust heat to ensure a steady flow of steam. Steam vegetables until just tender. If a steamer is unavailable, place vegetables into a metal sieve. Place sieve over a saucepan of boiling water. Add more boiling water to the steamer or saucepan if necessary. Cover with aluminium foil to keep in the steam. Steam vegetables until just tender. Take care when removing the foil. Serve immediately.

MICROWAVING

Cut vegetables to a similar size. Place in a shallow microwave dish with a small amount of water and cover. If no lid is available, cover with microwave-safe plastic film. Stir once during cooking time. After cooking, leave covered while standing. Standing time is about one-third of total cooking time. Always undercook as cooking continues while standing. Add salt and other seasonings after cooking (see pages 174–180).

ROASTING

Place oil in a roasting pan and heat in a hot oven. Dry pieces of prepared vegetables. Potato and kumara may be rolled in flour to give a crisp coating. Arrange vegetables around meat or place in roasting pan containing hot oil. Turn vegetables so they are well coated in oil. Roast in moderate oven. Turn vegetables halfway through cooking time. Cook until tender. Remove from roasting dish. Drain on absorbent paper and keep warm until ready to serve.

STIR-FRYING

Suitable vegetables are onion, carrot, mushrooms and all green vegetables. Cut vegetables into bite-sized pieces. A variety of shapes like sticks and rounds makes a stir-fry more interesting. A vegetables may be stir-fried by itself or any combination may be cooked together. Heat a small amount of oil in a frying pan or wok. Add vegetables that require longer cooking first, e.g. broccoli, carrot, cauliflower, onion. Stir occasionally. Partially cook then add remaining vegetables which require shorter cooking. Cook until tender but crisp.

BEETROOT

3 medium beetroot, trimmed and
   washed
2 tablespoons sugar
$^{1}/_{4}$ cup boiling water

$^{3}/_{4}$ cup DYC malt vinegar
$^{1}/_{2}$ teaspoon salt
black pepper

Put beetroot into a saucepan. Cover with cold water. Bring to the boil and cook for 45 minutes or until beetroot are tender. Drain, then rinse under cold running water. Top and tail then slip skins off. Slice and place in serving dish. Dissolve sugar in boiling water. Add vinegar, salt and pepper to taste. Pour this over sliced beetroot. Serve cold.
Serves 6.

BROCCOLI WITH ALMONDS

500 g broccoli, cut into florets
2 tablespoons butter
2 tablespoons lemon juice

salt
black pepper
2 tablespoons toasted sliced almonds

Cook broccoli in boiling salted water until tender. In another small saucepan, melt butter. Add lemon juice, salt and pepper. Drain broccoli. Add almonds to butter mixture. Spoon over broccoli.
Serves 4–6.

CAULIFLOWER CHEESE

1 cauliflower, whole
25 g butter
2 tablespoons Edmonds *standard plain*
    flour
2 cups milk

$^3/_4$ cup grated tasty cheese
salt
white pepper
$^1/_2$ teaspoon dry mustard

Cook cauliflower in boiling salted water until tender. While cauliflower is cooking, melt the butter in a saucepan. Stir in flour and cook until frothy. Gradually add milk, stirring constantly until mixture boils and thickens. Remove from heat. Add $^1/_2$ cup of the cheese, salt and pepper to taste, and mustard. Drain cauliflower and transfer to an ovenproof serving dish. Pour sauce over the cauliflower. Sprinkle with remaining cheese. Cook at 190°C for 20 minutes or until golden.
Serves 4–6.

CHINESE STIR-FRIED VEGETABLES

2 tablespoons oil
1 tablespoon finely grated root ginger
2 medium onions, quartered and
    separated
2 carrots, finely sliced
$^1/_4$ cauliflower, cut into florets
1 cup liquid chicken stock
1 cup sliced beans

2 stalks celery, sliced diagonally
1 red or green pepper, diced
3 courgettes, sliced
$^1/_4$ cabbage, shredded
1 cup bean sprouts
1 teaspoon chicken stock powder
1 tablespoon soy sauce
2 to 3 spring onions, sliced

Heat oil in a large frying pan or wok. Add ginger, onions, carrots and cauliflower. Stir to coat in oil. Add stock, bring to boil and cook for 3 minutes. Add beans, celery, pepper and courgettes. Cook, stirring occasionally until just tender. Add cabbage and bean sprouts. Cook for 1 to 2 minutes. Sprinkle with stock powder and soy sauce. Stir to combine. Serve garnished with spring onion.
Serves 4–6.

COURGETTES PROVENÇAL

1 tablespoon oil
1 onion, sliced
2 cloves garlic, crushed
500 g courgettes, thinly sliced

$^1/_2$ teaspoon salt
black pepper
3 large tomatoes, blanched and
    chopped

Heat oil in a large saucepan. Add onion and garlic. Cook until onion is clear. Add courgettes, salt and pepper to taste. Stir. Add tomatoes. Cover and cook over a low heat until tender.
Serves 4–5.

To wash, cut the core from lettuce or cabbage. Drain well and store in
a plastic bag or plastic storage container in the refrigerator to crisp.

CURRIED VEGETABLES

50 g butter
1 onion, sliced
2 potatoes, diced
2 teaspoons hot Indian curry powder
1 tablespoon lemon juice
1 tablespoon Edmonds standard plain
  flour
salt

black pepper
1 cup water
3 to 4 cups of chopped or sliced
  vegetables — e.g. carrots, beans,
  green pepper, courgettes,
  mushrooms, celery, broccoli,
  cauliflower

Melt butter in a large saucepan. Cook onion and potato gently for 5 minutes, stirring frequently. Add curry powder, lemon juice, flour, salt and pepper to taste, and cook for 1 minute. Add water and remaining vegetables. Cover and simmer gently for 5 to 8 minutes or until vegetables are tender.
Serves 4.

TO MICROWAVE:
Reduce water to $1/2$ cup. Put butter in a large dish and cook on High Power (100%) for 30 seconds. Add onion and potato and cook for 1 minute. Add curry powder, lemon juice, flour, salt and pepper to taste, and cook for 1 minute. Add water and remaining vegetables. Cover and cook for 6 minutes, stirring after 3 minutes.

HASH BROWN POTATOES

1 kg old potatoes, chopped
50 g butter

2 rashers bacon, finely chopped
1 tablespoon chopped chives

Cook potatoes in boiling salted water until tender. Drain well then leave to cool. Mash. Put butter in a large frying pan. Add bacon and cook until crisp. Using a slotted spoon, remove bacon from pan. Do not discard fat. Spread potatoes over base of frying pan. Press down until even. Cook over a low heat for 25 minutes or until underside is deep golden brown. Turn, using a spatula, and cook other side. Scoop potato out of pan and into heated serving dish. Sprinkle with bacon and chives.
Serves 6.

HONEY-GLAZED CARROTS AND PARSNIPS

2 to 3 medium carrots, sliced diagonally
1 to 2 medium parsnips, sliced
  diagonally
2 tablespoons honey

1 tablespoon lemon juice
1 tablespoon butter
2 teaspoons toasted sesame seeds

Cook carrots and parsnips in boiling salted water until just tender. Drain. Add honey, lemon juice and butter. Shake saucepan so mixture coats carrots and parsnips. Serve sprinkled with toasted sesame seeds.
Serves 4–6.

ITALIAN GREEN BEANS

500 g green beans, sliced diagonally
2 tablespoons oil
1 clove garlic, crushed

2 to 3 tomatoes, blanched and
  chopped
salt
black pepper

Cook beans in boiling salted water until just tender. Drain. Heat oil in a saucepan. Add beans, garlic, tomatoes, salt and pepper to taste. Simmer gently for 5 minutes or until beans are cooked and tomatoes soft.
Serves 4–6.

TO MICROWAVE:
Cook beans in a little water on High Power (100%) for 7 minutes or until just tender. Drain. Combine all ingredients and cook for 2 to 3 minutes.

KUMARA AND ORANGE

2 medium kumara, chopped
2 tablespoons brown sugar
1 tablespoon butter

1 teaspoon grated orange rind
$^1/_4$ cup orange juice
1 tablespoon chopped chives

Cook kumara in boiling salted water until tender. Drain well. Add brown sugar, butter, orange rind and juice to kumara. Return saucepan to heat. Bring to the boil. Reduce heat. Continue cooking until orange mixture thickens and kumara is glazed. Garnish with chives.
Serves 6.

ORANGE AND GINGER CARROTS

4 to 6 medium carrots, cut into sticks
1 teaspoon ground ginger
$^1/_2$ cup orange juice
2 tablespoons water

$^1/_2$ teaspoon salt
2 tablespoons brown sugar
2 tablespoons butter

Put carrots, ginger, orange juice, water, salt, brown sugar and butter into a saucepan. Simmer uncovered for 8 to 10 minutes or until carrots are just tender and liquid has reduced to a glaze.
Serves 4–6.

TO MICROWAVE:
Reduce orange juice to 2 tablespoons and omit water. Put carrots, ginger and orange juice in a microwave-proof dish. Cook on High Power (100%) for 5 to 7 minutes or until just tender. Add salt, brown sugar and butter. Cook for 1 minute.

PEPPERS (ROASTED)

Red and green peppers

Place peppers on the oven rack near the top of the oven and roast at 210°C for 20 to 30 minutes or until the skins are browned. Turn frequently during roasting. Place a tray or piece of foil on the rack under the peppers to catch the drips. Leave peppers on a board for 10 minutes before peeling off skins. Use in salads or serve with French Dressing (page 189).

Place fresh vegetables in the refrigerator crisper to store.
Wash just before use.

POTATO SKINS WITH LEMON DRESSING

4 large potatoes	2 tablespoons oil

DRESSING
1/4 cup Mayonnaise (page 184)	1 tablespoon chopped parsley
1 clove garlic, crushed	1 teaspoon grated lemon rind

Wash potatoes well. Cut lengthwise into eight pieces. Heat oil in a roasting dish. Carefully add potatoes, turning to coat the cut surfaces with oil. Cook at 200°C for 30 minutes or until golden and cooked through. Drain on absorbent paper. Serve hot with dressing.
Serves 6–8.

DRESSING
Combine all ingredients.

RATATOUILLE

1/4 cup olive oil	1 large onion, sliced
6 medium tomatoes, blanched and chopped	2 cloves garlic, crushed
	1 green pepper, sliced
1/2 teaspoon salt	250 g courgettes, sliced
black pepper	1 eggplant, chopped
1/4 teaspoon sugar	

Heat half the oil in a small saucepan. Add tomatoes, salt, pepper to taste, and sugar. Cook for 10 minutes or until sauce consistency, stirring frequently. Heat remaining oil in a large frying pan or saucepan. Add onion and garlic and cook until onion is clear. Stir in green pepper, courgettes and eggplant. Cover and cook slowly until vegetables are tender, stirring frequently. Add tomato mixture to the vegetables. Stir to combine. Serve hot.
Serves 6.

SCALLOPED POTATOES

4 medium potatoes, thinly sliced	salt
1 small onion, finely sliced	white pepper
1 cup grated cheese	1 cup milk

Place a layer of potatoes in a 20 cm diameter casserole dish. Sprinkle with some onion, cheese, salt and pepper to taste. Repeat until ingredients are used, ending with a cheese layer. Pour milk over potato mixture. Cover and cook at 180°C for 30 minutes. Remove lid and continue cooking for a further 10 to 15 minutes or until potatoes are cooked.
Serves 4.

Top: Ratatouille (pg 168), Centre: Stuffed Mushrooms (pg 171),
Bottom: Chinese Stir-Fried Vegetables (pg 165)

STUFFED BAKED POTATOES

4 medium potatoes
2 tablespoons oil
$1/2$ cup milk
2 tablespoons butter
salt

black pepper
2 tablespoons chopped parsley
$1/2$ cup grated tasty cheese
$1/2$ teaspoon paprika

Scrub potatoes and brush with oil. Bake at 180°C for 1 to 1$1/4$ hours or until soft. Cut a lengthwise slice from top of each potato. Scoop out potato without breaking skins. Mash potato, milk, butter, salt and pepper to taste, and parsley. Spoon mixture into potato skins. Sprinkle with cheese and paprika. Bake at 180°C for 5 to 10 minutes or until hot and cheese has melted.
Serves 4.

TO MICROWAVE
Cook potatoes on High Power (100%) for 12 to 16 minutes. Continue as above. Return to microwave and cook for 1 to 2 minutes.

STUFFED CHEESY TOMATOES

6 large tomatoes
2 spring onions, finely sliced
$1/2$ cup soft breadcrumbs
1 cup grated tasty cheese

1 tablespoon chopped fresh basil or
  1 teaspoon dried basil
salt
black pepper

Cut tops off tomatoes. Scoop out pulp. Remove core and reserve rest of pulp. Combine tomato pulp, spring onions, breadcrumbs, cheese, basil, salt and pepper to taste. Spoon filling into tomatoes. Bake at 180°C for 10 minutes or until hot and cheese has melted.
Serves 6.

TO MICROWAVE:
Prepare as above. Cook on High Power (100%) for 2 to 3 minutes.

STUFFED MUSHROOMS

12 large mushrooms
3 rashers bacon
25 g butter
2 tablespoons onion, finely chopped

1 cup soft breadcrumbs
$1/2$ teaspoon salt
black pepper
1 tablespoon melted butter

Remove stems from mushrooms and chop stems finely. Remove rind from bacon. Chop bacon. Heat butter in a small frying pan. Add onion, mushroom stems and bacon. Cook until onion is clear. Remove from heat. Add breadcrumbs, salt and pepper to taste. Mix until well combined. Brush outside of mushroom caps with melted butter. Grill the butter side for 2 minutes. Turn over and spoon crumb mixture into mushroom cavities. Grill until filling is golden. Serve hot.
Serves 6.

SWEET AND SOUR RED CABBAGE

2 tablespoons butter
1/2 red cabbage, shredded
2 apples, peeled and grated
1/4 cup DYC white vinegar

3 tablespoons brown sugar
salt
black pepper

Melt butter in a saucepan. Add cabbage and apple. Cook for 5 minutes. Stir occasionally. Add vinegar and brown sugar. Season with salt and pepper to taste. Cover and cook gently for 20 minutes or until tender, stirring occasionally.
Serves 4–6.

SWEETCORN FRITTERS

3/4 cup Edmonds standard plain flour
1 teaspoon Edmonds baking powder
1/2 teaspoon salt
black pepper

1 egg
440 g can cream-style corn
2 tablespoons oil

Sift flour, baking powder, salt and pepper to taste into a bowl. Add egg, mixing to combine. Stir in sweetcorn. Heat oil in a frying pan. Drop tablespoonsful of corn mixture into pan. Cook until golden then turn and cook other side. Drain on absorbent paper. Serve hot.
Serves 4–6.

VEGETABLE FLAN

PASTRY

1 1/2 cups Edmonds wholemeal flour
1/2 teaspoon salt
1 teaspoon Edmonds baking powder
  or use 1 sheet Edmonds Savoury
  Short Pastry

100 g butter
1/4 cup water, approximately

FILLING

2 medium potatoes, grated
2 courgettes, grated
1 large onion, grated
1 cup grated pumpkin
1 clove garlic, crushed
1/2 cup grated tasty cheese

1/4 cup chopped parsley
2 tablespoons chopped chives
1/4 cup relish
salt
black pepper
4 egg whites

Put flour, salt and baking powder into a bowl. Rub butter into dry ingredients until mixture resembles fine breadcrumbs. Add enough water to mix to a smooth, firm dough. Knead lightly and form into a ball. Cover and chill for 15 minutes. On a lightly floured board, roll out dough and line a 22 cm pie plate or use ready rolled sheet. Spoon prepared filling into pastry base. Bake at 190°C for 40 minutes or until golden.
Serves 6–8.

FILLING
Combine vegetables, garlic, cheese, parsley, chives and relish, mixing well. Season with salt and pepper to taste. In another small bowl, beat egg whites until stiff but not dry. Carefully fold egg whites into vegetable mixture.

VEGETABLE FRITTERS

$^1/_2$ cup Edmonds *standard plain flour*
$^1/_2$ *teaspoon salt*
$^1/_2$ *teaspoon curry powder*
$^1/_2$ *teaspoon* Edmonds *baking powder*
$^1/_4$ *cup grated onion*
$^1/_2$ *cup milk*

1 cup grated vegetables — e.g.
  beetroot, courgette, pumpkin, carrot,
  kumara
1 egg white
2 tablespoons oil

Sift flour, salt, curry powder and baking powder into a bowl. Stir in onion. Gradually add milk, mixing until smooth. Batter should be the consistency of thick cream. Stir in vegetables of your choice. In another small bowl, beat egg white until stiff but not dry. Carefully fold egg white into vegetable mixture. Heat oil in a frying pan. Drop tablespoonsful of vegetable mixture into pan. Cook until golden then turn and cook other side. Drain on absorbent paper. Serve hot.
Serves 4–6.

VEGETABLE STIR-FRY

2 tablespoons olive oil
1 tablespoon finely chopped root
  ginger
2 cloves garlic, crushed
2 small onions, quartered and
  separated
250 g broccoli, cut into florets
$^1/_4$ cauliflower, cut into florets

1 small bunch spinach, washed, stems
  removed
230 g can bamboo shoots, drained
230 g can water chestnuts, drained
$^1/_2$ cup baby corn
$^1/_2$ cup liquid chicken stock, boiling
2 to 3 spring onions, sliced

Heat oil in a large frying pan or wok. Add ginger, garlic and onions. Stir to coat with oil. Cook for 1 minute. Add remaining vegetables and toss to combine. Stir in stock. Bring to the boil. Cover and cook for 3 minutes or until vegetables are just tender, stirring occasionally. Garnish with spring onions.
Serves 4.

COOKING FRESH VEGETABLES

T — Tablespoon, t — teaspoon, C — cup, MW — microwave

N.B. Microwave times for 600–700 watt oven. All cooking times High Power (100%) unless otherwise stated.

Most vegetables can be cooked using various methods. Select the method that best suits the end need. Times for cooking are a guide only as they are affected by the maturity of vegetables and the size of pieces — the older and larger, the longer time needed. Very large volumes of vegetables in one pot also take longer times. Cut vegetables into pieces of similar size for even cooking. Personal preference will decide how tender each vegetable should be when cooked. Test this by piercing with a sharp fork or skewer. Avoid overcooking green vegetables. They should retain a good green colour. Starchy vegetables, such as potatoes and kumara, should be cooked until tender throughout.

Vegetable	Preparation	Cooking Methods and Times	Serving Suggestions
Artichokes (Globe)	If necessary soak in salted water for 30 minutes to remove insects. Trim outer leaves and stem.	BOIL: To stop browning, add lemon juice to water and cook for 20–25 minutes or until leaf comes away easily when pulled. Place upside down to drain.	• Hot — with butter, lemon sauce, Cheese or Hollandaise Sauce. • Cold with French Dressing.
(Jerusalem or Root)	Scrub and trim or peel.	BOIL: Cook for 12–20 minutes. ROAST: Cook around meat for 35–45 minutes.	• Toss in butter. • Curry, Parsley or Tomato Sauce.
Asparagus	Remove woody ends or remove outer skin from lower end with potato peeler.	BOIL: Cook for 5–10 minutes (lying in boiling water), OR tie in bundles and cook for 8–10 minutes with stem end in water. MW: Have similar length spears. Place tips to centre of dish. Add 2T water. Cook 500 g for 5–8 minutes. STIR-FRY: Cut into 5 cm pieces and cook in a little butter or oil.	• Hot with butter, lemon, Cheese or Hollandaise Sauce. • Cold in salad or with French Dressing. • Buttered crumbs, chopped parsley and chopped hard-boiled egg are all suitable garnishes.

Vegetable	Preparation	Cooking Methods and Times		Serving Suggestions
Aubergine (eggplant)	Use whole, sliced or diced. Peel if preferred. Sprinkle with salt or put in lightly salted water and leave for about 30 minutes. Drain and pat dry.	MW:	Add 2T butter. Cook 500 g for 6–8 minutes.	• Sprinkle with grated tasty or parmesan cheese.
		FRY:	Dip slices in flour or beaten egg then breadcrumbs and fry in oil or butter.	• With Cheese or Tomato Sauce.
		GRILL:	Dip slices in flour, brush with melted butter then grill.	• Stuff before baking.
		BAKE:	Brush whole with oil and cook in moderate oven for 30 minutes or until tender.	
Beans — Green, Runner and Butter	Trim ends and string if necessary. Cut into pieces, slice diagonally or leave whole.	BOIL:	Cook for 5–12 minutes depending on type and age.	• With butter.
		MW:	Add 2T water. Cook 500 g for 7–14 minutes.	• Cold in salads.
		STIR-FRY:	Cook cut or sliced in oil or butter until tender-crisp.	
Beetroot	Trim stalks to 2 cm from beet. Wash well. Leave skins and roots on.	BOIL:	Cover with water and cook for 30–60 minutes. Drain, rinse in cold water and slip skins off.	• Hot — Add a little butter or serve with a Sweet and Sour or orange sauce.
		MW:	Pierce skin with sharp knife. Add 2T water. Turn twice during cooking. Cook 500 g for 15–20 minutes.	• Cold — Slice and serve with vinegar, lemon juice or French Dressing.
Broad Beans	If young and small, cook whole in pods. Remove beans from older pods.	BOIL:	Cook whole young pods for 5–10 minutes.	• Butter, Parsley or Cheese Sauce.
		MW:	Add 2T water. Cook 250 g for 6–9 minutes on 90% power.	• With bacon.
Broccoli	Trim stalks and divide heads into florets.	BOIL:	Cook for 5–10 minutes.	• Lemon, Cheese or Hollandaise Sauce.
		STEAM:	Cook for 10–15 minutes.	• Butter and lemon juice.
		MW:	Place in dish with stalks to outer edge. Add 2T water. Cook 500 g for 7–10 minutes. If stalks thick, cut cross in base.	• Buttered breadcrumbs.

Vegetable	Preparation	Cooking Methods and Times		Serving Suggestions
Brussels Sprouts	Remove damaged leaves. Cut small cross in base of sprout.	BOIL: STEAM: MW:	Cook for 5–10 minutes. Cook for 10–15 minutes. Add ¼ cup water. Cook 500 g for 7–10 minutes.	• Cheese Sauce or a little butter. • Chop, add cream and curry powder.
Cabbage	Remove damaged leaves. Shred coarsely or finely.	BOIL: MW: STIR-FRY:	Plunge into rapidly boiling water and cook for 3–5 minutes. Drain thoroughly. Cook ½ medium cabbage (shredded) for 5–7 minutes. Cook in 1T butter or oil.	• Add a little butter or squeeze of lemon juice. • Add finely chopped spring onion or cooked ham.
Capsicums (green and red sweet peppers)	Remove seeds. Use whole, halved or sliced as desired.	BAKE/ ROAST: STIR-FRY:	Oven-cook whole or halves, stuffed or plain, for 30–40 minutes. Sliced, in oil until tender-crisp.	• Over rice. • As a garnish for grilled meats.
Carrots	If young, scrape and leave whole. Older, peel and slice, dice, cut into strips or grate.	BOIL: STEAM: MW: STIR-FRY:	Cook for 10–15 minutes. Cook for 10–20 minutes. Add 2T water. Cook 250 g for 4–5 minutes. Cut into matchsticks or grate. Cook in a little butter or oil.	• Toss in a little butter and chopped parsley. Add 2T orange juice and 1T honey. • Add brown sugar and ground ginger. • If older, mash.
Cauliflower	Cut into florets or leave whole. If whole cut a cross in base of stalk.	BOIL: STEAM: MW:	Florets — cook for 5–10 minutes. Whole — cook for 10–15 minutes. Florets — cook for 10–15 minutes. Whole — cook for 15–20 minutes. Florets — add 2T water. Cook 500 g for 6–8 minutes. Whole — wrap in plastic film and cook 500 g for 8–10 minutes.	• Parsley, Cheese or Curry Sauce. • Sprinkle with grated cheese and place under grill. • Sprinkle with mixture of buttered breadcrumbs, chopped hard-boiled egg and chopped parsley.
Celery	Cut into 2–3 cm pieces or sticks. Remove strings from older stalks.	BOIL: MW: STIR-FRY:	Cook for 8–10 minutes. Add 1T water and 1T butter. Cook 500 g for 4–6 minutes. Cook in 2T butter or oil until tender.	• Parsley or Cheese Sauce.

Vegetable	Preparation	Cooking Methods and Times	Serving Suggestions
Choko	Hold in a clean teatowel to peel. Cut in half, remove the seed and slice.	BOIL: Cook for 8–10 minutes. STEAM: Cook for 10–15 minutes. MW: Add 1T water or butter. Cook 250 g for 3–4 minutes. ROAST: Cook halves around meat for about 40 minutes.	• Add butter and chopped parsley. • Cheese, Lemon or Curry Sauce. • Cold in salads.
Courgette (Zucchini)	If small, trim ends and leave whole. Cut in half lengthwise, slice, cut in strips or grate.	BOIL: Cook for 3–4 minutes. STEAM: Cook for 5–10 minutes. MW: Add 1T butter or water. Cook 250 g for 3–4 minutes. STIR-FRY: Cook in a little butter or oil until just tender.	• Sprinkle with chopped parsley, chives or grated cheese. • Cold in salads.
Kumara	Scrub and leave skin on. Peel and halve or cut into desired size.	BOIL: Cook for 15–20 minutes. STEAM: Cook for 20–30 minutes. MW: Roll pieces in butter. Cook 500 g for 8–10 minutes. In jacket, prick skin, put on paper. Cook 500 g for 9–12 minutes. ROAST: Cook around meat for 45–60 minutes. BAKE: Cook at 180°C for 45–60 minutes.	• Mash and flavour with salt and pepper, butter and milk. • Orange rind and juice. • Split open jacket when cooked and season with butter and salt.
Leeks	Remove roots and tough outer leaves. Trim tops. Wash well and slice finely or in 3–4 cm pieces.	BOIL: Cook for 10–15 minutes. STEAM: Cook for 10–20 minutes. MW: Add 2T water. Cook 500 g for 6–8 minutes. STIR-FRY: Finely sliced in butter or oil until tender-crisp.	• Cheese or Parsley Sauce. • Butter and a little lemon juice.
Marrow	Peel (optional), remove seeds and slice or dice.	BOIL: Cook for 5–8 minutes. STEAM: Cook for 8–10 minutes. MW: Add 1T water and 1T butter. Cook 250 g for 4 minutes. BAKE: Add 2–3T water, 1T butter and cover. Cook for 30–40 minutes. ROAST: Cook around meat for 35–45 minutes.	• Cheese or Parsley Sauce. • Stuff whole or large pieces before baking.

Vegetable	Preparation	Cooking Methods and Times		Serving Suggestions
Mushrooms	Wipe with a damp cloth. Do not peel unless skin is thick or damaged. Slice. If small, leave whole.	MW:	Add 1T butter. Cook 250 g for 2-3 minutes.	• Sprinkle with chopped parsley, chives or a little lemon juice.
		GRILL:	Brush with melted butter and cook until tender.	• In cream sauce.
		FRY:	Cook in hot oil or butter.	
		POACH:	Simmer in water with squeeze of lemon juice.	
		STIR-FRY:	Cook in butter or oil until tender-crisp.	
Onions	Remove outer skin. Leave whole, cut in half, slice or dice.	BOIL:	Leave whole and cook for 20-30 minutes.	• Cheese or Parsley Sauce.
		STEAM:	Leave whole or cut in half. Cook for 30-40 minutes.	
		MW:	Slice and add 2T water or 1T butter. Cook 500 g for 5-8 minutes.	
		FRY:	Slice, dice or leave tiny onions whole and cook in butter or oil. Leave whole or cut in half.	
		ROAST:	Par-boil, put around meat and cook for 45-60 minutes.	
Parsnips	Peel and slice or cut lengthwise. Remove core from older parsnips.	BOIL:	Cook for 10-15 minutes.	• Mash. Add 1T sugar, 1T lemon juice.
		STEAM:	Cook for 15-25 minutes.	• Sprinkle with chopped parsley.
		MW:	Add 2T water. Cook 500 g for 6-8 minutes.	• Mash with equal amount cooked carrots.
		ROAST:	Par-boil, put around meat and cook for 40-50 minutes.	
Peas	Shell peas.	BOIL:	Cook for 6-10 minutes. (If desired add sprig of mint.)	• Add a little butter.
		MW:	Add 1T water and 1T sugar. Cook 500 g for 4-6 minutes.	

Vegetable	Preparation	Cooking Methods and Times		Serving Suggestions
Potatoes	If new, wash and scrape. If old, peel or scrub and leave skins on.	BOIL:	New — cook for 15–20 minutes. (If desired add sprig of mint.) Old — cook for 20–25 minutes.	• Old — mash with a little milk, butter and pepper. • New — toss in butter and sprinkle with chopped parsley or mint. • Baked — cut top and press open. Top with butter, sour cream or yoghurt.
		STEAM:	Cook for 30–35 minutes.	
		MW:	To boil, add ½ cup water and cook 500 g for 8–10 minutes. To bake, prick the skin. Turn once during cooking and allow 3–4 minutes per potato.	
		ROAST:	Cook around meat for 1–1½ hours.	
		BAKE:	Brush with oil or melted butter. Cook for 1–1½ hours.	
Pumpkin, Buttercup, Butternut	Cut into wedges. Remove seeds. If baking or roasting, leave skin on if desired.	BOIL:	Cook for 10–15 minutes.	• Mash with a little butter and pepper. • Add ginger, orange rind or herbs to vary flavour.
		STEAM:	Cook for 20–30 minutes.	
		MW:	Add 2T water and cook 500 g for 5–6 minutes.	
		ROAST:	Cook around meat for 40–50 minutes.	
		BAKE:	½t each butter and brown sugar on each wedge. Cook for 40–50 minutes.	
Silverbeet	Shred leaves and cut stalks into slices.	BOIL:	Cook for 5–10 minutes.	• Chop or purée. • Season with lemon juice or nutmeg.
		MW:	Add 2T water. Cook 250 g for 3–4 minutes.	
Spinach	Wash well.	BOIL:	Place in covered saucepan and cook for 5–8 minutes in water that clings from washing. Drain well.	• Chop or purée. • Add pinch nutmeg and 1T cream. • Add lemon juice.
		MW:	Do not add extra water. Cook 250 g for 2–3 minutes.	

Vegetable	Preparation	Cooking Methods and Times		Serving Suggestions
Swedes	Peel and cut into slices or dice. Grate for baking.	BOIL:	Cook for 15–20 minutes.	• Mash with butter and pepper. • Mash and add chopped parsley.
		MW:	Add 2T water. Cook 250 g for 5–6 minutes.	
		ROAST:	Cook around meat for about 1 hour.	
		BAKE:	Add 1T butter to grated swede. Cover, cook for 30 minutes.	
Sweetcorn	Large cobs can be halved.	BOIL:	Remove husks and cook for 5–12 minutes.	• Serve with butter and pepper. • Serve with herb butter.
		MW:	Leave husks intact. Place cobs directly on glass tray and allow 3–4 minutes for each cob.	
Tomatoes	Cut in half or slice thickly. If small leave whole.	MW:	Cook 250 g for 2 minutes.	• Sprinkle with chopped chives, basil or parsley.
		BAKE:	Cook for 8–12 minutes.	
		GRILL:	Cook for 5 minutes.	
		FRY:	Cook halved or sliced for 3–5 minutes.	
		STEW:	Cook halved or sliced gently until juices run then simmer until tender. Thicken if desired.	
Turnips	Peel and slice or quarter. If small leave whole.	BOIL:	Cook for 6–12 minutes.	• Toss in butter. • Parsley Sauce. • Glaze with butter and sugar.
		MW:	Add 4T water. Cook 500 g for 6–8 minutes.	
Yams	Wash.	BOIL:	Cook for 10–15 minutes.	• Serve with orange sauce. • Add butter and chopped mint.
		MW:	Add 2T water. Cook 250 g for 5–6 minutes.	
		ROAST:	Cook around meat for 35–45 minutes.	
		BAKE:	Cook for 35–45 minutes.	

LETTUCE TYPES

Green oak	— narrow, crinkly-edged green leaves.
Red oak	— narrow, crinkly-edged leaves, bronze-red at edges and green in centre.
Red sails	— large leaves, green at centre and bronze-red toward edges.
Lollo rosso	— almost flower-like with frilled leaves that are red on the tips and green on the inside of the leaf.
Cos	— long, crunchy leaves with a sharp flavour. Also known as Romaine.
Iceberg	— large, crisp cup-shaped leaves well suited for wrapping or holding fillings.
Butterhead or Buttercrunch	— has rounded, flattish, soft-textured leaves that form a close rosette in the centre.

BEAN SALAD

1/2 cup dried kidney beans
1/2 cup dried haricot beans
1/2 cup dried lima beans
1/2 teaspoon salt
1/2 cup French Dressing (page 189)

2 teaspoons sugar
1 clove garlic, crushed
1/4 cup chopped parsley
1 small onion, sliced

Cover beans with water and soak overnight. Drain. Cover with water and simmer gently for 40 minutes or until tender. Add salt. Drain and cool. Combine French Dressing, sugar and garlic. Pour this over beans. Add parsley and onion. Toss to combine. Chill for at least 2 hours before serving.
Serves 6–8.

VARIATIONS
Any of the following can be added:
1 green pepper, finely chopped
1 cup drained whole-kernel corn

1/2 cup sliced celery

BEETROOT SALAD

4 to 6 cooked beetroot, sliced or cubed
6 spring onions, sliced
1/4 cup chopped parsley
2 tablespoons sugar

2 tablespoons hot water
salt
pepper
1/2 cup DYC malt vinegar

Put beetroot into a bowl. Add spring onions and parsley. Dissolve sugar in hot water and pour over beetroot. Add salt, pepper and vinegar. Chill before serving.
Serves 6–8.

Use a variety of lettuce types to add interest and colour to a salad.

CARROT SALAD

3 cups grated carrot
1 cup grated cheese
$^1/_2$ cup raisins or sultanas

$^1/_2$ cup roasted peanuts
$^1/_2$ cup natural unsweetened yoghurt

Combine all ingredients. Chill. If wished, serve on a bed of lettuce leaves.
Serves 4–6.

VARIATIONS
Any of the following can be added:
1 to 2 tablespoons toasted sesame
   or sunflower seeds
2 apples, grated

$^1/_4$ to $^1/_2$ cup coconut
$^1/_4$ to $^1/_2$ cup chopped parsley

CHICKEN AND AVOCADO SALAD

2 avocados, sliced
2 tablespoons lemon juice
2 cups cooked diced chicken or
   smoked chicken
$^1/_4$ cup sliced celery

$^1/_4$ cup raisins
2 oranges, peeled and sliced
$^1/_4$ cup Mayonnaise (page 190)
lettuce leaves

Toss avocados in lemon juice. Combine avocado, chicken, celery, raisins, oranges
and Mayonnaise. Toss to combine. Place on a bed of lettuce leaves. Chill before
serving.
Serves 4–6.

COLESLAW

4 cups finely shredded cabbage
1 green pepper, finely sliced
$^1/_2$ cup diced celery
1 tablespoon finely chopped onion

$^1/_4$ to $^1/_2$ cup French Dressing,
   Mayonnaise, Yoghurt or Blue
   Cheese dressing (pages 189 and
   190)

Combine cabbage, pepper, celery and onion. Pour dressing over coleslaw. Toss
to combine. Chill before serving.
Serves 6–8.

VARIATIONS
Any of the following can be added:
1 cup grated carrot
1 cup grated cheese
$^1/_2$ cup chopped walnuts or peanuts
$^1/_2$ cup raisins, sultanas, chopped
   dates or chopped dried apricots

1 orange, peeled and diced
$^1/_2$ to 1 cup pineapple pieces
1 apple, finely diced
2 tablespoons chopped parsley
1 teaspoon caraway seeds

*To wash, cut the core from lettuce or cabbage. Drain well and store in
a plastic bag or plastic storage container in the refrigerator to crisp.*

EGG SALAD

3 courgettes, thinly sliced
1/4 cup chopped parsley
6 hard-boiled eggs
3/4 cup Mayonnaise (page 190)

1 clove garlic, crushed
salt
black pepper

Combine courgettes and parsley in a bowl. Shell and chop the eggs. Add to courgettes. Combine Mayonnaise and garlic. Season to taste with salt and pepper. Pour dressing over salad. Stir to combine. Chill before serving.
Serves 4–6.

KUMARA SALAD

2 large kumara
3 spring onions, chopped
1/4 cup Mayonnaise (page 190)
1/4 cup sour cream

1/2 teaspoon curry powder
salt
1 tablespoon chopped walnuts

Cook kumara in boiling, salted water until just tender. Drain and leave to cool. Cut into 2.5 cm cubes. Combine kumara and spring onions in a serving bowl. In another bowl, combine Mayonnaise, sour cream, curry powder and salt to taste. Pour this over kumara. Toss to coat. Garnish with walnuts.
Serves 4.

MUSHROOM SALAD

500 g mushrooms, thinly sliced
1/2 cup chopped parsley

5 spring onions, chopped
1/2 cup French Dressing (page 189)

Combine mushrooms, parsley and spring onions. Pour French Dressing over salad. Chill for at least 2 hours before serving, stirring occasionally.
Serves 6–8.

VARIATIONS
Any of the following can be added:
2 to 3 firm tomatoes, cut in wedges   1/4 cup chopped walnuts

PASTA SALAD

1¹/₂ to 2 cups Diamond *macaroni or*
  shell pasta, etc.
2 to 3 spring onions, sliced
¹/₂ cup sliced celery

1 green pepper, sliced
3 to 4 tomatoes, cut in wedges
¹/₂ cup French Dressing (page 189)
  or Mayonnaise (page 190)

Cook pasta according to packet directions. Drain well and leave to cool. Add spring onions, celery, pepper and tomatoes. Pour dressing over salad. Toss to combine. Chill before serving.
Serves 4–6.

VARIATIONS
Any of the following can be added:
1 red pepper, sliced
2 hard-boiled eggs, chopped
1 cup grated cheese

3 rashers bacon, cooked and diced
  or 1 can tuna or salmon, flaked

POTATO SALAD

2 to 3 cups diced cooked potato
2 to 3 spring onions, sliced
2 hard-boiled eggs, chopped

1 to 2 teaspoons finely chopped mint
¹/₂ to 1 cup Mayonnaise, French or
  Yoghurt Dressing (pages 189 and
  190)

Gently combine all ingredients. Chill before serving.
Serves 4–6.

VARIATIONS
Any of the following can be added:
1 green or red pepper, sliced
1 tablespoon chopped chives or
  parsley
2 to 3 rashers bacon, cooked and diced

¹/₄ cup toasted sunflower or sesame
  seeds
¹/₄ cup sliced gherkins
4 radishes, sliced

RICE SALAD

1 cup long grain rice
¹/₂ cup raisins or sultanas
1 green or red pepper, sliced

¹/₂ to 1 cup pineapple pieces
¹/₄ cup French Dressing (page 189)

Cook rice according to packet directions. Drain and cool. Add raisins, pepper and pineapple to rice. Pour dressing over rice. Toss to combine. Chill before serving.
Serves 6–8.

VARIATIONS
Any of the following can be added:
¹/₂ cup sliced olives
2 hard-boiled eggs, diced
¹/₂ to 1 cup sliced celery

¹/₄ cup gherkins, sliced
¹/₂ cup chopped peanuts
¹/₂ cup whole kernel corn

SMOKED SALMON SALAD

1/2 telegraph cucumber
1 red lettuce
1 avocado, sliced
100 g smoked salmon

4 hard-boiled eggs, quartered
1/2 cup fresh Herb Dressing made
    with lemon or lime juice (page 190)

Cut cucumber into thin strips. Arrange lettuce leaves, cucumber and avocado on four serving plates. Top with smoked salmon and hard-boiled eggs. Pour Herb Dressing over salad.
Serves 4.

SPINACH SALAD

1 bunch spinach
6 to 8 mushrooms, sliced
2 spring onions, sliced
1 orange, peeled and segmented

3 rashers bacon, cooked and diced
1/4 cup French Dressing (page 189)
2 hard-boiled eggs, chopped
1/4 cup toasted flaked almonds

Tear spinach into bite-sized pieces and place in salad bowl. Add mushrooms, spring onions, orange segments and bacon. Chill before serving. Add French Dressing and toss. Garnish with eggs and flaked almonds.
Serves 4–6.

TABBOULEH

1 cup burghul (cracked wheat)
2 tablespoons chopped fresh mint
1 cup chopped parsley
2 tomatoes, chopped

2 tablespoons oil
1/4 cup lemon juice
salt
pepper

Put wheat into a bowl. Cover with boiling water. Leave to stand for 30 minutes. Stir and drain if necessary. Add the mint, parsley, tomatoes, oil, lemon juice, salt and pepper to taste. Stir to combine. Chill before serving.
Serves 6.

TOMATO SALAD

6 medium tomatoes, sliced
4 spring onions, chopped
1/4 cup chopped parsley
2 cloves garlic, crushed
2 tablespoons lemon juice

4 tablespoons oil
black pepper
1/4 teaspoon sugar
1/4 teaspoon salt

Arrange tomatoes on flat serving dish. Sprinkle with spring onions and parsley. Combine garlic, lemon juice, oil, pepper, sugar and salt. Pour this over salad. Chill for 15 minutes before serving.
Serves 4–6.

TOSSED GREEN SALAD

1 lettuce
selection of salad vegetables — e.g.
young spinach, finely chopped
mint, parsley, chives or basil,
watercress, finely sliced celery

or green pepper, sliced cucumber,
bean sprouts
2 to 4 tablespoons French or Mustard
Dressing (page 189)

Tear lettuce into bite-sized pieces and place in a salad bowl. Add other prepared vegetables. Add French Dressing and toss.
Serves 4–6.

WALDORF SALAD

2 to 3 apples, cut into cubes
2 to 3 oranges, peeled and cut into
cubes
1 to 2 cups diced celery

$1/2$ cup walnut pieces
$1/2$ cup dressing — use Mayonnaise
(page 190), $1/2$ Mayonnaise and
$1/2$ natural yoghurt, cream or sour
cream

Combine apples, oranges, celery and walnuts. Pour dressing over salad. Chill before serving.
Serves 4–6.

VARIATIONS
Any of the following can be added:
$1/2$ cup raisins or chopped dates
$1/2$ to 1 cup pineapple pieces
$3/4$ cup cubed cheese

1 to 2 bananas, sliced
$1/2$ to 1 cup grapes

WINTER SALAD

2 cups broccoli florets, cooked
2 cups cauliflower florets, cooked
$1/2$ cup sliced celery

4 mandarins, divided into segments
$1/2$ cup French Dressing (page 189)

Combine broccoli, cauliflower, celery and mandarins. Pour dressing over salad. Toss to combine. Chill before serving.
Serves 6–8.

VARIATIONS
Any of the following can be added:
$1/4$ cup chopped walnuts
1 cup bean sprouts

1 to 2 apples, diced
1 cup beans, cooked

Top Left: Coleslaw (pg 182), Top Right: Tabbouleh (pg 185),
Bottom: Chicken and Avocado Salad (pg 182)

AVOCADO DRESSING

¹/₂ a ripe avocado, roughly chopped
1 tablespoon lime juice or lemon
*   juice*
¹/₄ cup oil

¹/₂ teaspoon sugar
salt
black pepper

Put avocado into food processor or blender. Process until smooth. Add lime juice, oil and sugar. Process to combine. Season with salt and pepper to taste.
Makes ¹/₂ cup.

BLUE CHEESE DRESSING

50 to 100 g blue vein cheese
1 cup sour cream or ³/₄ cup cream
*   and ¹/₄ cup DYC white vinegar*

1 clove garlic, crushed
2 to 3 tablespoons milk

Mash cheese with fork. Add sour cream, garlic and milk. Beat or blend until smooth.
Makes 1¹/₂ cups.

COOKED SALAD DRESSING

1 tablespoon butter
3 tablespoons sugar
1 teaspoon dry mustard
1 teaspoon salt

2 eggs
¹/₂ cup DYC malt vinegar
2 to 3 tablespoons milk

Soften butter. Add sugar and beat to a cream. Add mustard and salt. Beat in eggs. Stir in vinegar slowly. Bring slowly to the boil, stirring constantly. Before serving, thin with milk to the consistency of cream.
Makes 1 cup.

FRENCH DRESSING (VINAIGRETTE)

³/₄ cup oil
¹/₄ cup DYC white, wine or
*   cider vinegar or lemon juice*
¹/₄ teaspoon dry mustard
salt

black pepper
1 clove garlic, crushed
1 tablespoon chopped parsley, chives
*   or fresh basil*

Put all ingredients into a screw-top jar. Shake well to combine.
Makes 1 cup.

MUSTARD DRESSING
Add 2 teaspoons wholegrain mustard.

HERB DRESSING

1 tablespoon chopped fresh chives
2 tablespoons chopped fresh parsley
2 teaspoons chopped fresh thyme
$^1/_2$ teaspoon grated lemon rind
$^1/_4$ cup DYC white or wine vinegar or
   lemon juice

$^1/_2$ cup oil
$^1/_2$ teaspoon salt
black pepper
$^1/_4$ teaspoon sugar

Put all ingredients into a screw-top jar. Shake well to combine.
Makes 1 cup.

MAYONNAISE

1 egg yolk
$^1/_2$ teaspoon salt
$^1/_4$ teaspoon dry mustard
pinch of cayenne pepper

1 tablespoon DYC malt vinegar or
   lemon juice
1 cup oil

Mix egg yolk, salt, mustard and cayenne pepper in a bowl. Add vinegar. Add oil
drop by drop, beating constantly with a whisk or beater. As mixture begins to
combine add remaining oil in a fine stream while beating. If mixture is too thick,
add more vinegar.
Makes 1 cup.

QUICK BLENDER MAYONNAISE

2 eggs
1 tablespoon DYC white or wine
   vinegar or lemon juice
$^1/_2$ teaspoon dry mustard

$^1/_2$ teaspoon salt
pinch of cayenne pepper
1 cup oil

Put eggs, vinegar, mustard, salt and cayenne pepper into food processor or blender
and process until combined. Continue blending while adding oil in a thin, steady
stream, blending until thick. If too thick, add extra vinegar.
Makes 1$^1/_4$ cups.

UNCOOKED (CONDENSED MILK) SALAD DRESSING

397 g can sweetened condensed milk
1 cup DYC malt vinegar

1 teaspoon salt
2 teaspoons dry mustard

Stir all ingredients until combined. Leave to stand for a few minutes to thicken
before using.
Makes about 2 cups.

YOGHURT DRESSING

1 cup natural unsweetened yoghurt
salt
pepper

1 tablespoon lemon juice
$^1/_4$ teaspoon dry mustard

Stir all ingredients until combined. Chill before using.
Makes 1 cup.

Use olive oil in dressings as a healthy alternative and for good flavour.

APPLE SAUCE

3 to 4 large cooking apples, peeled and
   chopped
1 tablespoon water

1 tablespoon butter
2 cloves or few drops lemon juice
sugar

Put apples, water, butter and cloves into a saucepan. Simmer until apples are
pulped. Blend or beat with a fork until smooth. Add sugar to taste.
Makes about 1$^1/_2$ cups.

BÉARNAISE SAUCE

3 tablespoons DYC *wine vinegar or
   tarragon vinegar*
6 peppercorns
1 bay leaf
$^1/_4$ small onion, chopped

2 egg yolks
75 to 100 g butter
salt
pepper
1 tablespoon chopped parsley

Put vinegar, peppercorns, bay leaf and onion into a small saucepan. Bring to the
boil and reduce to 1 tablespoon. Strain and reserve liquid. Place yolks and reserved
liquid in a double boiler and lightly beat. Gradually add butter in small pieces,
beating until sauce is thick enough to show the marks of whisk. Do not allow
to boil or sauce will curdle. Season with salt and pepper to taste. Add parsley.
Keep warm.
Makes about $^3/_4$ cup.

COCKTAIL SAUCE

1$^1/_2$ tablespoons DYC *spiced vinegar*
1 teaspoon prepared mustard
$^1/_2$ cup Mayonnaise (page 184)
2 tablespoons oil
2 hard-boiled eggs, chopped

1 tablespoon chopped cucumber
1 tablespoon chopped parsley
salt
pepper

Combine all ingredients in a bowl. Adjust seasoning to taste.
Makes $^1/_2$ cup.

CUMBERLAND SAUCE

$^1/_2$ cup redcurrant jelly
1 tablespoon finely chopped onion
1 tablespoon lemon juice
$^1/_2$ cup orange juice

1 tablespoon shredded orange rind,
   blanched
1 tablespoon port

Gently heat red currant jelly in a saucepan. Add onion, lemon juice, orange juice,
rind and port. Bring sauce to the boil.
Makes 1 cup.

*If a very smooth sauce is wanted, place sieved mixture in a blender or
food processor to get preferred consistency.*

GREEN PEPPERCORN SAUCE

50 g butter
2 tablespoons lemon juice
2 tablespoons green peppercorns,
  rinsed
4 egg yolks

$^1/_4$ cup cream
2 tablespoons sour cream
1 teaspoon prepared mustard
salt
pepper

Melt butter in a saucepan. Add lemon juice. Stir in peppercorns, egg yolks, cream, sour cream and mustard. Cook over gentle heat until sauce thickens. Do not allow sauce to boil. Season with salt and pepper to taste.
Makes $^3/_4$ cup.

HOLLANDAISE SAUCE

50 g butter
1 tablespoon lemon juice
2 egg yolks

$^1/_4$ cup cream
$^1/_2$ teaspoon dry mustard
$^1/_4$ teaspoon salt

Melt the butter in a double boiler. Add lemon juice, egg yolks and cream. Cook, stirring constantly, until thick and smooth. Do not boil or sauce will curdle. Remove from heat. Add mustard and salt and beat until smooth.
Makes $^3/_4$ cup.

MINT SAUCE

$^1/_4$ cup finely chopped mint leaves
boiling water
1 tablespoon sugar

$^1/_2$ cup DYC malt vinegar
salt

Put mint into a jug. Cover with boiling water. Add sugar and vinegar. Add salt to taste.
Makes $^1/_2$ cup.

MUSHROOM SAUCE

50 g butter
200 g mushrooms, sliced
3 tablespoons Edmonds standard
  plain flour

1 cup milk
salt
pepper
1 tablespoon chopped parsley

Melt butter in a saucepan. Add mushrooms and cook until mushrooms are soft. Stir in flour and cook until frothy. Gradually add milk. Heat until sauce boils and thickens, stirring constantly. Season with salt and pepper to taste. Stir in parsley.
Makes $1^1/_2$ cups.

MUSTARD SAUCE

1 egg
2 tablespoons sugar
1 tablespoon Edmonds *standard*
  plain flour
2 teaspoons dry mustard

1 cup water or liquid corned beef
  cooked in
1/4 cup DYC *malt vinegar*
salt
pepper

Beat egg and sugar together. Put into a saucepan. Add flour and mustard. Stir in water and vinegar gradually. Cook over a low heat until mixture thickens. Season with salt and pepper to taste, adding more sugar if necessary.
Makes 1 1/2 cups.

SATAY SAUCE

2 tablespoons oil
1 clove garlic, crushed
1 onion, chopped
1/4 to 1/2 teaspoon chilli powder
1/2 cup crunchy peanut butter

1 tablespoon soy sauce
1 tablespoon lemon juice
1 tablespoon brown sugar
3/4 cup coconut cream
salt

Heat oil in a saucepan. Add garlic, onion and chilli powder. Cook until onion is clear. Stir in peanut butter, soy sauce, lemon juice and sugar. Add coconut cream. Cook until mixture boils, stirring constantly. Season with salt to taste. Add more sugar if necessary.
Makes 1 1/4 cups.

SPICY BARBECUE SAUCE

1 cup tomato sauce
1/2 cup water
3 tablespoons golden syrup
1 teaspoon salt
2 teaspoons Worcestershire sauce

1/2 teaspoon curry powder
black pepper
1 clove garlic, crushed
1/4 cup dry red wine

Combine all ingredients. Leave to stand for 5 to 6 hours.
Makes 2 cups.

SWEET AND SOUR SAUCE

1 tablespoon oil
1 clove garlic, crushed
1 onion, chopped
1/4 cup tomato sauce
1 1/2 tablespoons Edmonds Fielder's
  cornflour

2 tablespoons sugar
3/4 cup liquid chicken stock
1 tablespoon DYC *white vinegar*
salt
pepper

Heat oil in a saucepan. Add garlic and onion. Cook until onion is clear. Combine tomato sauce and cornflour. Stir into onion mixture. Add sugar and gradually stir in stock. Bring to the boil, stirring constantly. Remove from heat. Add vinegar. Season with salt and pepper to taste.
Makes 1 cup.

TARTARE SAUCE

1 cup Mayonnaise (page 190)
1 tablespoon finely chopped capers
  or gherkins

1 tablespoon chopped parsley
1 tablespoon finely chopped onion

Combine all ingredients.
Makes 1 cup.

TOMATO AND BASIL SAUCE

2 tablespoons oil
1 clove garlic, crushed
1 onion, chopped
400 g can tomatoes in juice
1½ tablespoons Edmonds Fielder's
  cornflour

¼ cup tomato paste
1 teaspoon sugar
salt
pepper
1 tablespoon chopped fresh basil

Heat oil in a saucepan. Add garlic and onion. Cook until onion is clear. Purée tomatoes and juice in a food processor or blender. Strain through a sieve. Combine cornflour and tomato paste. Add tomato purée, tomato paste and sugar to saucepan. Bring to the boil. Season with salt and pepper to taste. Remove from heat. Stir in basil.
Makes 2 cups.

WHITE SAUCE

1st EDITION RECIPE

2 tablespoons butter
2 tablespoons Edmonds standard
  plain flour

1 cup milk
salt
pepper

Melt butter in a small saucepan. Stir in flour and cook until frothy. Gradually add milk, stirring constantly. Stir over a medium heat until sauce boils and thickens. Cook for a further 2 minutes. Season with salt and pepper to taste.
Makes 1 cup.

BÉCHAMEL SAUCE
Stud an onion with 6 cloves. Place onion in milk and bring almost to the boil. Strain. In a separate pan melt butter and continue as above. Add heated milk.

CHEESE SAUCE
Remove pan from heat. Stir in ½ cup grated tasty cheese after cooking sauce.

CURRY SAUCE
Add 1 to 2 teaspoons curry powder when adding flour.

EGG SAUCE
Add chopped whites of 3 hard-boiled eggs to sauce. Garnish with sieved yolks and chopped parsley.

ONION SAUCE
Add 1 sliced onion to butter and cook until clear. Continue as above.

PARSLEY SAUCE
Remove pan from heat. Add 2 to 4 tablespoons chopped parsley.

TOMATO SAUCE
Omit milk and use ½ cup tomato purée and ½ cup water.

BRANDY OR RUM SAUCE

2 tablespoons Edmonds Fielder's
   cornflour
2 tablespoons sugar
1½ cups milk

1 tablespoon butter
2 tablespoons brandy or rum
pinch of nutmeg

In a saucepan, mix cornflour, sugar and ¼ cup of the milk to a smooth paste. Add remaining milk. Cook for 2 to 3 minutes, stirring constantly until mixture boils and thickens. Remove from heat. Add butter, brandy and nutmeg.
Makes 1¼ cups.

BRANDY CUSTARD
Replace cornflour with Edmonds custard powder.

CARAMEL SAUCE

125 g butter
¾ cup brown sugar
1½ tablespoons Edmonds Fielder's
   cornflour

1 cup water
1 tablespoon golden syrup
½ cup cream

Melt butter and sugar in a saucepan, stirring constantly until sugar dissolves. Boil for 3 minutes, stirring occasionally. Remove from heat. In a bowl combine cornflour, water and golden syrup until smooth. Add to saucepan. Bring mixture back to the boil, stirring constantly. Boil for 2 minutes. Remove from heat. Add cream.
Makes about 2 cups.

CHOCOLATE SAUCE

1 tablespoon Edmonds Fielder's
   cornflour
¼ cup cocoa

1 cup milk
1 to 2 tablespoons sugar
1 tablespoon butter

In a saucepan, mix cornflour, cocoa and ¼ cup of the milk to a smooth paste. Add the remaining milk, sugar, butter and cook stirring constantly for 2 to 3 minutes or until thick and smooth.
Makes 1 cup.

CUSTARD SAUCE

1 tablespoon Edmonds custard
   powder
1 cup milk

1 egg, beaten
1 teaspoon sugar

In a saucepan, mix custard powder and 2 tablespoons of the milk to a smooth paste. Add the remaining milk, egg, sugar and cook stirring constantly until custard thickens. Do not boil.
Makes 1 cup.

VANILLA CUSTARD
Add ½ teaspoon vanilla essence.

BARBECUE MARINADE

2 tablespoons tomato sauce
1 teaspoon sugar
1 tablespoon soy sauce

$^1/_4$ cup chilli sauce
2 cloves garlic, crushed

Combine all ingredients in a bowl. Mix well. Place meat in mixture, coating well. Cover and leave to marinate for at least 1 hour. Suitable for steaks, chicken, lamb and pork.

BLACK PEPPERCORN MARINADE

2 tablespoons coarsely crushed black
  peppercorns
1 tablespoon chopped parsley

$^1/_4$ cup lemon juice
1 clove garlic, crushed

Combine all ingredients in a bowl. Mix well. Place meat in mixture, stirring to coat. Cover and leave for at least 1 hour. Cook meat with peppercorn mixture coating it. Suitable for steak, lamb and chicken.

CHINESE MARINADE

$^1/_4$ cup dry sherry
1 tablespoon soy sauce
1 tablespoon honey

2 cloves garlic, crushed
1 tablespoon grated root ginger

Combine all ingredients in a bowl. Mix well. Place meat in mixture, stirring to coat. Cover and leave to marinate for at least 1 hour. This is ideal for chicken wings. Brush wings liberally all over with marinade. Suitable for chicken and pork.

KIWIFRUIT MARINADE

2 kiwifruit, finely chopped
1 tablespoon honey

2 teaspoons grated root ginger
coarsely crushed peppercorns

Combine all ingredients in a bowl. Mix well. Place meat in mixture, stirring to coat. Cover and leave to marinate for at least 15 minutes, turning occasionally. Suitable for steaks and lamb chops.

WHITE WINE MARINADE

1 onion, finely chopped
1 cup dry white wine
$^1/_4$ cup oil
1 teaspoon grated lemon rind
1 tablespoon lemon juice

2 cloves garlic, crushed
2 tablespoons chopped parsley or
  chives
1 bay leaf

Combine all ingredients in a bowl. Mix well. Place fish or chicken in marinade and turn over to coat both sides. Cover and leave fish for 20 minutes and chicken for 1 hour. Suitable for fish and chicken.

BLUE CHEESE SPREAD

250 g wedge blue cheese
150 g pot cream cheese
1 small onion, chopped
2 tablespoons softened butter
1 tablespoon Worcestershire sauce

dash tabasco sauce
2 tablespoons dry sherry
Canapé Bases (see below)
toasted sliced almonds

Crumble blue cheese into the bowl of a food processor. Add cream cheese, onion, butter, Worcestershire and tabasco sauces and sherry. Process until smooth. Transfer to a bowl. Cover and refrigerate until firm. When ready to use, pipe or spread on canapé bases. Garnish with toasted sliced almonds.
Makes about 2 cups.

CANAPÉ BASES

toast bread or thin sandwich bread

Remove crusts from bread to be used as bases for canapés. Cut out rounds using a 2.5 cm round cutter or alternatively cut into small squares. Place bread on an oven tray. Bake at 150°C allowing 20 minutes for toast bread and 10 minutes for sandwich bread. Leave until cold before using. Store in an airtight container.

CHEESE BALL

250 g cream cheese
1 cup grated tasty cheese
1 pickled onion, finely chopped
2 tablespoons finely chopped parsley
2 tablespoons finely chopped gherkin
1 tablespoon tomato sauce

1 teaspoon Worcestershire sauce
few drops tabasco sauce
$1/4$ teaspoon paprika
$1/2$ cup chopped walnuts,
  approximately

Combine cream cheese and cheese in a bowl. Add pickled onion, parsley, gherkin, tomato, Worcestershire and tabasco sauces and paprika. Beat well to combine. Shape into a ball. Roll in chopped walnuts until well coated. Wrap and chill until firm. Serve with crackers.

CHEESE BISCUITS OR STRAWS

1 cup Edmonds *standard plain flour*
2 teaspoons Edmonds *baking powder*
⅛ teaspoon dry mustard
pinch of cayenne pepper

75 g butter
¾ cup grated tasty cheese
1 egg

Sift flour, baking powder, mustard and cayenne pepper into a bowl. Rub in butter until mixture resembles fine breadcrumbs. Stir in cheese. Lightly beat egg with a fork and add. Stir until mixture forms a stiff, pliable dough. On a lightly floured board roll out dough to 5 mm thickness. Cut out shapes using small pastry cutters. Alternatively, cut into fingers 1 × 5 cm. Place onto a greased oven tray. Bake at 190°C for 10 minutes or until pale golden. Transfer to a cooling rack. When cold store in an airtight container. Serve with dips or spreads.
Makes about 30.

CHICKEN LIVER PÂTÉ

500 g chicken livers
50 g butter
1 small onion, finely chopped
2 cloves garlic, crushed
sprig thyme
100 g butter, softened

2 tablespoons brandy
salt
pepper
clarified butter
1 bay leaf

Trim fat and membrane from livers. Set aside. Heat first measure of butter in a frying pan. Add onion and garlic and cook until onion is clear. Remove from pan and set aside. Add chicken livers to pan and quickly cook for 5 minutes or until livers are browned but still a little pink in centre. Put onion mixture and livers into the bowl of a food processor or blender. Process until finely chopped. Add thyme, second measure of butter, brandy and salt and pepper to taste. Process to combine. Spoon mixture into a serving dish, smoothing over the top surface. Melt clarified butter. Pour this over pâté. Set bay leaf on top. Allow to cool. Cover and chill overnight.
Makes about 2 cups.

DEVILLED ALMONDS

1 tablespoon oil
1 cup blanched almonds

⅛ teaspoon chilli powder,
  approximately
1 teaspoon salt

Heat oil in a frying pan. Add almonds and stir continuously until golden. Lift almonds from pan. Drain on absorbent paper. Combine chilli and salt. Toss almonds in this mixture to coat. Add more chilli if wished. Leave to dry.
Makes 1 cup.

DEVILS ON HORSEBACK

8 well-soaked or cooked prunes *4 rashers bacon, rind removed*

Remove stone from prunes. Cut each rasher of bacon in half. Wrap each prune in bacon. Secure with toothpick. Place on an oven tray. Grill on both sides until bacon is cooked. Serve warm.
Makes 8.

BACON-WRAPPED BANANAS

2 bananas *4 rashers bacon, rind removed*
lemon juice

Peel bananas and cut into 4 pieces. Brush with lemon juice. Cut each rasher of bacon in half. Wrap bananas in bacon. Secure with toothpicks. Grill on both sides until bacon is cooked. Serve warm.

MOUSETRAPS

toast bread *salt*
grated tasty cheese *pepper*
finely chopped onion *chopped parsley*
chutney

Toast the bread on one side only. Combine cheese and onion. Spread untoasted side of bread with chutney. Top with cheese mixture. Season with salt and pepper to taste. Place mousetraps on an oven tray. Grill until golden. Garnish with chopped parsley.

SALMON PÂTÉ

200 g can red salmon *2 teaspoons gelatine*
1 spring onion, finely sliced *2 tablespoons water*
¼ cup Mayonnaise (page 184) *fresh herbs*
pepper *lemon slices*

Drain and flake the salmon, reserving ¼ cup liquid. Put salmon and spring onion into a bowl. Mix in mayonnaise, reserved salmon liquid and pepper to taste. Combine gelatine and water. Leave to swell for 10 minutes. Dissolve gelatine over hot water. Stir into salmon mixture. Pour salmon mixture into a mould and cover. Chill until set then unmould onto a plate. Garnish with fresh herbs and slices of lemon.
Makes about 1½ cups.

SALMON PUFFS

1 sheet Edmonds Flaky Puff Pastry
1 egg yolk
1 tablespoon water
1/2 cup cream cheese

1/4 cup cream, whipped
100 g smoked salmon, chopped
1 tablespoon lemon juice
1 tablespoons chopped parsley
pepper

Cut out rounds from the pastry approximately 5 cm in diameter. Place pastry rounds onto an oven tray. Prick all over with a fork. Combine egg yolk and water in a bowl. Brush pastry rounds with egg mixture. Bake at 200°C for 8 to 10 minutes or until golden. Split rounds apart and allow to cool. Beat together cream cheese, cream, salmon, lemon juice, parsley and pepper to taste. Spread salmon mixture onto bottom rounds. Replace pastry tops.
Makes about 20.

SANDWICH FILLINGS

Combinations of brown and white sandwich breads make attractive club or regular sandwiches.

asparagus and mayonnaise
chopped celery and grated cheese
chopped hard-boiled eggs and sliced
    spring onions
chopped nuts and yeast extract
chopped oysters and lemon juice
cress and yeast extract
dates and lemon juice
freshly chopped mint and finely
    chopped pineapple
grated apples and grated chocolate
grated carrot and chopped parsley

grated cheese, chopped egg and
    parsley
grated cheese and finely chopped
    pineapple
grated cheese and freshly chopped
    mint
preserved ginger and lemon honey
raisins and lemon juice
sardines and lemon juice
sliced tomato and grated cheese
cream corn and grated cheese

SARDINE SAVOURY

106 g can sardines
1 teaspoon curry powder
1 teaspoon lemon juice

2 tablespoons chutney
chopped parsley
Canapé Bases (page 197)

Drain sardines. Remove and discard tails. Mash sardines in a bowl. Add curry powder, lemon juice and chutney. Mix to a paste. Spread on Canapé Bases. Garnish with parsley.
Makes about 12.

No 6. eggs are used in recipes in this book.

SAUSAGE ROLLS

500 g sausagemeat
1 small onion, finely chopped
¼ cup finely chopped parsley
2 tablespoons tomato sauce

400 g packet flaky pastry
1 egg yolk
1 tablespoon water

Combine sausagemeat, onion, parsley and tomato sauce in a bowl. Mix well. On a lightly floured board roll out pastry to a 40 × 30 cm rectangle. Cut lengthwise into three even strips 40 × 10 cm. Pipe the sausagemeat mixture lengthwise down each piece. Alternatively roll sausagemeat into 3 × 40 cm lengths with floured hands. Brush edges of pastry with a little water and roll pastry over sausagemeat to encase the filling. Combine egg yolk and water in a bowl. Brush sausage rolls with egg mixture. Cut to size required. Place on an oven tray. Bake at 220°C for 15 to 20 minutes or until golden. Serve hot or cold.

SAVOURY PITA BREADS

large pita bread
butter, softened
garlic, crushed

grated cheese
sesame seeds or poppy seeds

Cut the pita bread in half horizontally. Spread the split side with butter and garlic. Top with cheese and sesame seeds. Cut into wedges. Place on an oven tray. Cook at 190°C for 10 minutes or until golden. Serve hot or cold.

SAVOURY TARTLETS

2 rashers bacon, chopped
1 onion, finely chopped
2 eggs
1 cup milk
salt

pepper
4 sheets Edmonds *Flaky Puff Pastry*
1 tablespoon chopped parsley,
*   approximately*

Cook bacon and onion in a frying pan until onion is clear. Set aside to cool. In a bowl combine eggs, milk and salt and pepper to taste. Place pastry on a lightly floured board. Cut out rounds and use to line patty tins. Spoon a little of the onion mixture into each pastry case. Top with parsley. Spoon egg mixture over. Bake at 200°C for 15 minutes or until golden and set. Serve hot.
Makes about 24.

STUFFED CELERY

stalks celery

Trim and wash celery. Remove strings from older stalks. Fill the cavity with filling of your choice. Cut into 3 cm lengths.

FILLINGS:
cream cheese and chopped walnuts
cream cheese, crushed pineapple and
*   chopped ham*

crunchy peanut butter and cooked,
*   chopped bacon*
cottage cheese and red pepper

Rinse knife clean between each cut when cutting sausage rolls.

STUFFED EGGS

8 hard-boiled eggs
1 teaspoon curry powder
2 to 3 tablespoons Mayonnaise
  (page 190)

salt
chopped parsley
stuffed olives

Shell the eggs. Cut in half lengthwise. Carefully remove yolks and place in a bowl. Add curry powder, Mayonnaise and salt to taste to the yolks. Mash with a fork until creamy. Spoon or pipe egg yolk mixture back into cavity. Decorate with parsley and slices of stuffed olives.
Makes 16.

DIPS

Serve the dips in the following recipes with —

raw vegetables — carrots, broccoli,
  celery, cauliflower, courgettes
crackers

corn chips
toasted pita bread
French bread

AVOCADO DIP (GUACAMOLE)

1 ripe avocado
1/2 cup sour cream
2 teaspoons lemon juice
3 tablespoons oil

few drops tabasco sauce
1/4 to 1/2 teaspoon chilli powder
salt

Remove flesh from avocado and mash. Mix in sour cream, lemon juice, oil, tabasco sauce and chilli powder. Season with salt to taste. Cover. Chill until ready to serve.
Makes about 1 cup.

CHICK-PEA DIP (HUMMUS)

1 cup chick peas
1 spring onion, finely chopped
3 tablespoons tahini
  (sesame seed paste)
2 cloves garlic, crushed

2 tablespoons lemon juice
1/2 teaspoon salt
1 tablespoon parsley, finely chopped
2 tablespoons olive oil
extra oil

Put the chick peas into a bowl. Cover with boiling water. Stand for 1 hour. Drain. Cook in boiling, salted water for 1 hour or until tender. Drain and allow to cool. Put chick peas into a food processor or blender. Add onion, tahini, garlic, lemon juice, salt, parsley and oil. Process until smooth. More oil may be required to blend to a smooth paste. Chill until ready to serve.
Makes about 1 cup.

CORN AND TOMATO SALSA

1 onion, finely chopped
2 cloves garlic, crushed
450 g can whole peeled tomatoes,
 roughly chopped
1/2 cup whole corn kernels
1/2 green pepper, finely chopped
1 teaspoon cumin

1 teaspoon basil
1/2 teaspoon rosemary
1/2 teaspoon paprika
1/4 teaspoon chilli
1 tablespoon chives, finely chopped
1/2 teaspoon salt

Combine all ingredients in a saucepan and simmer for 5 minutes. Serve warm or cold with corn chips.
Makes about 2 cups.

ONION DIP

32 g packet onion soup mix
250 g pot sour cream
1 tablespoon finely chopped cucumber

2 tablespoons finely chopped red and
 green peppers

Combine soup mix and sour cream. Cover and chill for 1 hour before serving. Add cucumber and pepper just before serving.
Makes about 1 cup.

APRICOT MARSHMALLOW

425 g can apricot halves
2 teaspoons gelatine
¹/₄ cup water

2 egg whites
3 tablespoons sugar

Drain apricots, reserving four halves for garnish. Purée remainder. Set aside. Combine gelatine and water. Leave to swell for 10 minutes. Dissolve over hot water and keep warm. Beat egg whites until stiff peaks form. Gradually pour in gelatine, beating until very thick. Add sugar, 1 tablespoon at a time, beating well until sugar dissolves. Fold in apricot purée. Pour into serving dish or individual serving dishes. Chill until set. Decorate with reserved apricots.
Serves 6.

BANANA MARSHMALLOW
Omit the apricots and replace with 2 bananas, mashed. Garnish with banana slices.

BLANCMANGE

3¹/₂ tablespoons Edmonds Fielder's
cornflour
2 tablespoons sugar

2 cups milk
few drops vanilla, almond or lemon
essence

In a saucepan, mix cornflour, sugar and ¹/₄ cup of the milk to a smooth paste. Add the remaining milk and heat, stirring constantly until mixture boils and thickens. Remove from heat. Stir in essence of your choice. Pour into a wet mould. Chill until set. Unmould onto a serving plate. Serve with fruit.
Serves 4–6.

CHEESECAKE

250 g packet Digestive biscuits
1 teaspoon grated lemon rind

1 tablespoon lemon juice
75 g butter, melted

FILLING
2 teaspoons gelatine
2 tablespoons water
250 g pot cream cheese
250 g pot sour cream

¹/₂ cup sugar
2 tablespoons lemon juice
1 teaspoon lemon rind
1 teaspoon vanilla essence

Finely crush biscuits. Combine biscuit crumbs, lemon rind, juice and butter. Line the base and sides of a 20 cm spring-form tin with biscuit mixture. Chill while preparing filling. Pour filling into prepared base. Chill until set.
Serves 6.

FILLING
Combine gelatine and water. Leave to swell for 10 minutes. Beat cream cheese until soft. Add sour cream and beat until well combined. Add sugar, lemon juice, rind and vanilla. Beat until sugar has dissolved. Dissolve gelatine over hot water. Add to cheese mixture.

Top: Pavlova (pg 210), Centre: Fruit Flan (pg 208),
Bottom: Easy Chocolate Mousse (pg 207)

CRÈME CARAMEL

³/₄ cup sugar
¹/₂ cup water
2 cups milk

¹/₂ teaspoon vanilla essence
4 eggs
2 tablespoons sugar

Combine first measure of sugar and water in a heavy-based saucepan. Gently heat, stirring constantly until sugar has dissolved. Bring to the boil. Do not stir. Leave syrup to boil until golden. Divide syrup evenly among six individual ramekin dishes. Set aside. Heat milk until almost boiling. Remove from heat. Add vanilla. In a separate bowl beat eggs and second measure of sugar together until pale. Pour heated milk onto egg mixture. Stir to combine. Strain. Divide egg mixture evenly among the caramel-lined dishes. Place dishes in a roasting dish. Pour in enough water to come halfway up the sides of ramekin dishes. Bake at 180°C for 35 minutes or until custard is set. Remove from roasting dish and allow to cool. Chill overnight then unmould onto serving plates.
Serves 6.

EASY CHOCOLATE MOUSSE

150 g cooking chocolate
4 eggs, separated
300 ml cream

2 tablespoons sugar
cream
grated chocolate

Break chocolate into the top of a double boiler. Stir over hot water until chocolate has melted. Allow to cool slightly. Stir yolks into chocolate. Beat until thick and smooth. Beat cream until thick. Quickly fold chocolate mixture into cream. Beat egg whites until stiff but not dry. Gradually add sugar, beating until thick and glossy. Fold half egg white mixture into chocolate mixture until well mixed. Repeat with remaining egg white mixture. Pour into four or six individual dishes or one large one. Chill until firm. Serve decorated with whipped cream and chocolate.
Serves 4–6.

CHOCOLATE LIQUEUR MOUSSE
Add 1 tablespoon brandy, chocolate or coffee liqueur to melted chocolate.

FLUMMERY

85 g packet jelly crystals
1 cup boiling water

375 ml can evaporated milk, chilled
until very cold

Dissolve jelly crystals in boiling water. Cool. Beat evaporated milk until thick. Add jelly mixture. Continue beating until thick and well combined. Pour into serving dish. Chill until firm.
Serves 6.

YOGHURT FLUMMERY
Omit evaporated milk. Chill jelly until consistency of raw egg white. Beat until thick and foamy. Stir in 2 × 150 g pots fruit-flavoured yoghurt. Pour into serving dish. Chill until set.

FRUIT FLAN

200 g Sweet Shortcrust Pastry or 1 sheet Edmonds *Sweet Short Pastry*

FILLING
1 cup milk
2 egg yolks
2 tablespoons sugar

2 tablespoons Edmonds *custard powder*

TOPPING
fresh or canned fruit — e.g.
  kiwifruit, grapes, strawberries,
  peaches, sliced

GLAZE
¹/₄ cup apricot jam

2 teaspoons water

On a lightly floured board roll out pastry and use to line a 20 cm flan ring or use ready rolled sheet. Bake blind at 190°C for 25 minutes. Remove baking blind material and return to oven for 1 minute to dry out pastry base. Set aside until cold. When cold spread filling into prepared base. Arrange sliced fruit topping decoratively over custard. Spoon or brush glaze over fruit.
Serves 6.

FILLING
In a saucepan, whisk milk, yolks, sugar and custard powder to a smooth paste. Cook over a low heat, stirring until mixture thickens. Do not let mixture boil. Remove from heat. Cover and leave until cold.

GLAZE
Gently heat apricot jam and water together. Strain.

GINGER BAVARIAN CREAM

1 tablespoon gelatine
¹/₄ cup water
2 egg yolks
¹/₂ cup sugar

1 cup milk
1 teaspoon vanilla essence
300 ml cream
¹/₂ cup chopped crystallised ginger

Combine gelatine and water. Leave to swell for 10 minutes. Beat egg yolks and sugar until pale. Pour milk onto yolks. Stir. Pour milk mixture into the top of a double boiler. Cook over a low heat until mixture thickens and coats the back of a wooden spoon. Remove from heat. Dissolve gelatine over hot water. Add gelatine and vanilla to milk mixture. Pour into a bowl. Chill until consistency of raw egg white. Beat cream until thick. Fold cream and ginger into chilled mixture. Pour into a large wet mould or serving dish. Chill until firm.
Serves 6.

CITRUS BAVARIAN CREAM
Omit ginger and vanilla. Add 2 tablespoons grated orange or lemon rind.

Crush biscuits in a food processor, blender or place in a bag and crush with a rolling pin.

ICE-CREAM

4 eggs, separated
1/4 cup caster sugar
1/4 cup caster sugar

1 teaspoon vanilla essence
300 ml cream

Beat egg whites until stiff peaks form. Gradually add first measure of sugar, 1 tablespoon at a time, beating until sugar dissolves before adding the next tablespoon. In a separate bowl beat egg yolks and second measure of sugar until thick and pale. Add vanilla. Gently fold yolk mixture into egg white mixture. In another bowl beat cream until thick then fold into egg mixture. Pour mixture into a shallow container suitable for freezing. Freeze for 2 hours or until firm.
Serves 6.

VARIATIONS
Any of the following can be added after the cream:
1 cup chocolate chips
1 cup chopped nuts

1 cup puréed berry fruit — e.g.
strawberries, raspberries

ICE-CREAM PUDDING

50 g butter
1/4 cup sugar
1/4 cup Edmonds *standard plain flour*

1 egg
2 cups milk
1/2 teaspoon vanilla essence

Cream butter and sugar until pale. Stir in flour. Lightly beat egg with a fork. Add to creamed mixture. In a saucepan, mix creamed mixture and milk together. Cook over a low heat until mixture boils and thickens, stirring constantly. Remove from heat. Add vanilla. Pour into serving dish. Chill until set.
Serves 4.

MARINATED STRAWBERRIES

2 punnets strawberries, hulled
2 tablespoons icing sugar
2 teaspoons grated orange rind

1 tablespoon orange-flavoured liqueur
1/4 cup orange juice

Put strawberries into a serving bowl. Sprinkle icing sugar and rind on top. Pour liqueur and juice over strawberries. Stir to coat. Leave to marinate for 1 hour before serving.
Serves 4.

MELROSE CREAM

2 tablespoons Edmonds *custard*
  powder
1 tablespoon sugar

2 cups milk
85 g packet jelly crystals

In a saucepan mix custard powder, sugar and *1/4* cup of the milk to a smooth paste. Add remaining milk and cook, stirring constantly until mixture boils and thickens. Remove from heat. Cover and set aside. Make jelly according to packet directions. Allow to cool. Combine jelly and custard. Pour into a wet mould. Chill until set. Unmould onto a serving plate.
Serves 6.

ORANGE AND LEMON PUDDING

2 eggs, separated
$^1/_4$ cup sugar
$^1/_2$ cup orange juice

$^1/_4$ cup lemon juice
1 tablespoon gelatine
1 cup water

Beat egg yolks, sugar and juices together. Combine gelatine with 2 tablespoons of the measured water. Leave to swell for 10 minutes. Bring the remaining water to the boil. Pour onto the gelatine and stir to dissolve the gelatine. Pour onto the egg yolk mixture. Beat the egg whites until stiff and fold into the gelatine mixture. Mix well and pour into a wet two-and-a-half-cup capacity mould. Leave to cool, then refrigerate until set.
Serves 4.

PAVLOVA

3 egg whites
3 tablespoons cold water
1 cup caster sugar

1 teaspoon vinegar
1 teaspoon vanilla essence
3 teaspoons cornflour

Preheat oven to 150°C. Using an electric mixer, beat egg whites until stiff. Add water and beat again. Add sugar very gradually while still beating. Slow beater and add vinegar, vanilla and cornflour. Line an oven tray with baking paper. Draw a 22 cm circle on the baking paper. Spread the pavlova to within 2 cm of the edge of the circle, keeping the shape as round and even as possible. Smooth top surface over. Bake pavlova for 45 minutes, then leave to cool in the oven. Carefully lift pavlova onto a serving plate. Decorate with whipped cream and fresh fruit.
Serves 6.

PINEAPPLE SNOW

440 g can pineapple pieces
85 g packet pineapple jelly crystals

1$^1/_2$ cups boiling water
2 egg whites

Drain pineapple, reserving all the juice. Place pineapple into a serving dish. Place jelly crystals into bowl. Add boiling water. Stir to dissolve sugar. Add reserved pineapple juice. Chill until consistency of raw egg white. Beat egg whites until stiff. Combine egg whites and jelly. Beat together until thick. Pour over pineapple in serving dish. Chill until set.
Serves 6.

SHERRY TRIFLE

200 g packet trifle sponge
$^1/_4$ cup raspberry or apricot jam
$^1/_4$ cup sherry
425 g can fruit salad
4 tablespoons Edmonds *custard powder*
3 tablespoons sugar

2 cups milk
300 ml cream
$^1/_2$ teaspoon vanilla essence
1 tablespoon icing sugar
$^1/_4$ cup chopped nuts

Cut sponge in half horizontally. Spread cut surface with jam. Sandwich halves together. Cut into cubes then put into serving dish. Spoon sherry over sponge. Spoon fruit salad and juice evenly over sponge. Set aside. In a saucepan, mix custard powder, sugar and $^1/_4$ cup of the milk to a smooth paste. Add remaining milk and cook over a low heat, stirring constantly until mixture boils and thickens. Remove from heat, cover and leave until cool. Pour custard over fruit salad in serving dish. Chill until set. Beat cream, vanilla and icing sugar until thick. Decorate trifle with cream and nuts.
Serves 6.

VARIATION
Fresh berries, cherries or plums (stones removed) can be substituted for fruit salad.

SORBET

500 g fruit — e.g. grapes,
  boysenberries, plums, strawberries
$^1/_2$ cup sugar

1 cup water
$^1/_4$ cup lemon juice
2 egg whites

Purée fruit to be used. Strain and discard the skins and seeds. Set aside. In a saucepan combine sugar and water. Cook over a low heat, stirring constantly until sugar has dissolved. Remove from heat and allow to cool slightly. Combine sugar syrup, fruit purée and lemon juice. Pour into a shallow container. Put in freezer until mixture starts to freeze on top. Transfer mixture to a bowl. Add egg whites and beat until combined. Refreeze until set. Serve in chilled glasses.
Serves 6.

SPANISH CREAM

1 tablespoon gelatine
2 tablespoons water
2 eggs, separated

$^1/_4$ cup sugar
2 cups milk
1 teaspoon vanilla essence

Combine gelatine and water. Leave to swell for 10 minutes. In a bowl beat egg yolks and sugar until pale. Pour milk and egg mixture into the top of a double boiler. Cook over a low heat, stirring constantly until mixture thickens to coat the back of a wooden spoon. Remove from heat. Add vanilla. Dissolve gelatine over hot water. Stir gelatine into custard mixture. Chill until consistency of raw egg white. Beat egg whites until stiff. Fold into custard mixture. Pour into a wet mould. Chill until firm. Unmould onto a serving plate.
Serves 6.

APPLE PIE

200 g Sweet Shortcrust Pastry or
  2 sheets Edmonds Sweet Short
  Pastry

2 teaspoons sugar

FILLING
4 to 6 Granny Smith apples
1/2 cup sugar
25 g butter, melted

2 tablespoons Edmonds standard
  plain flour
1/4 teaspoon ground cloves

On a lightly floured board roll out pastry slightly larger than a 20 cm pie plate or use ready rolled sheet. Cut two 2.5 cm wide strips long enough to go around the edge of the pie plate. Brush with water. Spoon apple filling into centre of pie plate. Cover with remaining pastry. Press edges firmly together to seal. Cut steam holes in centre of pastry. Trim and crimp edges. Decorate pie with any pastry trimmings. Brush lightly with milk or water. Sprinkle with sugar. Bake at 200°C for 25 minutes or until pastry is golden. Test with a skewer if the apple is cooked. If not, reduce oven temperature to 180°C and cook until apple is tender.
Serves 6.

FILLING
Peel, core and slice the apples thinly. Combine sugar, butter, flour and cloves. Toss apples in this mixture.

BAKED APPLE DUMPLINGS

2 1/2 cups Edmonds standard plain flour
1/2 teaspoon salt
3 teaspoons Edmonds baking powder
50 g butter
1 cup milk

4 medium Granny Smith apples,
  peeled and cored
1 cup sugar
1 cup hot water

Sift flour, salt and baking powder into a bowl. Cut in butter until it resembles fine breadcrumbs. Add milk, mixing to a soft dough. Divide dough into four portions. On a lightly floured board roll out each portion of dough to a 20 cm square. Place an apple onto each dough square. Dampen edges with water. Sprinkle each apple with 1 teaspoon of the measured sugar. Carefully wrap the dough around each apple. Place apples in a greased ovenproof dish. Put water and remaining sugar into a saucepan. Heat gently, stirring constantly until sugar has dissolved. Pour this over apples. Bake at 190°C for 45 minutes or until pastry is golden and apples are cooked.
Serves 4.

Try not to stretch pastry when rolling and handling. It will shrink on cooking. If time permits, rest pastry before baking.

212

BAKED APPLES

1 tablespoon butter
2 tablespoons brown sugar

¼ cup sultanas or currants
6 Granny Smith apples

Cream butter and sugar until light and fluffy. Add sultanas. Peel apples one third way down. Core. Score apples with fork. Spoon mixture evenly into cavity. Place apples in an ovenproof dish. Add enough water to come 2 cm up dish. Bake at 160°C for 35 minutes or until apples are tender.
Serves 6.

BAKED CUSTARD

3 eggs
¼ cup sugar
2 cups milk, heated

½ teaspoon vanilla essence
pinch of nutmeg

In a saucepan, whisk eggs, sugar, heated milk and vanilla together. Pour custard into a 20 cm pie plate. Sprinkle with nutmeg. Set pie plate in a shallow pan of water. Bake at 150°C for 1 hour or until set. Serve hot or cold.
Serves 4.

BREAD AND BUTTER PUDDING

4 slices toast bread, cut into triangles
2 tablespoons currants
¼ cup sugar

2 teaspoons grated lemon rind
3 eggs
2 cups milk

Layer bread triangles, currants, sugar and lemon rind in an ovenproof dish. Beat eggs and milk together. Pour egg mixture over. Leave to stand for 15 minutes. Bake at 180°C for 30 minutes or until golden and set. Serve dusted with icing sugar.
Serves 4–6.

CHOCOLATE SELF-SAUCING PUDDING

100 g butter, softened
¾ cup sugar
1 egg
1 teaspoon vanilla essence

1¼ cups Edmonds standard plain flour
2 teaspoons Edmonds baking powder
1 tablespoon cocoa
2 cups boiling water

SAUCE
½ cup brown sugar
1 tablespoon Edmonds Fielder's
 cornflour

¼ cup cocoa

Beat butter, sugar, egg and vanilla together. Sift flour, baking powder and cocoa together. Fold into beaten mixture. Spoon mixture into a greased six to eight cup capacity ovenproof dish. Sprinkle sauce mixture over. Carefully pour boiling water over the back of a spoon onto the pudding. Bake at 180°C for 35 minutes or until pudding springs back when lightly touched.
Serves 6.

SAUCE
Combine all ingredients.

CHRISTMAS PUDDING

1 cup sultanas
1 cup raisins
1 cup currants
70 g packet blanched almonds
150 g packet mixed peel
1 cup shredded suet
1 cup Edmonds *standard plain flour*
1¹/₂ teaspoons Edmonds *baking powder*
1 teaspoon mixed spice

1 teaspoon cinnamon
¹/₄ teaspoon ground nutmeg
¹/₄ teaspoon salt
1¹/₂ cups soft breadcrumbs
1 cup brown sugar
2 eggs
2 teaspoons grated lemon rind
¹/₂ cup milk
1 tablespoon brandy

Put sultanas, raisins, currants, almonds and mixed peel into a large bowl. Add suet, mixing to combine. Sift flour, baking powder, mixed spice, cinnamon, nutmeg and salt into fruit mixture. Mix well. Add breadcrumbs and mix through. In a separate bowl beat brown sugar, eggs, lemon rind and milk together. Add to fruit mixture, mixing thoroughly to combine. Stir in brandy. Spoon mixture into a well-greased eight-to-ten-cup-capacity pudding basin. Cover with pleated greaseproof paper or foil. Secure with string, leaving a loop to lift out pudding when cooked. Place a trivet or old saucer in the bottom of a large saucepan half-filled with boiling water. Carefully lower pudding into saucepan making sure the water comes two-thirds of the way up the sides of basin. Cover and cook for 5 hours, making sure water is constantly bubbling. Check water level from time to time. Remove from saucepan. Leave until cold. Wrap well and store in refrigerator until ready to use. Steam for a further 2 hours before serving.
Serves 6.

CUSTARD TART

200 g *Sweet Shortcrust Pastry* or
1 sheet Edmonds *Sweet Short Pastry*

FILLING
2 eggs
1 cup milk

¹/₄ teaspoon ground nutmeg

2 tablespoons sugar

On a lightly floured board roll out pastry and use to line a 20 cm pie plate or flan ring or use ready rolled sheet. Do not prick the pastry. Bake blind at 200°C for 15 minutes. Remove baking blind material. Return pastry shell to oven for 1 minute to dry out pastry base. Reduce oven temperature to 180°C. Carefully pour filling into prepared base. Sprinkle with nutmeg. Return to oven and continue to cook for 20 minutes or until custard is set.
Serves 4–6.

FILLING
In a saucepan, whisk together eggs, milk and sugar. Cook, stirring, until almost boiling.

DOMINION PUDDING

![1st EDITION RECIPE]

50 g butter
¹/₂ cup sugar
1 egg
1 cup Edmonds *standard plain flour*

1¹/₂ teaspoons Edmonds *baking powder*
¹/₄ cup milk
2 tablespoons jam or raisins

Cream butter and sugar until light and fluffy. Beat in egg. Sift flour and baking powder together. Add to creamed mixture alternately with milk. Place jam or raisins in bottom of a well-greased two-cup-capacity pudding basin. Spoon mixture over. Cover with pleated greaseproof paper or foil. Secure with string. Steam for 1¼ hours or until pudding feels firm when lightly touched. Unmould onto a serving plate. Serve hot with *Edmonds* custard.
Serves 4–6.

EDMONDS VELVET CUSTARD

1 tablespoon Edmonds *custard powder*
2 teaspoons sugar

1 cup milk
1 egg, lightly beaten

In a saucepan, whisk custard powder, sugar, milk and egg together. Cook, stirring constantly until mixture boils and thickens.
Serves 4.

EDMONDS CUSTARD (POURING)

2 tablespoons Edmonds *custard powder*

2 teaspoons sugar
2 cups milk

In a saucepan, mix custard powder, sugar and ¼ cup of the milk to a smooth paste. Add remaining milk and gently heat, stirring constantly until mixture boils and thickens.
Makes 2 cups.

FRUIT CRUMBLE

2 cups stewed fruit — e.g. apples, plums, apricots
2 tablespoons brown sugar
1 cup Edmonds *standard plain flour*

1 teaspoon Edmonds *baking powder*
50 g butter
¼ cup sugar

Place stewed fruit in bottom of an ovenproof dish. Sprinkle with brown sugar. Sift flour and baking powder into a bowl. Cut in butter until it resembles coarse breadcrumbs. Stir in sugar. Spoon mixture over fruit. Bake at 190°C for 30 minutes or until pale golden.
Serves 6.

WHOLEMEAL CRUMBLE
Replace flour with wholemeal flour. Increase butter to 75 g.

WHOLEGRAIN OAT CRUMBLE
Reduce flour to ½ cup. Increase butter to 75 g. Stir in ½ cup wholegrain oats after sugar.

FRUIT BETTY
Omit flour and baking powder and replace with 2 cups soft breadcrumbs. Increase butter to 100 g and melt. Combine butter and breadcrumbs, cooking until pale golden and slightly crisp. Add remaining crumble ingredients. Layer apple mixture with breadcrumb mixture, finishing with a layer of breadcrumbs. Cook as above until golden.

Too much water will produce a tough pastry.

FRUIT SPONGE

2 cups hot stewed fruit — e.g.
  apples, boysenberries, apricots
sugar
125 g butter
1/2 teaspoon vanilla essence

1/2 cup sugar
2 eggs
1 cup Edmonds standard plain flour
2 teaspoons Edmonds baking powder
2 tablespoons milk

Place stewed fruit in an ovenproof dish. Sweeten with sugar to taste. Cover and keep hot. Put butter, vanilla and measured sugar into a bowl. Beat until pale and creamy. Beat in eggs one at a time, beating well after each addition. Sift flour and baking powder together. Fold into creamed mixture. Add milk and mix to combine. Spoon mixture over fruit. Bake at 190°C for 40 minutes or until sponge springs back when lightly touched. Serve hot dusted with icing sugar.
Serves 4–6.

HARLEQUIN PUDDING

50 g butter
5 tablespoons sugar
1 egg
3/4 cup Edmonds standard plain flour
2 tablespoons Edmonds custard powder

1 teaspoon Edmonds baking powder
1/4 cup milk
1 cup raisins
1 tablespoon cocoa

Cream butter and sugar together until light and fluffy. Add egg, beating well. Sift flour, custard powder and baking powder together. Fold into creamed mixture. Stir in milk. Place raisins in a well-greased two-cup-capacity pudding basin. Spoon half the mixture on top. Stir cocoa into remaining mixture. Spoon this on top of plain mixture. Cover with pleated greased paper or foil. Secure with string. Steam for 30 minutes or until mixture feels firm when touched. Unmould onto a serving plate.
Serves 4–6.

JAM TART

200 g Sweet Shortcrust Pastry or
  1 sheet Edmonds Sweet Short
  Pastry

1/2 cup jam, approximately
2 tablespoons milk, approximately
2 teaspoons sugar

Cut one-quarter from the pastry. On a lightly floured board roll out larger portion of pastry to a rectangle 25 × 15 cm or use 3/4 ready rolled sheet. Using the rolling pin, carefully lift pastry onto a greased oven tray. Spread lightly with jam, leaving a 2 cm edge all the way round. Roll the edge up so it is touching the jam. Roll out remaining pastry and cut into strips 2 × 16 cm or use rest of ready rolled sheet. Dampen ends of strips with water. Place the strips over jam tart, pressing the ends of the strips firmly to the pie edge. Brush strips with milk. Sprinkle strips with sugar. Bake at 200°C for 15 minutes or until golden. Serve warm or cold.
Serves 4.

LEMON MERINGUE PIE

BASE
200 g Sweet Shortcrust Pastry or 1 sheet Edmonds *Sweet Short Pastry*

FILLING
¼ cup Edmonds Fielder's cornflour
1 cup sugar
2 teaspoons grated lemon rind
½ cup lemon juice

¾ cup water
3 eggs, separated
1 tablespoon butter

TOPPING
¼ cup caster sugar

¼ teaspoon vanilla essence

On a lightly floured board roll out pastry to 6 mm thickness or use ready rolled sheet. Use to line a 20 cm flan ring. Trim off any excess pastry. Bake blind at 190°C for 20 minutes. Remove baking blind material. Return pastry shell to oven for 1 minute to dry out pastry base. While pastry is cooking make the filling. Pour filling into cooked pastry base. Spoon meringue topping over lemon filling. Return to oven and bake at 190°C for 10 minutes or until golden.
Serves 6.

FILLING
Blend cornflour, sugar, lemon rind and juice together until smooth. Add water. Cook over medium heat until mixture boils and thickens, stirring constantly. Remove from heat. Stir in yolks and butter.

TOPPING
Beat egg whites until stiff but not dry. Beat in sugar, 1 tablespoon at a time, until very thick and glossy. Stir in vanilla.

LEMON SOUFFLÉ

75 g butter
3 tablespoons Edmonds standard plain flour
¾ cup milk

2 teaspoons grated lemon rind
2 tablespoons lemon juice
¼ cup sugar
4 eggs, separated

Melt the butter in the top of a double boiler. Remove from heat. Stir in flour, mixing until smooth. Stir in milk, lemon rind and juice until smooth. Return to heat and cook until sauce is thick. Stir in sugar, stirring until it dissolves. Remove from heat. Allow to cool slightly. Beat egg yolks until pale. Add to sauce. Beat egg whites until soft peaks form. Fold half into sauce mixture. Repeat with remaining egg whites. Pour soufflé carefully into a greased soufflé dish. Bake at 190°C for 40 minutes or until mixture is well risen and golden. Serve immediately.
Serves 4–6.

CHOCOLATE SOUFFLÉ
Increase milk to 1 cup. Omit lemon rind and juice. Stir in 150 g grated cooking chocolate when adding sugar. Stir until chocolate has melted. Continue as above.

Always roll pastry away from you with light, even strokes. Do not press down hard with the rolling pin.

217

PANCAKES

1 cup Edmonds *standard plain flour*
⅛ teaspoon salt
1 *egg*

¾ cup milk
water

Sift flour and salt into a bowl. Add egg, mixing to combine. Gradually beat in milk, mixing to a smooth batter. Chill for 1 hour. Stir. The batter will thicken on standing. Add a little water if necessary to bring it back to the original consistency. Heat a greased pancake pan or small frying pan. Pour in just enough batter to cover base of pan. Cook until golden on underside. Release with knife around edges. Flip or turn and cook other side. Stack pancakes as you cook. Serve sprinkled with lemon juice and sugar.
Makes 8.

PECAN PIE

200 g Sweet Shortcrust Pastry or 1 sheet Edmonds *Sweet Short Pastry*

FILLING
100 g butter, softened
½ cup brown sugar
3 eggs

3 tablespoons liquid honey
3 × 70 g packets pecan nuts

On a lightly floured board roll out pastry and use to line a 22 cm flan tin or use ready rolled sheet. Bake blind at 200°C for 15 minutes. Remove baking blind material. Return pastry shell to oven for 1 minute to dry out pastry base. Reduce oven temperature to 180°C. Pour filling into cooked pastry base. Return to oven and bake for a further 30 minutes or until filling is set.
Serves 6.

FILLING
Cream butter and sugar until light and fluffy. Add eggs one at a time, beating well after each addition. Stir in honey and pecans.

QUEEN OF PUDDINGS

2 eggs, separated
2 cups milk
2 tablespoons sugar

1 cup soft breadcrumbs or cake
  crumbs
2 tablespoons raspberry jam
¼ cup sugar

Beat egg yolks, milk and sugar together. Place breadcrumbs in bottom of a greased ovenproof dish. Pour in egg yolk mixture. Bake at 160°C for 30 minutes or until set. Remove from oven and allow to cool. Increase oven temperature to 200°C. Spread jam on top. Beat egg whites until stiff but not dry. Gradually beat in sugar, 1 tablespoon at a time, until sugar has dissolved. Spoon or pipe meringue on top of pudding. Return to oven and bake at 200°C for 10 minutes or until golden.
Serves 4–6.

VARIATION
Add 1 teaspoon grated lemon rind and 1 teaspoon vanilla essence.

RICE PUDDING

1st EDITION RECIPE

5 tablespoons short grain rice
2 tablespoons sugar
3 cups milk

2 to 3 drops vanilla essence
1 teaspoon butter
$1/4$ teaspoon ground nutmeg

Place rice and sugar in the bottom of an ovenproof dish. Add milk and vanilla. Mix well. Add butter. Sprinkle nutmeg over surface. Bake at 150°C for 2 hours, stirring two to three times in first hour. This pudding should be creamy when cooked. Serves 4.

SAGO PUDDING

1st EDITION RECIPE

Omit rice and replace with 3 tablespoons sago.

STEAMED SPONGE PUDDING

50 g butter
$1/4$ cup sugar
1 egg
2 tablespoons apricot jam
1 cup Edmonds standard plain flour

1 teaspoon Edmonds baking powder
$1/8$ teaspoon salt
$1/2$ teaspoon Edmonds baking soda
$1/2$ cup milk

Cream butter and sugar until light and fluffy. Add egg, beating well. Stir in jam. Sift flour, baking powder and salt into creamed mixture then fold in. Dissolve soda in milk and add to mixture. Spoon mixture into a greased two-cup-capacity pudding basin. Cover with greased paper or foil. Secure with string. Steam for 30 minutes or until pudding feels firm to touch.
Serves 6.

GOLDEN SYRUP PUDDING
Place 1 tablespoon golden syrup at the bottom of pudding basin.

APPLE PUDDING
Mix $1/2$ cup stewed apple into mixture.

FIG OR PRUNE PUDDING
Mix $1/2$ cup chopped figs or prunes into mixture.

UPSIDE-DOWN PUDDING

125 g butter
$1/2$ cup sugar
2 eggs
1 cup Edmonds standard plain flour
2 teaspoons Edmonds baking powder
2 tablespoons milk

25 g butter, melted
$1/4$ cup brown sugar
1 teaspoon mixed spice
425 g can pear halves, drained, or
   8 pineapple rings

Cream first measure of butter and sugar until light and fluffy. Add eggs one at a time, beating well after each addition. Sift flour and baking powder together. Fold into creamed mixture. Stir in milk. Combine second measure of butter, sugar and mixed spice. Spread this mixture onto the base of a 20 cm round cake tin. Arrange pears cut side down or pineapple rings on the butter mixture. Spoon cake mixture over fruit. Bake at 180°C for 40 minutes or until cake springs back when lightly touched. Unmould onto a serving plate. Glacé cherries can be placed in the centre of each pear or pineapple.
Serves 6.

Brush avocados, apples and pears with lemon juice to prevent browning.

YOGHURT CREAM

200 g pot natural unsweetened
  yoghurt
1 tablespoon icing sugar

2 teaspoons grated orange rind
2 tablespoons whipped cream

Combine all ingredients. Mix well. Chill until ready to serve.
Serves 4.

Top: Apple Pie (pg 212), Centre: Edmonds Custard (pg 215),
Bottom: Upside Down Pudding (pg 219)

APPLE COCONUT FLAN

1 packet Edmonds
  Butter Cake Mix
1 cup coconut
125 g butter

2 cups stewed apple
1 teaspoon grated lemon rind
1 cup water
$^1/_4$ cup lemon juice

Put contents of cake mix packet and coconut into a bowl or food processor. Process to combine. Cut in butter until it resembles coarse breadcrumbs. Combine apple and lemon rind. Place stewed apples in the bottom of a large greased ovenproof dish. Spoon cake mixture evenly over apples. Combine water and lemon juice. Pour this over cake mixture. Bake at 180°C for 55 minutes or until pale golden and firm to touch. Serve hot or cold.
Serves 8–10.

APRICOT ISLANDS

1 packet Edmonds Butter
  Cake Mix
2 eggs
$^1/_2$ cup water

50 g butter, softened
8 canned apricot halves
70 g packet sliced almonds

Put cake mix, eggs, water and butter into an electric mixer bowl. Mix at low speed until the ingredients are combined. Beat for 2 minutes at medium speed. Scrape down sides of bowl occasionally. Place apricots cut side uppermost in well-greased patty pans. Spoon a tablespoonful of cake mixture into cavity of each apricot. Sprinkle sliced almonds over. Bake at 180°C for 15 minutes or until cake springs back when lightly touched. Serve warm or cold. Use remaining mixture to make cup cakes.
Serves 4.

BANANA PANCAKES

2 cups Edmonds Pancake and Pikelet
  Mix
1$^1/_2$ cups milk

1 large ripe banana, mashed
$^1/_4$ cup finely chopped walnuts
$^1/_2$ teaspoon ground nutmeg

Make pancake mix according to packet directions, using only the measured 1$^1/_2$ cups milk. Stir in banana, walnuts and nutmeg. Cook pancakes according to packet directions. Serve with whipped cream.
Serves 6.

BLACK FOREST CHEESECAKE

1 packet Edmonds *Continental
  Cheesecake Mix*
4 tablespoons melted butter
³/₄ cup cold milk

¹/₂ cup chopped cherries
100 g cooking chocolate, melted
¹/₂ cup whipped cream
grated chocolate

Put contents of biscuit base sachet into a bowl. Mix in butter. Press crumbs firmly over base and sides of a greased 20 cm pie plate or over the base and halfway up sides of a spring-form tin. Chill. Into an electric mixer bowl place milk and contents of filling sachet. Beat on low speed until all ingredients are moistened. Beat on medium speed for 3 minutes or until thick and creamy. Fold cherries and chocolate through cheesecake mixture. Pour into prepared crumb shell. Chill until firm. Serve decorated with whipped cream and grated chocolate.
Serves 6–8.

DUTCH LAYERED PANCAKES

500 g Granny Smith apples, peeled
  and chopped
¹/₄ cup sugar
¹/₂ teaspoon cinnamon

1 cup Edmonds *Pancake and Pikelet
  Mix*
2 teaspoons icing sugar

Put apples, sugar and cinnamon into a saucepan. Cook until apples are pulpy. Mash with a potato masher until smooth. Make pancakes according to packet directions. Place a pancake on a serving dish. Spread with a little apple mixture. Repeat, topping the stack with a pancake. Chill until cold. Dust with icing sugar. Cut into wedges to serve.
Serves 4–6.

EASY FRUIT SPONGE

3 cups stewed fruit
1 packet Edmonds *Butter
  Cake Mix*

2 eggs
¹/₂ cup water
50 g butter, softened
icing sugar

Put stewed fruit into the bottom of a greased ovenproof dish. Put cake mix, eggs, water and butter into an electric mixer bowl. Mix at low speed until the ingredients are combined. Beat for 2 minutes at medium speed. Scrape down sides of bowl occasionally. Pour mixture over fruit. Bake at 180°C for 35 to 40 minutes or until sponge springs back when lightly touched. Serve dusted with icing sugar.
Serves 6.

LEMON COCONUT PUDDING

100 g butter, melted
4 eggs
1 cup Edmonds *Pancake and Pikelet Mix*
2 cups milk

1 cup sugar
$^1/_2$ cup coconut
1 tablespoon grated lemon rind
icing sugar

Beat all ingredients except icing sugar together. Pour into a greased shallow 22 cm ovenproof dish. Bake at 180°C for 1 hour or until centre feels firm to touch. Serve hot or cold, dusted with icing sugar.
Serves 6–8.

STEAMED PUDDING

2 tablespoons apricot jam or currants
1 packet Edmonds *Butter Cake Mix*

$^1/_2$ cup water
2 eggs
50 g butter, softened
Edmonds *custard (page 215)*

Spoon jam or currants into the bottom of a greased six-cup-capacity pudding basin. Put cake mix, water, eggs and butter into an electric mixer bowl. Mix at low speed until the ingredients are combined. Beat for 2 minutes at medium speed. Scrape down sides of bowl occasionally. Spoon mixture into prepared basin. Cover with pleated greaseproof paper. Secure with string. Steam for 1$^1/_4$ hours or until pudding feels firm to touch. Unmould onto a serving plate. Serve hot with *Edmonds* custard.
Serves 4–6.

HINTS FOR ALL BOILED SWEETS

1. **Use a large heavy-based saucepan** to allow sugar to rise when it boils.
2. **Make sure all sugar is dissolved on a low heat** before boiling, otherwise the finished product will be grainy.
3. **Only stir boiling syrup occasionally** to stop burning.
4. **When liquid reaches boiling point**, **cover with a lid for 2 to 3 minutes** to dissolve any crystals on the side of the saucepan.

Sugar cookery stages:
When testing to see if the correct stage of cooking has been reached, stop the cooking while testing by dipping the saucepan into cold water.

Temperatures

114°C	**Soft ball**	— Drop a small amount of syrup into very cold water. A soft ball forms that flattens on removal.
118°C	**Firm ball**	— Drop a small amount of syrup into very cold water. A firm ball forms that does not flatten on removal.
120°C	**Hard ball**	— Drop a small amount of syrup into very cold water. This forms a ball that is hard enough to hold its shape, yet plastic.
142°C	**Soft crack**	— Drop a small amount of syrup into very cold water. This separates into threads that are hard but not brittle.
150°C	**Hard crack**	— Drop a small amount of syrup into very cold water. This separates into threads that are hard and brittle.

5. **For fudges and coconut ice**, allow to cool. Beat until the syrup begins to thicken and loses its gloss. Pour immediately.

APRICOT BALLS

200 g dried apricots, chopped
$^{1}/_{2}$ cup orange juice
$^{1}/_{4}$ teaspoon citric acid
$^{1}/_{2}$ cup icing sugar

1 cup coconut
1 cup fine biscuit crumbs
$^{1}/_{2}$ cup coconut or melted chocolate

Put apricots, orange juice and citric acid into a saucepan. Cover and bring to the boil. Reduce heat and simmer for 10 minutes. Leave until cool. Purée apricot mixture in a food processor or blender. Transfer to a bowl. Add icing sugar, first measure of coconut and biscuit crumbs. Mix well. Measure tablespoonsful of mixture and roll into balls. Roll in second measure of coconut or dip in melted chocolate. Chill until set.
Makes about 20.

BRANDY BALLS

250 g packet Vanilla Wine biscuits
2 tablespoons currants
2 tablespoons chopped walnuts
1 egg
1/4 cup sugar

1 tablespoon cocoa
1 1/2 tablespoons brandy or sherry
125 g butter, melted
coconut or chocolate hail

Finely crush biscuits. Place crumbs into a bowl. Add currants and walnuts. Stir to combine. In another bowl lightly beat the egg with a fork. Add sugar and cocoa, stirring until thoroughly mixed. Add brandy. Pour this mixture into crumb mixture. Add melted butter, stirring until well combined. Measure tablespoonsful of mixture and shape into balls. Roll in coconut or chocolate hail. Chill until firm. Makes about 20.

BUTTERSCOTCH

1 teaspoon gelatine
1 tablespoon water
1/2 teaspoon cream of tartar

2 cups sugar
2/3 cup water
100 g butter

Combine gelatine and the first measure of water. Leave to swell for 10 minutes. Put cream of tartar, sugar and second measure of water into a large saucepan. Heat gently, stirring constantly until sugar dissolves. Dissolve gelatine over hot water. Quickly stir gelatine into sugar mixture and bring to the boil. Add butter. Do not stir. Let mixture boil until the soft crack stage. Pour mixture into a buttered tin. Cool slightly, then mark into squares. Cut when cold.

CHOCOLATE FUDGE

2 cups sugar
2 tablespoons cocoa
1/2 cup milk

25 g butter
1/2 teaspoon vanilla essence

Put sugar and cocoa into a saucepan. Mix to combine. Add milk and butter. Heat gently, stirring constantly until sugar has dissolved and butter melted. Bring to the boil. Do not stir. Let mixture boil until the soft ball stage. Remove from heat. Add vanilla and leave to stand for 5 minutes. Beat with a wooden spoon until thick. Pour into a buttered tin. Mark into squares. Cut when cold.

CHOCOLATE TRUFFLES

50 g butter
100 g cooking chocolate
1 cup icing sugar, approximately

1 tablespoon rum
1 teaspoon cocoa
coconut

Put butter and chocolate into a saucepan. Heat gently, stirring until butter and chocolate have melted. Add 1/2 cup of the icing sugar. Stir until mixture is thick enough to handle. Stir in rum and cocoa. Add enough of the remaining icing sugar to make a stiff mixture. Measure tablespoonsful of the mixture and shape into balls. Roll in coconut. Chill until firm. Makes about 15.

When dipping food in melted chocolate, place on a skewer before dipping in chocolate. Leave on foil until chocolate is hard.

COCONUT ICE

3 cups icing sugar
1/2 cup milk
25 g butter

1/4 teaspoon salt
3/4 cup coconut
few drops red food colouring

Put icing sugar, milk, butter and salt into a saucepan. Heat gently, stirring constantly until sugar dissolves. Bring to the boil. Do not stir. Let mixture boil until the soft ball stage. Add coconut. Remove mixture from the heat and allow to cool for 10 minutes. Divide mixture in half. Add a few drops of food colouring to one portion and beat until mixture starts to thicken. Pour into a buttered tin. Beat the white portion until it starts to thicken. Spread this mixture on top of pink mixture. Allow to cool. Cut into squares.

FLORENTINE CARAMELS

2 1/2 cups sugar
2 tablespoons coconut
1 teaspoon ground ginger
1 tablespoon golden syrup

25 g butter
1/2 cup milk
1 teaspoon vanilla essence

Put sugar, coconut and ginger into a saucepan. Mix to combine. Add golden syrup, butter and milk. Heat gently, stirring constantly until sugar dissolves. Bring to the boil. Do not stir. Boil mixture until the soft ball stage. Remove from the heat. Add vanilla and beat until thick and creamy. Pour into a buttered tin. Mark into squares. Cut when cold.

HOKEY POKEY

5 tablespoons sugar
2 tablespoons golden syrup

1 teaspoon Edmonds baking soda

Put sugar and golden syrup into a saucepan. Heat gently, stirring constantly until sugar dissolves. Increase the heat and bring to the boil. Boil for 2 minutes. Stir occasionally, if necessary, to prevent burning. Remove from heat. Add baking soda. Stir quickly until mixture froths up. Pour into a buttered tin immediately. Leave until cold and hard. Break into pieces.

MARSHMALLOWS

2 tablespoons gelatine
1/2 cup water
2 cups sugar
1 cup water

1 teaspoon vanilla or peppermint
  essence
coconut or icing sugar

Combine gelatine and first measure of water. Leave to swell for 10 minutes. Place sugar and second measure of water in a large saucepan. Heat gently, stirring constantly until sugar dissolves. Dissolve gelatine over hot water. Pour gelatine into sugar mixture and bring to the boil. Boil steadily for 15 minutes. Allow to cool until lukewarm. Beat well until very thick and white. Add vanilla or peppermint essence. Line a large tin with baking paper. Wet baking paper and pour mixture into the tin. Chill until set. Turn out of tin. Cut into squares and roll in coconut or icing sugar. Keep chilled.

Crush biscuits in a food processor, blender or place in a bag and crush with a rolling pin.

NUT TOFFEE

2 cups sugar
$^1/_2$ cup cream

2 tablespoons butter
$^1/_2$ cup chopped nuts

Put sugar, cream and butter into a saucepan. Heat gently, stirring constantly until sugar dissolves. Bring to the boil. Do not stir. Let mixture boil until the soft crack stage. Add nuts. Stir gently. Pour into a buttered tin. Mark into squares. Cut when cold.

RUSSIAN FUDGE

3 cups sugar
$^1/_2$ cup milk
$^1/_2$ cup sweetened condensed milk

125 g butter
$^1/_8$ teaspoon salt
1 tablespoon golden syrup

Put sugar and milk into a saucepan. Heat gently, stirring constantly until sugar dissolves. Add condensed milk, butter, salt and golden syrup. Stir until butter has melted. Bring to the boil and continue boiling to the soft ball stage, stirring occasionally to prevent burning. Remove from heat. Cool slightly. Beat until thick. Pour into a buttered tin. Mark into squares. Cut when cold. Vanilla essence or chopped nuts may be added to fudge before beating if desired.

TOFFEE

2 cups sugar
1 cup water

1 tablespoon DYC white vinegar
1 tablespoon butter

Put sugar, water, vinegar and butter into a saucepan. Heat gently, stirring constantly until sugar dissolves. Bring to the boil. Do not stir. Let mixture boil to the hard crack stage. Pour into a buttered tin. Mark into squares. Cut when cool.

TOFFEE APPLES

3 cups sugar
1 tablespoon DYC white vinegar
1 tablespoon butter
$^1/_2$ cup water
$^1/_2$ teaspoon cream of tartar

few drops red food colouring
8 apples, approximately
8 wooden ice-block sticks or wooden
  skewers

Put sugar, vinegar, butter and water into a saucepan. Heat gently, stirring constantly until sugar dissolves. Add cream of tartar and food colouring. Bring to the boil. Do not stir. Let mixture boil until the hard crack stage. While mixture is boiling, wipe the apples. Push an ice-block stick into each stem end. Remove pan from heat, tilt slightly then dip an apple into the toffee, turning to coat. Place on a sheet of baking paper or non-stick foil. Repeat with remaining apples. Leave until cold and set.

To stop caramel overcooking, place the saucepan in cold water once the caramel is ready.

TURKISH DELIGHT

2 tablespoons gelatine
³/₄ cup water
2 cups sugar
1 cup boiling water
¹/₂ teaspoon tartaric acid

few drops flavouring — e.g. rosewater
    or lemon or crème de menthe
few drops red food colouring
¹/₂ cup icing sugar
¹/₂ cup Edmonds *Fielder's* cornflour

Combine gelatine and first measure of water in a saucepan. Leave to swell for 10 minutes. Add sugar and boiling water. Stir until sugar and gelatine dissolve. Heat gently, stirring until mixture boils. Leave to boil for 15 minutes, stirring occasionally. Remove from heat. Add the tartaric acid, flavouring and colour. Line a large tin with baking paper. Wet baking paper and pour mixture into the tin. Leave to set for 24 hours. Combine icing sugar and cornflour. Cut into squares. Roll in cornflour mixture.

HINTS FOR JAM AND JELLY MAKING

PREPARATION

- **Select fruit which is well ripened, but not over-ripe.** Do not use fruit with rot. Remove damaged or bruised pieces of fruit.
- **Fresh or frozen fruit can be used.**
- **Wipe or wash and thoroughly drain** fruit as necessary before use.
- **Jars and lids for jams and jellies must be thoroughly clean and dry.** Wash in hot soapy water, rinse thoroughly and place in the oven at 120°C for 30 minutes. **Alternatively, sterilise jars and lids by boiling in water** in a large covered pan for 15 minutes. Leave the jars and lids in the covered pan until ready to use. Invert onto a clean teatowel to drain and dry just before filling.

COOKING

- **Use a large, heavy based saucepan or preserving pan** to avoid jams and jellies boiling over. **Never fill pan more than one-third full. Make jam in small rather than large amounts.** One and a half to two kilograms of fruit is a good average amount to handle.
- **Gently boil fruit until pulpy.** Less juicy fruits may need a little water added. **Add sugar slowly and stir until dissolved.** Once sugar is dissolved boil rapidly. Stir occasionally during this time to prevent jam sticking to bottom of saucepan.
- **Use a wooden spoon for stirring.**
- **Carefully skim scum from jelly during cooking.** This stops it breaking up and dispersing through jelly.
- **To strain jellies** use several thicknesses of fine cloth or a jelly bag. Jelly bags are available from kitchenware shops. If using a fine cloth, tie the cloth to the legs of an upturned chair. Place a bowl under the cloth. Pour the jelly into the cloth and leave to drain. **Do not squeeze the cloth or jelly bag** as this will give a cloudy jelly.

SETTING TEST

- **Ripeness of fruit, speed of boiling and size of pan will determine when the jam or jelly will set. This must be decided by testing.** Times given are only a guide. Test frequently to determine when setting point has been reached. Remove the pan from the heat while testing.
- **To test jam and jelly for setting:**
  1. Dip a wooden spoon into the jam or jelly and allow the mixture to drip. When two drips merge on the end of the spoon instead of running off the spoon, the mixture will set on cooling.
  2. Most jams and jellies will set at a temperature of 105°C.
  3. Put a little jam or jelly on a cold plate. Leave to cool slightly. The mixture will set if the surface wrinkles when touched and a channel formed (when a finger is drawn through) remains open.

PACKING

- **Jams and jellies should be poured into hot jars and covered immediately.** If this is not possible, cover the jars with a clean cloth and leave until thoroughly cold. Cover with lids, cellophane covers or with paraffin wax and a protective cover.

JELLY MAKING

1.5 kg fruit
2 to 4 cups water (soft fruits)
5 to 7 cups water (firm fruits)

3 to 3.5 litres water (hard fruits)
sugar

Mash small and soft fruit. Chop or slice large fruit, leaving cores and skin on as they are pectin rich. Add water according to type of fruit to just cover it. Add acid to low-acid fruits. Approximately 2 tablespoons lemon juice or $^1/_2$ teaspoon citric or tartaric acid is usually sufficient for most low-acid fruit. Cook fruit in a covered pan until completely pulped. Strain through a jelly bag or fine cloth. Measure juice and allow 1 cup sugar to 1 cup juice for strong jellying fruits, or $^3/_4$ cup of sugar to 1 cup juice for fruits with poorer jellying properties. Heat juice to boiling point. Remove from the heat and stir in sugar until dissolved. Return to heat and boil briskly until setting point is reached. Skim to remove scum. For most fruits this is quite a short time, about 15 minutes. Pour into sterilised jars at once.

SOFT FRUIT
berries, strawberries, red currants, grapes, plums

FIRM FRUIT
apples, guavas, crabapples, pineapple, feijoas, tamarillos

HARD FRUIT
oranges, grapefruit, quinces

Fruits of poorer setting quality should have apple and lemon added to the initial boiling for good results.

GOOD SETTING FRUITS (Rich in pectin and acid)

apples (sour varieties)	grapes
crabapples	grapefruit
boysenberries, loganberries and	lemons
raspberries	oranges (sour varieties)
currants, red and black	plums
gooseberries	passionfruit

FRUITS NEEDING ADDED ACID (Rich in pectin and low in acid)

feijoas	blackberries
melon	oranges (sweet varieties)
quinces	apples (sweet varieties)
*strawberries	

FRUIT NEEDING ADDED PECTIN SUCH AS APPLE OR LEMON
(Low in pectin, rich in acid)

apricots	tamarillos
*guavas	*strawberries
kiwifruit	pineapple

FRUIT NEEDING ACID AND PECTIN (Low in acid and low in pectin)

cherries	peaches
elderberries	pears
*guavas	*these fruits may require pectin and/ or acid depending on the variety and ripeness.

APRICOT JAM

2.75 kg apricots, halved and stoned *2$\frac{1}{2}$ cups water*
10 to 12 apricot kernels *12 cups sugar*

Crack a few apricot stones and remove kernels. Put apricots, kernels and water into a preserving pan. Cook slowly until fruit is pulpy. Add sugar. Stir until dissolved. Boil briskly for 30 minutes or until setting point is reached. Remove the kernels and pour jam into sterilised jars.
Makes about 10 × 350 ml jars.

BLACKBERRY AND APPLE JELLY

1 kg blackberries *water*
750 g apples, sliced, unpeeled and *sugar*
  uncored

Put blackberries and apples into a preserving pan. Add water to just cover fruit. Cook until fruit is pulpy. Strain through a jelly bag or fine cloth. Measure juice and return to pan. For each cup of juice, add $\frac{3}{4}$ cup sugar. Bring to the boil, stirring until sugar is dissolved. Boil briskly. Stir occasionally and test for setting after 10 to 15 minutes. When setting point is reached pour into sterilised jars.
Makes about 3 × 250 ml jars.

BLACKCURRANT JAM

1 kg blackcurrants *6 cups sugar*
2 cups water

Remove stalks from blackcurrants. Put blackcurrants and water into a preserving pan. Boil gently until fruit is soft. Add sugar. Stir until dissolved. Bring to the boil and boil rapidly for 15 minutes or until setting point is reached. Pour into sterilised jars.
Makes about 4 × 350 ml jars.

BLUEBERRY JAM

3 cooking apples, peeled, cored and *$\frac{1}{4}$ cup lemon juice*
  finely chopped or coarsely grated *4 cups sugar*
3 cups blueberries, fresh or frozen

Put apples, blueberries and lemon juice into a preserving pan. Boil until fruit is soft. Add sugar. Stir until dissolved. Boil briskly for 20 minutes or until setting point is reached. Pour into sterilised jars.
Makes about 4 × 350 ml jars.

CAPE GOOSEBERRY JAM

1 kg Cape gooseberries
1/2 cup water

1/4 cup lemon juice
3 1/2 cups sugar

Put gooseberries, water and lemon juice into a preserving pan. Boil until fruit is soft and broken up. Add sugar. Stir until dissolved. Boil briskly for 20 minutes or until setting point is reached. Pour into sterilised jars.
Makes about 4 × 350 ml jars.

DRIED APRICOT JAM

250 g dried apricots, roughly chopped
2 3/4 cups water
1/2 cup lemon juice

440 g can unsweetened crushed
  pineapple
3 1/2 cups sugar

Soak apricots in water for 12 hours. Bring to the boil and simmer in the soaking liquid for 20 minutes or until tender. Add lemon juice and crushed pineapple. Return to the boil. Add sugar. Stir until dissolved. Boil briskly with occasional stirring until setting point is reached. Pour into sterilised jars.
Makes about 3 × 350 ml jars.

KIWIFRUIT JAM

1 kg kiwifruit, peeled and chopped
1/2 cup water

1/2 cup orange juice
3 cups sugar

Put kiwifruit, water and orange juice into a preserving pan. Boil until fruit is soft and pulpy. Add sugar. Stir until dissolved. Boil briskly for 30 minutes or until setting point is reached. Pour into sterilised jars.
Makes about 3 × 350 ml jars.

LEMON HONEY

1st EDITION RECIPE

4 lemons
125 g butter

2 cups sugar
4 eggs, beaten

Grate only the yellow part of the lemon (avoid white part as it is bitter). Squeeze the lemons and strain the juice. Melt the butter in the top of a double boiler. Stir in sugar and lemon juice until sugar is dissolved. Add eggs and lemon rind. Place over boiling water and cook, stirring all the time until mixture thickens. Pour into sterilised jars. Store in the refrigerator.
Makes about 4 × 250 ml jars.

MARMALADE

4 large grapefruit, minced, chopped
    or thinly sliced
2 large lemons, minced, chopped or
    thinly sliced

3.5 litres water
sugar

Cover grapefruit and lemons with water and stand overnight. Next day boil for 45 minutes or until fruit is soft and pulpy. Allow to cool a little. Measure pulp and return to pan. Bring to the boil. For each cup of pulp, add 1 cup sugar. Stir until dissolved. Boil briskly, stirring occasionally until setting point is reached. Pour into sterilised jars.
Makes about 10 × 350 ml jars.

MINT AND APPLE JELLY

1 kg cooking apples, washed and
    chopped
water
sugar
1 lemon

$^{1}/_{2}$ cup firmly packed mint leaves,
    finely chopped (retain stalks)
$^{1}/_{2}$ cup wine vinegar
green food colouring

Put apples into a large saucepan. Add water to just cover the fruit. Cover and simmer until completely pulpy. Strain through a jelly bag or fine cloth overnight. Measure juice into a saucepan and allow 1 cup sugar to 1 cup juice. Grate the yellow part of the lemon. Tie up the mint stalks and lemon rind in a piece of muslin and add to the juice. Squeeze the lemon and strain its juice. Add this juice and vinegar to the saucepan. Heat slowly, stirring occasionally to dissolve the sugar. When the sugar has dissolved bring the jelly to the boil. Add mint leaves and boil rapidly for about 5 minutes or until setting point is reached. Remove muslin bag. Stir in a few drops of green colouring. Pour into sterilised jars.
Makes about 2 × 250 ml jars.

PLUM JAM

2 kg plums, halved and stoned
$1^{1}/_{2}$ cups water

7 cups sugar

Put plums and water into a preserving pan. Boil until soft and pulpy. Add sugar. Stir until dissolved. Boil briskly for 15 minutes or until setting point is reached. Pour into sterilised jars.
Makes about 6 × 350 ml jars.

RASPBERRY JAM

3 cups raspberries, fresh or frozen   *2³/₄ cups sugar*

Put the berries into a preserving pan and cook slowly until juice runs from them. Bring to the boil. Add sugar and stir until dissolved. Boil briskly for 3 to 5 minutes. Pour into sterilised jars. This jam firms up after a few days' storage.
Makes about 2 × 350 ml jars.

LOGANBERRY JAM
Omit raspberries and replace with loganberries.

BOYSENBERRY JAM
Omit raspberries and replace with boysenberries.

STRAWBERRY JAM

1 kg strawberries, hulled   *1¹/₂ teaspoons tartaric acid*
6 cups sugar

Put strawberries into a preserving pan. Crush lightly with a potato masher or fork. Add sugar and stir in thoroughly. Bring to the boil and boil for 5 minutes. Add tartaric acid and boil rapidly for a further 5 minutes. Pour into sterilised jars.
Makes about 3 × 350 ml jars.

SWEET ORANGE MARMALADE

1.25 kg sweet oranges   *1.5 litres water*
2 lemons   *sugar*

Squeeze the juice from the oranges and lemons. Tie pips in a piece of muslin. Finely shred the skins. In a preserving pan, gently boil juice, skins, pips and water for about 1 hour until the skins are tender. Cool a little. Measure pulp and return to pan. Bring to the boil. For each cup of pulp, add 1 cup sugar. Stir until dissolved. Boil briskly for 20 minutes or until setting point is reached. Remove muslin. Pour into sterilised jars.
Makes about 5 × 350 ml jars.

TAMARILLO JAM

1.25 kg tamarillos, blanched, skinned   *2 cups water*
* and chopped*   *sugar*
500 g cooking apples, peeled and   *¹/₄ cup lemon juice*
* chopped*

Put tamarillos, apples and water into a preserving pan. Boil until pulpy. Cool a little. Measure pulp and return to pan. Bring to the boil. For each cup of pulp, add 1 cup sugar. Add lemon juice. Stir until sugar is dissolved. Boil briskly for 30 minutes or until setting point is reached. Pour into sterilised jars.
Makes about 7 × 350 ml jars.

PICKLES, CHUTNEYS AND SAUCES

- **Vegetables and fruit for pickling must be of good quality**, well ripened, but not over-ripe. For chutney and relish they can be riper than for pickles. Well-ripened fruits are best for sauces. Never use diseased produce.
- **Wash, drain and dry vegetables and fruit before use.**
- **When salting vegetables always use a non-metallic bowl.**
- **Vinegar is an important ingredient** as it acts as a preservative. Always use the amount of vinegar stated in the recipe.
- **Lengthy cooking is needed to thicken chutneys, relishes and sauces.** Frequent stirring is needed to avoid the mixture catching on the bottom of the pan.
- **Pack chutneys, relishes and sauces into hot sterilised jars or bottles.** Leave chutneys and relishes to go cold and cover with sterilised lids. Preferably use a non-metallic lid.
- **For a smooth sauce place in a food processor or blender.**
- **Label preserves and store in a cool, dark place.** All pickles, chutneys and sauces improve with a few weeks' storage before use.

APRICOT OR PEACH SAUCE

3 kg apricots or peaches, peeled stoned and chopped
1 kg apples, peeled, cored and chopped
750 g tomatoes, chopped
4 onions, chopped
6 cloves garlic, crushed

2 litres DYC *malt vinegar*
2 tablespoons salt
2 cups sugar
3 teaspoons ground cloves
3 teaspoons white pepper
3 teaspoons ground ginger
$\frac{1}{2}$ teaspoon cayenne pepper

Put all the ingredients into a preserving pan. Boil steadily with occasional stirring for $2\frac{1}{2}$ hours or until completely pulpy. Press through a colander or coarse sieve. Return to pan and boil until preferred thickness. Pour into sterilised bottles and seal. Makes about 2 litres.

BEETROOT CHUTNEY

1 kg beetroot
500 g onions
$2\frac{1}{2}$ cups DYC *malt vinegar*
1 tablespoon salt
2 cups sugar

1 teaspoon ground allspice
1 teaspoon white pepper
1 teaspoon ground ginger
$\frac{1}{2}$ cup Edmonds *standard plain flour*
$\frac{1}{2}$ cup DYC *malt vinegar*

Cook unpeeled beetroot for 30 minutes or until skins slip off easily. Mince or finely chop onions and beetroot. Put into preserving pan with first measure of vinegar. Boil until onion is tender. Add salt, sugar, allspice, pepper and ginger. Boil for 25 minutes, stirring occasionally. Mix flour and second measure of vinegar to a smooth paste. Stir into pan and boil for 5 minutes. Pack into sterilised jars. Makes about 3 × 350 ml jars.

CASHMERE CHUTNEY

1 kg cooking apples, cored,
    unpeeled and chopped, or green
    gooseberries, topped and tailed
2 cups DYC malt vinegar,
    approximately
1 clove garlic, crushed

2 cups dates, chopped
2 cups raisins
125 g root ginger, grated
4 cups brown sugar
1 tablespoon salt
$^1/_2$ teaspoon cayenne pepper

Put apples and enough vinegar to almost cover fruit into a preserving pan. Cook until fruit is soft. Add garlic, dates, raisins and ginger to the pan. Stir in sugar, salt and cayenne pepper. Boil with frequent stirring for 30 minutes or until chutney is thick and jam-like. Pack into sterilised jars.
Makes about 4 × 350 ml jars.

FRUIT CHUTNEY

2 kg apples or plums or tamarillos,
    peeled and cored or stoned, then
    chopped
500 g onions, chopped
2 cups raisins
1 clove garlic, crushed
4 cups brown sugar

2 teaspoons salt
1 teaspoon ground cloves or mixed
    spice
$^1/_2$ teaspoon cayenne pepper
4 cups DYC malt vinegar,
    approximately

Put fruit, onion, raisins, garlic, sugar, salt, cloves and cayenne pepper into a preserving pan. Add enough vinegar to almost cover. Stir well. Boil gently with frequent stirring for 2 hours or until chutney is thick and jam-like. Pack into sterilised jars.
Makes about 6 × 350 ml jars.

KIWIFRUIT CHUTNEY

2 onions, chopped
2 apples, peeled and chopped
1 clove garlic, crushed
$^1/_2$ cup raisins
$^3/_4$ cup brown sugar

1 cup DYC malt vinegar
$^1/_2$ teaspoon ground ginger
$^1/_2$ teaspoon allspice
$^1/_4$ teaspoon ground cloves
500 g kiwifruit, peeled and chopped

Put onions, apples, garlic, raisins, sugar, vinegar, ginger, allspice and cloves into a preserving pan. Boil gently for about 30 minutes or until mixture is soft and thickened. Add kiwifruit. Continue cooking for a further 20 minutes or until chutney is thick and jam-like. Pack into sterilised jars.
Makes about 2 × 350 ml jars.

MUSTARD PICKLE

4 cups cauliflower florets
4 cups pickling onions
4 cups diced green tomatoes
4 cups diced cucumber
1¼ cups salt
2 litres water

1 cup Edmonds *standard plain flour*
4 teaspoons dry mustard
1½ tablespoons turmeric
½ teaspoon cayenne pepper
1 cup sugar
1 litre DYC *malt vinegar*

Put the prepared vegetables in a large non-metallic bowl. Dissolve the salt in water and pour it over the vegetables. Leave to stand for 24 hours. Drain thoroughly. Mix together flour, mustard, turmeric, cayenne pepper and sugar. Stir in a little of the measured vinegar to make a smooth paste. Gradually add remaining vinegar. Bring to the boil in a large preserving pan, stirring until mixture thickens. Add vegetables and boil for 5 minutes or until vegetables are heated through. Pack into sterilised jars.
Makes about 10 × 350 ml jars.

PEACH CHUTNEY

2.25 kg peaches, peeled, stoned and
    chopped
500 g onions, chopped
2 cups raisins
1 cup mixed peel
½ cup crystallised ginger, chopped

2 cups brown sugar
1 tablespoon salt
1 tablespoon curry powder
½ teaspoon cayenne pepper
3½ cups DYC *malt vinegar*

Put all ingredients into a preserving pan. Stir and bring to the boil. Boil steadily with frequent stirring for 1 hour or until mixture is thick and jam-like. Pack into sterilised jars.
Makes about 4 × 350 ml jars.

PICKLED ONIONS

1.5 kg pickling onions
½ cup salt
water

3 dry chillies, approximately
6 peppercorns, approximately
DYC *malt or white vinegar*

Place onions in a non-metallic bowl. Sprinkle with salt. Add cold water to cover onions. Stand for 24 hours. Drain and rinse in cold water. Drain again and pack into jars. To each jar add 1 chilli and 2 peppercorns. Add vinegar to cover onions. Seal with non-metallic lids or corks. Store for 4–6 weeks before using.
Makes about 3 × 500 ml jars.

PICKLED VEGETABLES

12 shallots or pickling onions, peeled
1 cucumber, peeled and diced
1 cup sliced celery
1 cup sliced green beans
2 cups cauliflower florets

1 red pepper, sliced
6 tablespoons salt
500 ml DYC spiced vinegar,
   approximately

Prepare vegetables so pieces are of similar size. Put onion, cucumber and celery in one non-metallic bowl; the beans and cauliflower in another and the red pepper in a third. Sprinkle red pepper with 1 tablespoon salt and divide the remaining salt between the other two bowls. Cover and leave to stand for 12 hours. Next day drain off liquid formed. Rinse in cold water and drain again. Put the cauliflower and beans into a wire basket or sieve and blanch in boiling water for 2 minutes. Drain well. Mix all vegetables together and pack into sterilised jars. Pour spiced vinegar over to cover. Seal with non-metallic lids. Keep for a minimum of 3 weeks before using.
Makes about 2 × 500 ml jars.

PLUM SAUCE

1st EDITION RECIPE

2.75 kg plums
1.75 litres DYC malt vinegar
3 cups brown sugar
50 g garlic
2 teaspoons ground pepper

2 teaspoons ground cloves
2 teaspoons ground ginger
1 teaspoon ground mace
1/2 teaspoon cayenne pepper
1 tablespoon salt

Put all the ingredients into a preserving pan. Bring to the boil, stirring frequently. Boil steadily until mixture is pulpy. Press through a colander or coarse sieve. Return sauce to pan and boil for 2 to 3 minutes. Pour into sterilised bottles and seal.
Makes about 1.5 litres.

SPICED VINEGAR

2.25 litres DYC malt vinegar
1 cup sugar
2 tablespoons black peppercorns
2 tablespoons whole cloves
1 tablespoon whole allspice

4 cm piece root ginger
2 tablespoons salt
1 tablespoon mustard seeds
2 teaspoons crushed nutmeg pieces

Put all ingredients into a saucepan. Boil gently for 10 minutes. Leave to cool and either strain and use, or leave to steep for several days then strain and use. The latter method gives a richer flavour. Sugar can be omitted if an unsweetened vinegar is desired.
Makes about 2.25 litres.

SWEET PICKLED GHERKINS

4 kg gherkins
1/2 cup salt
6 cups water
2.25 litres DYC malt vinegar

5 cups brown sugar
25 g whole mixed pickling spice
10 cm piece cinnamon stick
1 teaspoon whole cloves

Using a piece of coarse cloth or sugar sack, rub the gherkins to remove any roughness. In a non-metallic bowl mix salt and water together. Add gherkins. Leave to soak for 24 hours. Next day combine vinegar, sugar, pickling spice, cinnamon and cloves and boil for 5 minutes. Drain gherkins and pour boiling water over to completely cover. Drain. Pack while still hot into sterilised jars. Pour hot vinegar mixture over to cover gherkins. Seal at once with non-metallic lids. Keep for a minimum of 3 weeks before using.
Makes about 9 × 500 ml jars.

TOMATO CHUTNEY

2.25 kg green or firm tomatoes,
  chopped
6 onions, chopped
1.25 kg apples, peeled and chopped
2 cups seedless raisins
1 cup crystallised peel

4 cups brown sugar
4 cups DYC malt vinegar
2 tablespoons salt
1 teaspoon black peppercorns
2 teaspoons whole cloves
2 chillies

Put tomatoes, onions, apples, raisins, peel, sugar, vinegar and salt into a preserving pan. Tie peppercorns, cloves and chillies in muslin and add. Bring to the boil, stirring. Boil steadily with frequent stirring for about 2 hours or until mixture is thick and jam-like. Remove spice bag. Pack into sterilised jars.
Makes about 6 × 350 ml jars.

TOMATO PURÉE

2 kg ripe tomatoes, blanched and
  skinned

2 teaspoons salt

Put tomatoes and salt into a saucepan. Cook for 30 minutes or until pulpy. Strain through a sieve. Return to the saucepan and boil for 10 to 15 minutes. Pack into small preserving jars and process in a water bath for 15 minutes. Volume depends on how much liquid is boiled off. If non-acid tomatoes are used, add 1/2 teaspoon citric acid for each 1 litre purée.

To skin tomatoes, place in boiling water for 30 seconds then plunge into cold water.

TOMATO RELISH

1.5 kg tomatoes, blanched, skinned
   and quartered
4 onions, quartered
2 tablespoons salt
2 cups brown sugar
2¼ cups DYC malt vinegar

3 chillies
1 tablespoon dry mustard
1 tablespoon curry powder
2 tablespoons Edmonds standard
   plain flour
¼ cup DYC malt vinegar

Put tomatoes and onions into a non-metallic bowl. Sprinkle with salt and leave for 12 hours. Drain off liquid formed. Put vegetables, sugar, first measure of vinegar and chillies into a preserving pan. Boil gently for 1½ hours, stirring frequently. Mix mustard, curry, flour and second measure of vinegar to a smooth paste. Stir into relish. Boil for 5 minutes. Pack into sterilised jars.
Makes about 4 × 350 ml jars.

TOMATO SAUCE

1st EDITION RECIPE

3.5 kg tomatoes, chopped
1 kg apples, peeled and chopped
6 onions, chopped
3 cups sugar
4 cups DYC malt vinegar

2 tablespoons salt
½ to 1 teaspoon cayenne pepper
1 teaspoon black peppercorns
1 teaspoon whole allspice
2 teaspoons whole cloves

Put tomatoes, apples, onions, sugar, vinegar, salt and cayenne pepper into a preserving pan. Tie peppercorns, allspice and cloves in muslin and add. Boil steadily for about 2 hours or until completely pulpy. Discard whole spices. Press through a colander or coarse sieve. Return to pan and boil for 2 minutes. Pour into sterilised bottles and seal.
Makes about 1.75 litres.

BOTTLING

Bottling is a method of preserving food in sealed jars so that no harmful organisms can enter the jars and organisms already present are destroyed. It is easier and safer to freeze vegetables, fish and meat since the bottling process for these non-acid foods is very complex to ensure a totally safe product.

There are two main methods used to bottle fruit — the open pan and water bath methods.

FRUIT FOR BOTTLING

Fruit should be firm, well ripened and blemish free. Avoid preparing too much fruit at a time. Wash and prepare according to type. Peel, core or stone. Cut and if likely to discolour, place in water with a little salt or lemon juice to reduce browning.

GUIDE TO AMOUNT OF FRUIT TO NUMBER OF JARS

4 Kg FRUIT	No. 1 LITRE JARS	4 Kg FRUIT	No. 1 LITRE JARS
apples	4–6	pears	
apricots	6	halved	4–5
berries	5	sliced	3–4
cherries	6–7	plums	4–5
peaches		tomatoes	
whole	5–6	whole	4–6
sliced	3–4	puréed	2–3

The size, evenness and cut will vary the yield.

GUIDE TO AMOUNT OF SYRUP REQUIRED

PRESERVING JAR	WHOLE FRUIT	FRUIT HALVES
1 litre	2 cups	$1\frac{1}{2}$ cups
500 ml	$1\frac{1}{4}$ cups	$\frac{3}{4}$ cup

Fruit can be packed in syrup or water. Syrup will give a better colour and flavour. Make syrup before preparing fruit. Dissolve the sugar in water then bring to the boil.

SYRUPS	SUGAR	WATER	USE
Thin	1 cup	3 cups	light fruits
Medium	1 cup	2 cups	most fruits
Heavy	1 cup	1 cup	hard fruits, berries

Syrups can be flavoured with lemon or orange rind or spices according to fruit. Honey, raw or brown sugar or artificial sweeteners can be used if preferred.

EQUIPMENT NEEDED FOR BOTTLING

- Preserving jars — check that they are free from chips or cracks.
- Screwbands and new seals.
- A large saucepan or preserving pan with a lid for waterbath processing. The pan must be deep enough to hold several jars standing on a rack and to allow water to come 2–3 cm above the jar.
- Preserving jar tongs for handling hot jars. Jars must be sterilised by heating in 120°C oven for 30 minutes. Seals are prepared by standing them in boiling water for 5 minutes.

BOTTLING METHODS

OPEN PAN METHOD — OVERFLOW METHOD

Prepare jars: sterilise in boiling water for 15 minutes in a covered pan. Leave in covered pan or place in the oven at 100°C. Sterilise metal seals. Boil in water for 5 minutes. Leave in water. Prepare syrup.

Prepare the fruit and cook in sufficient syrup or water to cover, as for stewing. Reserve extra syrup; bring to the boil. Work with one jar at a time. Almost fill the hot jars with boiling fruit. Fill to just below the rim with boiling syrup. Wipe the rim with a scalding cloth. Immediately cover with the sterilised metal seal and screw the band on tightly.

Leave to cool. Remove the band when a seal is formed (the dome will be depressed). Wipe jars to remove any stickiness.

WATERBATH

COLD PACK METHOD

Fill the waterbath with sufficient water to cover the jars by 2–3 cm. Place a rack on the base. Heat water to almost boiling. Place clean jars in an oven heated to 100°C. Prepare and heat syrup. Prepare fruit. Sterilise the metal seals by boiling them in water for 5 minutes.

Pack the uncooked fruit firmly into the hot jars to within 1 cm of the top. Cover with boiling syrup. Remove any air bubbles with a knife blade. Wipe the jar rims.

Cover with the metal seals and screw on the bands. Lower the jars into the water bath. Cover. Heat rapidly to boiling point, then adjust the heat to maintain a steady boil. Count the time for processing from when the water returns to the boil.

Check one or two jars. The food should look cooked. Remove the jars to a board. Cool away from draughts.

Remove the screw bands when a seal is formed (the dome is depressed). Wipe the jars to remove any stickiness.

HOT PACK METHOD

This differs from cold pack only in that the fruit is partly cooked in syrup before being packed into jars. It is suitable for very firm fruits and for pulps and juices. The processing time is shorter.

TOMATOES

Tomatoes are bottled as pulp or bottled in water, flavoured with a little salt and/or sugar, or in tomato juice. Since many tomatoes are low in acid it is recommended that for all bottled tomato products, either $^1/_2$ teaspoon citric acid or 2 tablespoons lemon juice or vinegar is added to each 1 litre jar of tomatoes.

WATERBATH PROCESSING CHART IN MINUTES

FRUIT	COLD PACK	HOT PACK
apples		
raw pieces	20	10
stewed pulp	—	15
apricots	25	15
cherries	25	15
currants	20	10
feijoas	35	15
fruit salad	Time according to firmest fruit	
kiwifruit	30	15
nectarines	25	20
peaches	25	20
pears	35	25
plums	20	10
quinces	45	30
rhubarb	15	5
tamarillos	30	15
tomatoes, whole	40	15
JUICES AND PULPS		
fruit juices	15	10
passionfruit	10	5
tomato juice	—	15
tomato pulp	—	15

OVEN METHOD
This method is no longer recommended for processing. The dry heat is very slow to penetrate the food, therefore it cannot be assumed that the temperature reached in the centre of each jar is high enough to prevent spoilage.

PROCESSING IN PRESSURE COOKER OR AUTOMATIC PRESERVERS
These are suitable and it is recommended that the manufacturer's instructions are followed. Fruit not covered with syrup will discolour on storage.

STORAGE
Label the jars and store in a cool, dry, dark place.

Use level cup and spoon measures.

PASSIONFRUIT PULP

1 cup passionfruit pulp   *¹/₂ to ³/₄ cup sugar*

Heat pulp and sugar together, stirring until sugar is dissolved. Bring to the boil. Pour into small sterilised preserving jars. Seal and process in a waterbath for 5 minutes.
Makes about 1 cup.

RUMPOT

seasonal fruits   *dark rum*
sugar

Select a large container, preferably opaque as light spoils the colour of fruit. Use only perfect, ripe fruit, starting in spring with gooseberries and strawberries, and ending in autumn with pears, and later mandarins. Small fruit is left whole, large fruits peeled, cored and cut in sections. Few or many varieties can be used. Use about 200 grams of each fruit and allow 100 grams of sugar for each 200 grams of fruit. Place fruit in container. Sprinkle with sugar. Cover with rum to a depth of 1 cm above fruit. Stir gently next day to dissolve sugar. Repeat with each fruit as it comes into season. Keep container covered. Keep at least 3 weeks before using. Serve the fruit for dessert. The flavoured syrup can be served as a liqueur.

WHOLE TOMATOES

tomatoes, blanched and skinned   *citric acid*

Pack tomatoes into sterilised preserving jars. Add ¹/₂ teaspoon citric acid to each 1 litre jar of tomatoes. No liquid is necessary. Seal and tighten down screwband hand tight. Process in a waterbath for 40 minutes.

DEHYDRATING

- Drying food is increasingly practical with dehydrators and fan ovens making the process easy. Follow manufacturer's directions for processing food in these appliances.
- Select good-quality food in peak condition. Prepare and cut to uniform size for even drying. Test to check that fruit is dry. Take a piece from the dryer and cool. Fruit should feel pliable and leathery. There should be no visible moisture when the dried fruit is pressed between the fingers. Vegetables should be crisp and brittle. The size of load, thickness of product, humidity and temperature of the area all affect the drying time. Store dry product in containers that are moisture-proof and have secure lids. Keep dry food in a cool, dry, dark area.

TO DRY HERBS

Dry on stalk at a temperature of no more than 40°C. Once dry, leaves can be easily stripped off stems. Store in an airtight plastic or glass container in a cool, dark, dry area. When wanted for use, crumble or crush.

FRUIT LEATHERS

Use fully ripe fruit and purée in a blender. Add sugar only to very tart fruit. Spread 2 cups purée over dehydrator solid tray or mesh tray covered with plastic wrap. Keep the centre area thinner than outer edge as centre dries more slowly. When leather is no longer sticky in the centre it is ready. Exceptions are cherry and boysenberry which remain sticky even when they are dry. Always remove leather from tray while warm. Roll in plastic wrap and store in a tightly sealed container in a cool place.

- Lightly oil the dehydrator tray for easy removal of the leather.
- For apricot, peach, nectarine or pear, once puréed, bring to boil before drying. This reduces discolouration. For apple, add lemon juice to apple purée before drying.

FREEZING

Freezing food at a temperature of −15°C or less is a means of storage which prevents the growth of yeast, moulds and bacteria and ensures that biochemical and chemical reactions are greatly restricted. This provides safe, convenient and easy-to-use foods all year round.

Follow manufacturer's instructions for detailed freezer information.

FOR FREEZER SUCCESS

Choose good quality products as their quality will be retained but not improved while frozen. Use good quality moisture-proof packing materials, and label and date all items to prevent wastage. Pack in sizes convenient for use. Avoid very large units — it is better to use two packs. Use food before its recommended storage time expires. Thaw foods in refrigerator or use a microwave.

REFREEZING

Do not refreeze food which has completely thawed. If ice crystals are still visible refreeze and use as soon as possible.

PACKAGING

- Adequate packaging ensures frozen food will maintain its quality. It prevents damage, avoids food drying out and prevents freezer burn.
- Heavy duty plastic bags without holes are suitable for most types of food.
- Aluminium foil containers are useful for precooked foods. Cover with a lid or seal inside a plastic bag.
- Aluminium foil sheets can be used for wrapping oddly shaped items. Seal with freezer tape or inside a plastic bag.
- Plastic containers, boxes and bowls with tight-fitting lids make excellent containers for liquids, semi-soft and delicate foods.
- Glass jars (with a 2 to 5 cm headspace left for expansion), tins and casserole dishes can also be used.
- Twist ties, rubber bands and string are useful for sealing bags.
- Square shapes use freezer space most effectively. Irregularly shaped packages can be placed in square containers for freezing then removed and stacked for storage.
- Always remove the air from plastic bags or frost formation will cause the food to dry out and develop 'off' flavours. Use a vacuum pump or squeeze the air out by hand, then seal tightly.
- When using plastic or other rigid containers leave a headspace of 2 to 5 cm to allow for expansion.

FREE-FLOW

Use to freeze food in individual units. Suitable for berries, peas, sliced vegetables, corn kernels, chicken pieces, sausages, chops, diced meat. Spread prepared food in a single layer on a tray or shallow dish. Freeze until solid then pack into freezer bags or suitable containers. Remove the quantity wanted for use then reseal.

FOODS THAT DO NOT FREEZE

- Cooked egg white alone or in made dishes. It toughens, e.g. scotch eggs, stuffed eggs.
- Stuffed poultry — (high risk of food poisoning) as stuffing freezes very slowly.
- Custards and unwhipped cream — these tend to curdle and separate on thawing.
- White sauce, gravy or other sauces thickened with flour will be thin on thawing. Use cornflour for sauces which are to be frozen.
- Jellies and gelatine dishes — break down and separate on thawing.

- Meringue toppings — weep and crack on thawing.
- Mayonnaise — separates on thawing.
- Salad greens and vegetables to be eaten raw, such as lettuce and other leaf greens, cucumber, tomatoes, celery, spring onions and radishes are not suitable for freezing. However spinach, celery and tomatoes can be frozen and then used for cooking, e.g. casseroles, stews etc. as their softened texture will be appropriate for this use.

STORAGE TIME RECOMMENDATIONS

ITEM	TIME IN MONTHS	ITEM	TIME IN MONTHS
fruit	8–12	pâté	2
vegetables	4–8	ice-cream	
fish	2	in plastic	2
shellfish	2	in cardboard	1
commercially frozen	3	sandwiches	2
meat		pastry	2–3
offal	2	bread/buns	1–2
sausages	2	casseroles	1
sliced bacon	1	pancakes	2
raw ham	3	muffins	3
chops and steak	6	scones	1
mince	4	pies	2
roasts	4–8	soups	3
diced meat	3–6	stock	2
chicken		plated meat dinner	2
whole unstuffed	12	fruit cake	12
chicken pieces	6	cakes	3
		pavlova	2 weeks

Longer storage will result in a poorer quality product with flavour and texture deterioration.

INDEX

INDEX

INDEX

If you have any questions or comments
about the recipes in this book, please write
to:

Consumer Advisory Centre
Goodman Fielder
PO Box 58-422
Greenmount
Auckland 2141

NOTES